GERALD ASARIA

Challenge

LONE SAILORS OF THE ATLANTIC

TRANSLATED BY
FRANK GEORGE

MAYFLOWER BOOKS
NEW YORK

Library of Congress Cataloging in Publication Data
Asaria, Gérald
    Challenge, lone sailors of the Atlantic

    Translation of Les héros solitaires de l'Atlantique.
    Bibliography: p.
    1. Observer Transatlantic Singlehanded Sailing Race—History.
    2. Seamen—Biography. I. Title.
GV832.A8213   797.1′4   79-10041
ISBN 0-8317-1242-2

PHOTO ACKNOWLEDGEMENTS
James Andanson/Sygma, page 128; A.P., 53; APIS, 53; Gérald Asaria, 5, 12-13, 14, 18-19, 22 137, 138-9, 141, 170, 172; J.-M. Barrault, 168-9; Besstrashnyj, 161; J.-P. Biot/*Paris-Match*, 142-3; Daniel Camus/*Paris-Match,* 86; Alain Colas/Sygma, 116-17, 152-3; *Daily Express,* 52-3, 59, 60; *Daily Telegraph,* 83, 88-9, 90-1, 92-3; De Greef/Neptune Nautisme, 114-15; Gérard Pesky, 168-9; J.-C. Deutsch/*Paris-Match*, 123, 124; Roy Dickens, 66; E.C.A., 86; Christian Février, 72, 154-5, 158; Robert Fogliani, 47, 129; Freon, 144-5; Gamma, 71, 86; Daniel Gilles/Neptune Nautisme, 129; Alain Gliksman/Neptune Nautisme, 17; Guillau, 87; Patrick Jarnoux/*Paris-Match,* 104-5, 107, 108-9, 110; Olivier de Kersauson, 4, 146-7, 150-1; Dominique Lauga, 17; Michèle Lavalette, 8-9; Philippe Letellier/*Paris-March*, 74-5; *Observer Magazine,* 6, 20-1, 55, 58, 63, 64-5, 67, 69; Roger Picherie/*Paris-Match,* 82; Royal Navy, 111; *Rudder Magazine,* 41; Paul Slade/*Paris-Match,* 76-7, 79; Chris Smith/*Observer*/Transworld, 15, 16, 94-5, 96, 130-1; *Sydney Sun Herald,* 61, 119; U.P., 53; Roger Viollet, 42, 43, 45, 46; *Yachting* (U.S.A.), 39, 40, 45; Mystic Seaport Museum Inc., Mystic, Connecticut, 26-7.

The photographs on the pages listed below were taken from the following books: page 28, *Atlantic Adventures* by Humphrey Barton (Adlard Coles, London); 30, 31, 33, 34, *Lone Voyager* by Joseph E. Garland (New York 1963, photos by Philip Kuuse); 36, 37, 39, *Le Capitaine Slocum, Roi de la Mer* by Victor Slocum (Amiot-Dumont); 44, *Seul à travers l'Atlantique* by Alain Gerbault (Grasset, Paris).

ACKNOWLEDGEMENTS
This book was written with the technical collaboration of Olivier de Kersauson. The author would also like to thank: Claud Baïotti and Michel Smith for historical documentation; Jean Merlin for technical help; Jean Noli; Miss Angela Green, Miss Balcon, Chris Smith and Frank Page of the *Observer Magazine;* Michel Sola, Noël Tortevoy and Michel Goron of *Paris-Match; Yachting Magazine,* New York; *Rudder Magazine,* New York; Miss Sandra Hart; Mystic Seaport Museum, Connecticut; Cdt Luc-Marie Bayle of the Musée de la Marine, Paris; Sygma, Paris; and the Newport Public Library, Newport, Connecticut.

This book is dedicated to Alain Colas.

Contents

Preface

Until 1976 the single-handed race across the Atlantic stood alone among contests under sail. While others were subject to meticulous rules the Ostar (Observer Single-handed Transatlantic Race) was remarkable for their absence; the choice of boat was completely open so that the ingenuity of the contestants has a free rein. It is an added attraction to have to think about the kind of vessel you really need to win the race, but flights of fancy do no good unless they are backed up by sound seamanship and a clear understanding of what a single-handed voyage across the North Atlantic from east to west may involve. The difficulties of the passage are very real and in selecting this course the organizers of the race had certainly no thought of sending the contestants off on an easy jaunt.

For my part, it is a race I like very much because I find that it includes everything. The qualities of sportsmanship and seamanship that it calls for make it a unique contest, and no doubt that is why it has proved such a success. Many would like to see big changes but as far as I am concerned I do not want them, because then the Ostar would not be the Ostar.

I am very glad that this book and the important collection of photographs it contains have now been dedicated to single-handed voyages across the Atlantic and to the Ostar.

Eric Tabarly, winner of the Ostar in 1964 and 1976

Tabarly's Pen Duick VI *during the fifth Ostar, 1976*

Introduction

The finest single-handed race

The haze that had shrouded the roadstead for the past two days cleared before a light south-easterly breeze. Then under a colourless but clearing sky there appeared a remarkable spectacle – the 125 yachts that were to compete in the fifth single-handed Transatlantic Race were getting ready for the start, in three classes according to size. After weeks of preparation, adjustment and finishing touches, after a last wakeful night, the 125 solitary mariners anxiously awaited the sound of the starting gun that would set them on the wildest and most daring race ever devised.

There had never been so many contestants as on that dawn of 5 June 1976, never so many sophisticated craft. There was to be a ruthless settling of accounts between the mono-hulls and the multi-hulls. Everybody knew that this fifth Ostar would be a hard-fought battle in which the victor would be recognized as sovereign of the seas.

Having left Plymouth's Millbay Dock in the evening of 4 June the big yachts had spent the night at anchor off Drake's Island. Alain Colas with his giant 72-metre *Club Méditerranée*, a veritable liner under sail, had been named favourite by the British bookmakers. He was also favourite with the spectators, who did not know whether to admire most the ship or the man. Colas was outspoken, and on the eve of departure after his press conference had said 'anyone can have second place'. Such unfortunate and boastful remarks immediately aroused the ill will of his rivals, and

Spirit of Surprise, the tiny catamaran in which Ambrogio Fogar meant to sail the 4,200-mile southern route

of many others who had been irritated by the display of publicity that had surrounded the building of that endless blue hull.

Typically, Eric Tabarly had less to say. It was known that he did not think much of Colas' chances because he considered the rigging of the heavy four-master to be too light. Nor indeed did Tabarly think much of his own chances; with his *Pen Duick VI* scarcely modified for single-handed sailing he hoped only to get an honourable mention. For him there were four particularly strong rivals for the prize: *I.T.T.-Océanic* which Yvon Fauconnier had got into excellent shape and which, with her 33-metre length, would go very well close-hauled; *Kriter III* was a particularly fast catamaran that a sailor like Jean-Yves Terlain could drive hard if the weather was right and if he took the southern route; *Spirit of America* with the American Michael Kane at the helm was a very seaworthy trimaran that answered to the lightest winds; and then there was Mike McMullen in his trimaran *Three Cheers* who was so sure of himself that he had only taken on supplies for twenty days. In the event it was quite another story; even if the experts agreed that Mike McMullen could cross the Atlantic in under three weeks, the fifth 'race of the century' took a tragic turn for him on 1 June.

Like the other contestants Mike was working against time to give his boat a few finishing touches; his young wife Elizabeth was helping him by rubbing down the bottom with an electric sander. The tide was out but there were still a few inches of water under the boat. She had been warned of the danger of using electrical equipment so near the water and to keep the lead dry she had put it round her neck. Suddenly the sander slipped and she instinctively picked it up; the blinding flash that followed was fatal.

At the funeral McMullen, with a set face, spoke no words of complaint or regret. To this giant Royal Marine commando, expert skier and hardened mountaineer, who had already survived one capsize in his trimaran, harsh ordeals were commonplace. Yet some of his friends thought he might be taking it too hard. Although they knew that he was more determined than ever to carry off the prize that Elizabeth had wanted to see him win, they and everyone else could not but wonder whether he could possibly face the ordeal.

For if the Ostar of 1976 was more than ever before a rally of fine boats, it was above all a muster of brave men. Alongside a fine trimaran like *Cap 33* or a 236-foot monster like *Club Méditerranée*, one of the Italians sailed a contraption of two floats barely 50 centimetres wide and joined together with booms along the waterline. It could hardly be called a catamaran. But the confident smile of Ambrogio Fogar, her helmsman, almost made one forget that he meant to cross more than 4,000 miles of ocean in two frail and hollow bits of wood, where he could neither find shelter nor lie at length. This fifth Ostar featured every kind of boat, including the unusual *Jester*, the invention of Colonel Hasler who had devised this fantastic race with her in mind in 1960, and women and men of high resolve like Valentine Howells, the bearded giant who had been one of the five contenders in that first, little publicized Ostar.

At noon on 5 June 1976 the wind was rising a little when the starting gun fired. The thousands of spectators lining the cliffs at Picklecombe Point south of Cawsand Bay greeted it with a cheer. In the Sound the hundreds of yachts and motor boats sounded their

Twelve o'clock, Saturday, 5 June 1976. One hundred and twenty-five of the most beautiful yachts in the world face the Atlantic. Accompanied by hundreds of other

boats are Club Méditerranée *(left),* Pen Duick VI *(centre) and* Cap 33 (right)

Pen Duick VI, *32-ton ketch, draft 3.4 metres, height of masts 27 metres and 18 metres, sail area 700 square metres – the cruiser designed for a crew of fourteen in*

which Tabarly sailed the Atlantic alone

'Jumbo-Yacht', 'Cathedral of the Seas', 'Ocean Giant', 'Liner under Sail', the names applied to Club Méditerranée, *the biggest yacht ever built for single-handed*

sailing: 260 tons, draft 5.6 metres, four 32.5-metre masts, sail area 1,000 square metres

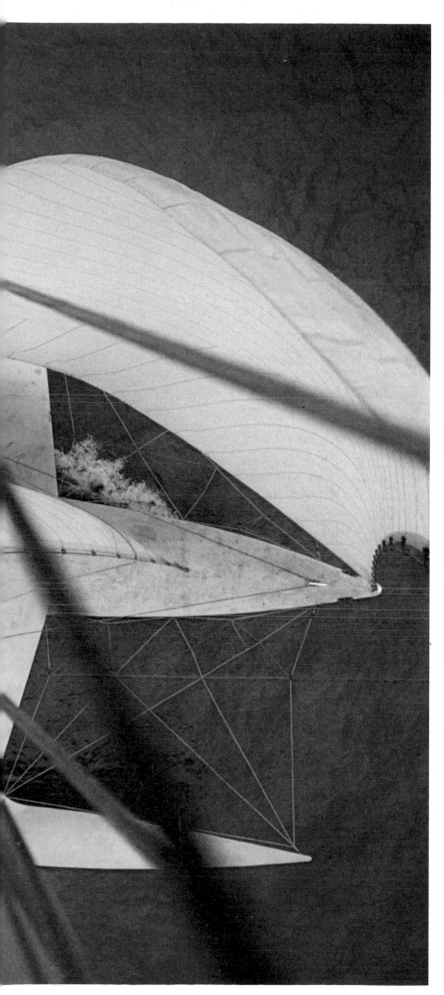

Mike McMullen in the 46-foot multi-hull Three Cheers, weighing only 3 tons, was the British hope for the 1976 Ostar. His young wife, whom he had just married, helped him to get the already famous trimaran ready for the race, but three days before the start she dropped an electric sander into the sea and was killed by the shock. In spite of his sorrow Mike McMullen took part in the race; his friends feared that this might be his last voyage

Two profiles already famous in sailing legend: the little junk-rigged Jester *which Blondie Hasler (left), the founder of the Transatlantic Race, sailed in 1960 and 1964 and which Mike Richey (above) sailed in 1968 and 1972 before taking part in the fifth race*

Right: The burly Valentine Howells, known as the 'bearded lady' since the 1960 race because of his first name, was, at the age of fifty, once again to challenge the Atlantic

sirens and fog horns to salute the contestants as they crossed the line. From the emotions and rivalries it had aroused it was already clear that this fifth Ostar would be keenly contested and hard, dangerous even, for one felt that not a few of the competitors lacked the necessary experience for such a course.

First in the field, *Spirit of America,* with her big jib in the colours of the American flag, was off like an arrow and gained speed famously. Next came the multi-hulls, *Three Cheers, Kriter III* and *The Third Turtle,* while *I.T.T.-Océanic, Pen Duick VI* and *Club Méditerranée* seemed to lose ground, handicapped by the light airs. They all headed south-east to pick up the wind off-shore and go about.

In these first few minutes of what was to be a long and exacting race the onlookers were already trying to judge form and assess chances. The impressive sprint by the multi-hulls seemed unbeatable when suddenly Tabarly tacked and headed south-west. He was the only one to choose the inshore passage. The skippers in the boats astern thought he had made a mistake, that he would

The race is about to begin; the unknown and unclassified mingle with the giants. Michael Flanagan in Galloping Gael *(sail number 6) contemplates* Club

Méditerranée *before they go out of the Sound. He was to be one of the brave men never to return to land*

have the tide against him and that under the land he would lose what little wind there was, but in fact Tabarly had made a good move. For several days, under the pretext of trying out *Pen Duick VI*, he had been spying out the land and determining the limits of the tidal streams. Less than an hour after the start, while *Club Méditerranée* was coasting along and the others were still heading away from the land, Tabarly had rounded the south-west headland and found himself alone in the lead; the stratagem had worked. Within two hours he had established a lead of seven miles. Confounding the pundits, the 1964 winner had begun to show his strength. *Pen Duick VI*, which had already covered some 50,000 miles in every ocean, was in fine fettle and the stoutest and most seaworthy of them all.

But on that first day Tabarly became aware of a serious defect that almost persuaded him to abandon the race. As he wrote in the log in which he recorded the most important events of the voyage:

My troubles began on the very first day. The generator that should have fed the automatic pilot obstinately refused to start although it had been in good working order when we tested it at Brest; there was a short-circuit somewhere. The start was at noon and I am worried because an automatic pilot is absolutely essential. Without it, to handle for weeks so powerful a boat as *Pen Duick VI* would call for an effort that would floor a Hercules.

We set off. The light south-westerly wind was practically on the nose for rounding the Lizard. I was just astern of Fauconnier's *I.T.T.-Océanic* and just ahead of Terlain's *Kriter III*. I went about to clear *I.T.T.*, and *Club Méditerranée* too which was coming up on the starboard tack. The boats full of sightseers scattered in front of us like frightened chickens. Far ahead *Spirit of America* was tearing along, but in quite the wrong direction. I tacked when I was far enough ahead of Colas, immediately put on more speed than the others and would soon lose sight of them.

Plymouth was lost to sight in the haze and overtaking *Spirit of America* I was out in front alone. With the automatic pilot plugged in to my auxiliary generator I got ready to cook a dish of spaghetti with onions and eggs.

At midnight the fog was still getting thicker and after rounding the mark I set a course for the Scillies. The fog signal on Round Island would enable me to clear them. At 03.30, knowing that in these waters I need fear no close encounter, I decided to get some sleep.

The second big disappointment that day came when I plugged in the heading indicator alarm and it would not work. I looked at it in dismay for it had been with me since 1968, both in *Pen Duick IV* and *Pen Duick VI*. It was invaluable to a single-hander because it sets off a klaxon as soon as the boat goes off course. It was no use getting angry and cursing the thing, it just wouldn't work properly; as soon as it was engaged it set up a perpetual din.

Twelve o'clock, the starting gun fires and a black ketch goes about and takes the lead before fading into the silence of the ocean

Newport, Connecticut, June 1976: the small American metropolis of sailing awaits the lone sailors of the Atlantic

Just before the start Tabarly had said, 'I hope we get hard weather.' Pépé, as his crew named him, was to get what he asked for!

This fifth race across the Atlantic, which had begun in a spirit of high adventure, was to develop as the days went by into an extraordinary epic. Newport, the goal of the 125 craft, had never seemed as far away as it did in June 1976. None of them reached it within the expected time and, tragically, some never got there at all. This Ostar, which marked the bicentenary of the United States of America, was to be the hardest race ever run between single-handers, and indeed one of the strangest and loneliest ordeals of the sea. Despite its severe hardships and tragedies, it was also to be one of the most exciting and magnificent races in the long history of sail.

One

1876: Alfred Johnson The first man to cross the Atlantic single-handed

As on every other day of the year Alfred Johnson was quietly getting in his lines. The cold waters of the Grand Banks of Newfoundland had yielded their usual harvest of halibut. He was in no hurry to get back in spite of the impending storm, for he knew that his dory could stand up to any weather although she was no more than an open boat 16 foot overall. Such boats had outridden many a storm that could founder an ocean-going schooner. He had often asked himself whether his fine dory could not carry him across the Atlantic, and that question had now become a challenge. That morning in 1876 was not quite like other mornings for within a few weeks the United States of America would be 100 years old, a centenary which young America had every intention of honouring fully, a centenary that fired the imagination of every citizen to show the world that this was indeed a land of men.

There was an idea doing its rounds among the seamen of the New England shore that somewhere there might be found a man tough enough to sail alone across the wide seas that separated the New World from the land of their forebears. This would be the very thing to show the world the quality of the American sailor. A few days later Alfred Johnson was asking himself whether he was not indeed the man to meet the occasion, a challenge which was not perhaps so mad after all.

He turned his dory towards his home at Gloucester; the sea grew more violent with the rising wind and while he bailed he muttered to himself: 'I shall have to deck her over a bit if I am to carry provisions for the voyage; and as for her rig she must have at least four sails – a mainsail, a foresail, a jib and perhaps a big square sail for following winds. She must carry ballast too if she is to be seaworthy because the Atlantic can be pretty rough.'

And so, early in 1876, Johnson decided to take a trip to Liverpool, the home of his ancestors. He decked in and ballasted his dory like a fishing smack and raised the sole to form a sort of bilge which, according to his expert friends, might also serve as a watertight compartment.

He fitted out at Gloucester. The weather was fine on 15 June, but his first week at sea gave him little satisfaction. His compass proved unreliable, which may well have been due to the iron ballast, which he restowed when he put into port again on 22 June. On the 25th bystanders on the quay at Shake Harbour in Nova Scotia were amused to see him put in there and the fisher folk thought his *Centennial* the most fantastic centenary folly of their American neighbours. Full to bursting the little craft had a freeboard up to the gunwales of barely 18 inches and just room for a man to stretch his legs among the sails and stores. 'If *Centennial* doesn't sink he'd be wise to turn back right away,' they said, and in spite of his friends' high opinion of young Alfred there were few who thought he had a chance of surviving the voyage. There was no chorus of farewells and not a single newspaper sent a reporter to witness the last hours on land of that simple fisherman.

They were still talking about him that evening in the little taverns along the quay after *Centennial* had disappeared over the horizon, but generally in the past tense, as they did of that Red Indian whose story some of them remembered over their ale.

According to some of these ancient mariners, long ago in the Kingdom of Spain, in the Middle Ages when nobody knew what shape the earth was, a man was found one day washed up on the beach, lying beside a primitive boat hollowed from a tree trunk. 'His skin was the colour of copper,' they said, 'not sun-burnt but like that of our Indians over here; it must have been some years before Christopher Columbus came our way. The man spoke some incomprehensible language and at first they thought he was in a delirium. He was taken to their bishop but died very soon

Alfred Johnson, who on 25 June 1876 left Shake Harbour, Nova Scotia, and sailed single-handed to Liverpool, England, arriving on 17 August

afterwards. Later it was thought that he might have been one of our American Indians who had crossed the Atlantic, but he took his secret with him to the grave. As for that poor Johnson, well he's gone and it's far from certain that he will ever fetch up some day, far away, like that Indian did.'

Thirty-four days had come and gone since 25 June and Alfred Johnson was still alive and indeed almost within reach of his goal. Although he had with him no modern navigation instruments apart from a simple boat compass, he reckoned that Cape Clear, his intended landfall, was not more than 250 miles away. He knew at all events that he was unlikely to run aground since he practically never slept through the night, bracing himself against the sides of the dory to steer when it was really rough. He had been able to husband his meagre rations, rendered the more spartan when he had lost overboard in a squall everything that was not stowed away below. He had survived a violent squall that had forced him to lower the short mast and make it fast before putting out a sea anchor to moderate the onslaught of wind and wave. The old stratagem worked and on 2 August he was again in full command of the boat; the squall didn't shake him or make him turn back. But Johnson had underestimated what the ocean might have in store, for a devastating storm now arose. The 16-foot cockleshell was tossed about in every direction and again he had to lower the mast and put out the sea anchor. But it was no use, *Centennial* broached

Newport in 1876

to, heeled over and capsized; he could do no more. Then followed the desperate ordeal of shipwreck. Johnson hung on, struggling to save himself from drowning.

For what seemed an interminable length of time he strove to get the dory upright again for his life depended on it, and with an effort born of despair he succeeded in righting her in spite of the heavy ballast. Exhausted, he dragged himself on board and surveyed the extent of the damage. The bitts had held the mast; the sails were full of water, but that didn't matter. What was serious was that there was now hardly any fresh water left on board and the last of the food that had not gone overboard was soaked in sea water. The wind and the rain increased in violence.

Five days later, 150 miles off Cape Clear, the crew of the brig *Alfredon* sighted what they took at first to be wreckage. They found the American, bearded, emaciated and soaked to the skin, and made ready to take him on board. But he would have none of it and only accepted some of their bread and fresh water and, without leaving the dory, again turned her head towards Europe.

He was sighted by several other vessels as he sailed through more heavy weather. First of all there was the three-masted barque of the Mexico – Liverpool line whose captain vainly tried to persuade the intrepid mariner to stay on board and quietly take to his boat again a few miles off Cape Clear. Of course he refused, and went on his way. The brig *Maggie Gander* shortened sail and kept

26

him in sight for a while. When he was finally given an exact position by the *Prince Lombardo* he was only fifty-three miles from Wexford Head.

On 10 August 1876 he sighted the western coast of Pembrokeshire and the *Centennial* quietly put into the little port of Abercastle. The Welshmen who saw this living skeleton step from his dory had no idea what he had achieved in those forty-six days. Nobody then thought it possible for a man to cross the Atlantic except in a ship of some size.

After only two days' rest Johnson set off again and reached his ancestral home of Liverpool on 17 August, where he discovered several members of his family and spent his time with them, quite unnoticed by the rest of the world. The voyage had taken so long that it was too late for him to send *Centennial* back to America in time for the United States centenary exhibition.

The America of 1876 failed to acclaim Alfred Johnson as a hero and there was no triumphant return to his native land for that poor halibut fisherman. Nevertheless, he had accomplished an extraordinary feat and in so doing had shown that an American sailor was as good as any English sailor whatsoever – but on the American seaboard they knew that very well already! Not one newspaper published a single line about him, for that was before the era of idols of the press, so when he got home it was back to his fishing lines. No doubt his exploit was a talking point in the East Coast taverns for years to come and he was pleased to find himself dubbed 'the centennarian'. He never committed his experiences to writing for the vogue for personal memoirs was still to come. His single-handed voyage was unique, but it was not an exciting race; such a race had yet to be conceived.

This remarkable illustration, taken from a retouched photograph or an old print worn with age, is one of the rare treasures held by the Mystic Seaport Museum, Connecticut. It shows Alfred Johnson at the helm of his 18-foot dory Centennial *when he was preparing for his transatlantic voyage*

Two

1891: William Andrews and Si Lawlor The first transatlantic race

On this occasion people flocked to Boston to witness the start of the longest boat race ever. The nineteenth-century town, the preserve of American aristocracy, was already the principal port of Massachusetts and in June 1891 the challenge thrown down by the sons of two of the leading families, the Lawlors and the Andrews, had caused quite a stir. The usually solemn local press was full of it. Fifteen years had gone by since Johnson's famous voyage, fifteen years during which not a few mariners had attempted with varying degrees of success to follow that halibut fisherman. Some had paid for their rashness with their lives, some had got no further than the mouth of the bay and the story of their misadventures no further than the columns of local news. But this was to be quite an event if only because of the personalities of the two contestants.

William Andrews was no casual amateur for he already held one Atlantic record, having made history in 1878 by an Atlantic crossing in a boat only 19 feet overall. Against everyone's advice he had set out to beat the record of that extraordinary husband and wife team, Mr and Mrs Thomas Carpo, who to the amazement of all the old hands in America and Europe had crossed the ocean a few weeks earlier in the *New Bedford*, a cockleshell of 19½ feet. And so in the *Nautilus*, some 7 inches shorter than the *New Bedford*, he also, with his younger brother Asa as crew, succeeded in braving the dangers of the sea. The Andrews brothers were resolved not to perish from hunger or thirst, for they had taken on plenty of provisions and even ballasted her with barrels of fresh water that could be refilled with sea water when empty. Leaving South Boston on 7 June 1878, they rounded the Lizard on 30 July before putting into the sandy inlet of Mullion Cove.

Provoked by the feat of Frederich Norman, who in the 16-foot *Little Western* in 1880 had given himself the pleasure of beating the record for 'the smallest boat to cross the Atlantic', Andrews set out once more, this time alone in the *Dark Secret* of 14 feet 3 inches overall; some contemporary accounts even say 12 feet 9 inches. There are indeed several contradictory accounts of his departure, although nearly 30,000 spectators had come to see *Dark Secret* take to the water on 17 June 1888. It is also true that this time the undertaking was sure to be noticed, because it was sponsored by the *New York World*.

After two months of struggle Andrews gave up, this time defeated by *Dark Secret*'s want of stability and by the growing fatigue of sixty days and sixty nights of solitary navigation. But all the same he succeeded in interesting the public in the attempt, thanks to an idea that had made the project possible and which almost a hundred years later enabled Alain Colas to finance the building of a 236-foot yacht. Throughout the voyage he sent in reports to the newspaper, having taken with him a supply of little waterproof bags into which he slipped short extracts from his log before passing them over to the ships he met with.

This setback had done nothing to deter the William Andrews of 1891. Now thirty-eight years old and feeling that he had gained an experience in seamanship that he lacked in his earlier attempts, the former piano maker made ready for another voyage, but this time in a slightly bigger boat, a 15-footer called *Mermaid*, smaller indeed than the record-breaking *Little Western* and only a little longer than *Dark Secret*. As ever, Andrews clung to the idea of the retractable centre-board and it was this that puzzled observers, who remarked that *Mermaid* might be the ideal boat for shallow waters, with her flat bottom and a centre-board you could easily raise where it shoaled, but for an ocean voyage simply ridiculous because there were no shoals to worry about, and most of all because a centre-board would reduce the hull resistance and also make her less watertight. This was almost the only point of

William Andrews (right) and his brother Asa

difference between the boats of the two contenders in the race.

Lawlor had also chosen a boat of very modest size for this first of all the Atlantic races. To beat his rival he wanted a boat that was light and handled well even in a moderate sea. In this he was assisted by his father, an eminent naval architect already well known for his more serious work. He designed a 15-foot plaything for his son; with arms extended one's hands were over her sides. She had a suitable rig and only her name, *Sea Serpent*, was out of keeping. 'One would have thought,' as people laughingly said when they saw Si Lawlor's boat, 'that she was more like a little maggot!' They asked themselves if Lawlor Junior had not gone mad, for hitherto they had regarded him as a serious-minded young man, particularly after his fine voyage two years before from New York to le Havre, although his boat *Neversink*, no less than 30 feet in length, was almost swamped on several occasions.

But, learning nothing from past experience, Lawlor had decided to tempt fate in a vessel where there was not only insufficient stowage for a reasonable amount of food and fresh water but even for bedding. The only possible explanation for such apparent folly lies in the deep-seated rivalry between the two men.

Both *Sea Serpent* and *Mermaid,* which got just as much publicity, had every reason to arouse the surprise and admiration of the good people of Boston. They became the favourite topics of conversation among seafarers of the East Coast, while their size and design fanned the fever of speculation that grew and grew once they had made up their minds to attempt the Atlantic.

Late in the evening of 23 June 1891 there were still many people waiting at the end of the quay for a last glimpse of the two small sails on the horizon, and on the way home bets were being freely laid. But Lawlor had few backers for he had chosen the northern route, the route fraught with storm and danger that Johnson had followed in *Centennial*. Andrews in *Mermaid* had chosen the southern route, to Spain by way of the Azores, longer but more prudent. All the same, those who backed Andrews lost their money.

Fifty-five long days after the start Andrews was still far from land, weary and almost at the end of his supply of food. He still had 700 miles to go before reaching Spain. The southerly winds had been exceptionally light and he no longer had any illusions — unless Lawlor had met with some serious reverse he must already be safe in harbour. Then things took a turn for the worse. The storm which sprang up on 18 August almost proved fatal to *Mermaid*; she turned over with her centre-board up like a blade of grass and he hung on to it with the last of his strength. After minutes that seemed like days he managed to right her. He was alive – but for how long? He had escaped drowning, but there was nothing left on board, no food and not a drop of water to drink. He had long since left the main shipping lanes and to encounter another vessel was his only chance of survival.

The first day of burning sun crept slowly by without a sail in sight and that night Andrews still gazed into the darkness in vain. Another day and another night came and went, the minutes dragged on, and with each day his failing strength ebbed away. Almost five days and nights had gone by before he closed his eyes and wondered for the last time whether Lawlor had fared any better.

By then Lawlor had already been comfortably installed in a pleasant English house for the past seventeen days; it had taken him no more than forty-five days to reach the coast of Cornwall, on 5 August 1891, and after that even his critics were forced to admire the achievement of the ship-builder's son. In those seventeen days he had plenty of time to talk about the crossing, which, however, he described as 'without incident'.

In this Lawlor may be classed with the modern type of hero who never has much to say about the difficulties he meets with at sea. An account of the voyage discovered by Humphrey Barton and quoted in his book *Atlantic Aventurers* reveals quite a different story. A contemporary issue of the *Western Morning News* reveals that on 1 July Lawlor gave himself a nasty fright when, belaying a rope with insufficient care, he soon found himself overboard in the middle of the ocean. Fortunately for him the sea was fairly smooth and, as throughout the voyage, he had a line about his waist and made fast to the boat. With some effort he was able to get back on board.

Seventeen days later, when he was running before a squall, he was unable to prevent *Sea Serpent* from being knocked down by a heavy sea. She filled rapidly and Lawlor sprang onto the keel to get her upright. Once again the safety harness saved his life. He was wearing three jackets and rubber sea boots, very heavy when full of water, and he lost his hold on the keel; it was only thanks to the harness that he was able to grasp the gunwale and with immense effort hoist himself into the half-swamped boat.

Again, on 24 July, Lawlor had taken advantage of a light breeze to allow himself a well-earned rest. At midnight he was awakened by a rasping sound which he thought might be some big fish frisking against the bottom of the boat. When he tried to get to sleep again he felt *Sea Serpent* shaking violently and once on deck he realized that he was involved with a giant shark, or perhaps some unknown cetacean, that was trying to wreck or break up his frail craft – the account speaks only of 'a monster' that was doing its best to send *Sea Serpent* and her skipper to the bottom.

Lawlor got hold of a rocket, wrapped it in a newspaper and lit the five-second fuse. He threw the lot overboard in the direction of the monster, which flung itself at him just as the charge went off with a deafening roar. 'There was a great commotion in the water, it did not blow the shark's head off but it put him to flight.'

The winner of the first Transatlantic Race is sparing of details in his narrative and perhaps this was because even the remarkable adventures he survived were nothing in comparison with what Andrews had to endure. It was the steamship *Elbruz* that saved the life of his unfortunate rival.

On 22 August the *Elbruz,* cruising off the coast of Spain, sighted what seemed to be an abandoned wreck. The captain immediately altered course towards her and discovered an apparently lifeless body lying in the bottom of the boat. William Andrews was at his last gasp, but they got him on board and managed to bring him back to life. The Boston sailor's life was spared on that occasion, but both he and Lawlor were doomed, years later, to meet their deaths in the Atlantic.

Andrews never admitted defeat and three years later set sail once more in an even smaller vessel, the *Sapolio*, 14½ feet overall. He did not want to risk losing his stores and gear this time and she was almost fully decked. Those who saw her for the first time called her the 'floating cradle' and the name stuck, but all the same he made a successful crossing and, although it took him eighty-four days, he broke the record for the smallest boat yet to do so. This was his last major exploit before he was lost at sea without a trace.

Ten years after the famous race Lawlor also decided to brave the Atlantic again, this time to mark the dawn of the twentieth century. And this time his wife sailed with him, but they were never to be seen again.

With this first race across the ocean Lawlor and Andrews inscribed their names upon the scroll of heroes of the Atlantic and, without knowing it, they were the pioneers of what was to become, seventy years later, the greatest of all yacht races. To their contemporaries, however, it was another man, Howard Blackburn, who was the hero at the turn of the century.

Above and above right: On 25 February 1883 Howard Blackburn and Tom Welch were on their way to retrieve their fishing lines when a storm swept them away from the fishing schooner. They were unable to regain the vessel: Tom Welch died and Blackburn lost all his fingers as a result of frostbite – he had let his hands freeze to the oars to enable him to continue rowing

Right: Blackburn setting out on 7 June 1903 to cross the Atlantic in his 17-foot dory America

Three

1883-1901: Howard Blackburn An indestructible Newfoundlander

On 1 January 1901, one man tried to organize a second transatlantic race. Just ten years after the race between Lawlor and Andrews, Howard Blackburn made known through the newspapers his intention to challenge any other sailor from Boston to Lisbon, he even deposited the stake money with the Gloucester Yacht Club. The start of what he hoped would be the first real ocean challenge was fixed for the afternoon of 9 June 1901. But alas he sailed alone, for nobody took up the challenge. Not one of the braggarts who often held forth over a glass of bourbon in the Eastern Yacht Club was prepared to match the stake.

One cannot really blame them, for that Newfoundlander seemed indestructible, and at the age of forty-two bore the indelible marks left by the legend that surrounded him. The man whom nobody would challenge had lost all the fingers of both hands in the icy waters of the North Atlantic. But in spite of that, or perhaps because of it, he had never given up the sea. His exploits have become a saga, retold by Jean Merrien and Paul Budker, to whom we owe the following account.

On 25 February 1883 Howard Blackburn had set out in his dory from the schooner *Grace L. Fears* with his usual companion Tom Welch to get in their lines. It was a flat calm sea but they had not got in half the lines before the wind got up and began to blow harder; it shifted to the north-west and rose to gale force with driving snow that reduced the visibility to a few yards. Blowing from this quarter, the dory was soon down wind of the schooner and, the situation becoming dangerous, Blackburn and Welch got in their

lines in all haste, took to the oars and rowed with all their might towards the ship. They rowed for a long while in the half light of storm and snow until, thinking that they must have passed the schooner, they let go the grapnel and waited for the weather to clear so that they could rejoin their ship.

It snowed all night and with all their strength they could make no headway against wind and sea, but knowing that it was now a matter of life and death they again weighed anchor and took to the oars, rowing with a desperation born of the will to live. But the wind was so violent and the sea so rough that they could not keep the boat head to wind. The cold increased and the dory was so covered with ice that they jettisoned their cargo of fish to lighten her, all but one twenty pound mackerel; of course they had neither food nor fresh water on board for fishermen were not in the habit of taking any provisions with them when out working their lines.

The two men bailed all through the night and broke away the ice as it froze on to the boat. When the day dawned they found themselves alone on a stormy sea, adrift and already out of sight of the schooner. The seas were so heavy and the waves so high and threatening that the dory was in constant danger of filling and capsizing. After a while they succeeded in getting her head on to the waves and while Tom Welch steadied her with the oars Blackburn improvised a sea anchor.

To get on with the job he had taken off his gloves and thrown them in the bottom of the boat. Welch had meanwhile grabbed a bucket to bail out the water that was pouring in and by mischance Blackburn's gloves went overboard with the first bucketful. It was an irreparable loss although Blackburn did not worry about it at

---

Howard Blackburn: he became a legend in his time through his astonishing sea voyages

the time; he streamed his sea anchor and it had an immediate effect, so that the two men were at last able to enjoy a little relative quiet.

It was then that Blackburn discovered that he had lost all feeling in his hands. A thought flashed through his mind: 'If my hands freeze I shall not be able to hold an oar, but even if I am to lose my hands they can at least still be of some use to us.'

Without wasting time he rallied his remaining strength, bent his numbed fingers round the shaft of an oar and waited for them to freeze. In twenty minutes Blackburn's hands had stiffened into a shape that made it possible for him to hold an oar. He made sure of this by repeatedly forcing the shaft into the nerveless circles that had once been hands and found that he could row as well as his friend.

All that day they had to bail ceaselessly and break away the ice that grew so thick that it threatened to overturn the boat. Breaking the ice with frozen hands was a terrible task and Blackburn, who had cut his right hand, thought of using one of his stockings for a glove. It slipped from his injured hand and was lost, and before long he knew that the bare foot in his sea boot had frozen too. But, in order not to add to his friend's miseries, he said nothing of this to Welch.

The storm raged on and the heavy seas that broke over the dory made it necessary for the two castaways to continue to bail without ceasing. In the evening, his resistance sapped by hunger, thirst and exhaustion, Welch became delirious and begged for water. Blackburn could only give him pieces of ice to suck and try to cheer him up, but in vain; he died before morning. At dawn Blackburn found him stiff and cold, already shrouded in ice from the frozen spray.

Another day went by, and another night. With nothing to eat or drink and without sleep, he bailed away mechanically in the storm and the cold with his dead companion at his side. Almost bereft of hope he struggled on, feeling himself already cut off from the land of the living and stoically awaiting the wave that must swamp the boat and send them to the bottom.

On the third day the wind dropped and the sea moderated. At sunrise it was almost calm. Blackburn took in his sea anchor and started to row in what he thought was the direction of land. He managed the oars with the greatest difficulty but eventually succeeded in getting some way on the boat. The friction of the wood against his frozen hands, in his own words, 'tore away pieces of flesh as big as a half-dollar!'. But he felt no pain and rowed on until evening. Night came, he shipped his oars and lay to the sea anchor; fearing to sleep he crouched in the bottom of the boat, his arms around a thwart, rocking backwards and forwards all night and struggling against the drowsiness and fatal lassitude that he felt creeping over him. Dawn came at last and Blackburn set off again, toiling at the oars.

Towards midday, the land was at last in sight and in the afternoon he put into the narrow mouth of a small river where he made fast to a little jetty beside a deserted cabin. He had now been five days without food, water or sleep but that was not the end of the ordeal, for that desolate inlet had nothing to offer. He passed his first night on land stretched on the bare boards of the hut, cold, miserable and feeling that all was lost, but yet mustering sufficient

After he lost his fingers Blackburn was unable to go back to fishing and he opened a bar (above) in the main street of Gloucester, Massachusetts, its walls adorned with artists' impressions of his experience with Tom Welch. Later Blackburn set off to dig for gold in the Klondyke (right), but broke a leg. When he had recovered he returned to his first love, the sea, and built himself a boat in which to cross the Atlantic single-handed

strength to get up and walk about when he felt himself falling asleep.

Next day, aware of the necessity of finding some habitation where he could get help, he decided to row further up the river; weakened by all that he had been through and with frostbitten hands that would hardly hold the oars, he made slow progress and only on the following morning finally reached a fishing village.

Little River, as the place was called, had indeed not much to offer, for the poverty of its inhabitants was near to destitution. Nevertheless, they flocked to his aid and one of them, Frank Lishman, took him home and did what he could, for the place had neither doctor nor medicines. Thanks to his magnificent constitution Blackburn survived his terrible experience, but his hands were irreparably frostbitten and within two months he had lost all his fingers and the extremities of his thumbs as well as parts of his right foot and ears.

Now a cripple, he was unable to go back to fishing, but enough money was raised by subscription to enable him to open a bar, where his old friends would gladly join him in a glass of beer and talk of the things that interested them all – boats, fishing and the sea.

Blackburn patiently learnt to make the best use of what

remained of his hands and everyone in Gloucester thought that he would end his days quietly ashore, that his days at sea were over. But they could not have been more wrong.

One day he left Gloucester in a fishing schooner which a group of them had bought and fitted out for a voyage to the Klondyke to prospect for gold. The voyage itself, round North and South America, was uneventful, although of course they got their share of heavy weather rounding Cape Horn. They reached San Francisco without mishap, but there Blackburn broke his leg and had to return home overland. For the next eight months the people of Gloucester watched him hobbling about on crutches. Nobody imagined that this cripple was soon to astonish not only his countrymen but everyone, in the new world and the old, concerned with the sea.

When he had recovered the use of his legs and given up his crutches Blackburn set about building a boat with his own fingerless hands: length 29 feet 6 inches, beam 8 feet 6 inches, draught 5 feet. While he was building the boat he had no idea what he would do with her until one of the people who often came to watch him at work happened one day to remark that it would be amusing to sail from Gloucester in America to Gloucester in England. Blackburn liked the idea, and when his boat, which he

had christened *Great Western*, was launched and rigged he took on board enough of everything for a single-handed Atlantic crossing.

He set sail at 2 o'clock in the afternoon on 18 June 1899, and all Gloucester was there on the quay to see him hoist sail and handle the boat perfectly with his stumps of hands. He reached Gloucester in England on 18 August at 9 o'clock in the morning, after sixty-one days at sea, to a rousing welcome which he little expected; it did not seem to him that he had done anything out of the ordinary. For him sixty-one days was mere dawdling – pleasure sailing. He sold *Great Western* in London and took passage back to the United States determined to do better next time.

Blackburn was a disappointed man when he again set out in June 1901, for he had found no other contestant in the race of which he had dreamed. But for want of a competitor he now set himself a

sterner challenge, a race against time. With his new yacht *Great Republic,* which had been specially built for it, he would establish a new record for the ocean crossing. But he was unlucky.

First of all he was unlucky with other vessels, for he was following the steamship route and they could not see him in foggy weather – *Great Republic* was even smaller than *Great Western*, only 24 feet 6 inches. On several occasions he narrowly missed being run down and one steamer passed him so close that her wake broke over him. The danger called for the greatest vigilance and he had to keep awake all the time until he finally settled for a safer, less frequented route that would unfortunately not break any records. Then at last he could revert to his usual 'leisurely' routine of nineteen hours on watch and five in semi-somnolence.

Then he was unlucky with the wind, which died away off the Azores before rising to such force that he had to run under trysail only; but at least it was blowing in the right direction and Blackburn sailed on through the storm. But two days later he had to heave to and had just accomplished this with some difficulty when a freighter, pitching and rolling in an alarming way, came as close to *Great Republic* as was prudent. 'Shall we take you on board?' hailed an officer from the bridge above him. 'No thanks,' he shouted back. 'Well, you'll soon change your mind,'

Above: Posing for Adolph Kupinel at the wheel of Cruising Club *in Gloucester harbour. At seventy Howard Blackburn was still a colourful figure in the United States*

Right: Blackburn's Great Republic, *the 25-foot sloop with clipper bow and boom extending beyond the transom in which he tried to establish a new transatlantic record in 1901*

they shouted, 'so we'll keep company with you for a bit.' The big steamer kept station on the little yacht, waiting for the lone mariner to abandon ship. Seeing this, Blackburn got under way again and resumed his course. For twenty minutes the steamer followed *Great Republic,* which her skipper was handling with difficulty among the high breaking seas. Then, seeing that the little sloop needed no help from them, the ship resumed its south-easterly course but not before saluting the intrepid navigator with three blasts on her whistle.

When he left Gloucester people thought Blackburn would be lucky if he made Europe within fifty days, but thirty-eight days after his departure he sighted Cape Espichel, some fifteen miles south of the mouth of the Tagus, after a voyage of 3,000 miles. On 18 July at 2 o'clock in the afternoon, exactly thirty-nine days out of Gloucester, his star-spangled flag flying proudly at the peak, he picked up a mooring in Lisbon harbour.

Great Republic came back to the States on board a steamer, and Blackburn put her behind his shop where any interested customer could come to look at her. But the little sloop, like her skipper, could not endure idleness for long and hearing of the Great Lakes Blackburn fitted her out and set sail again, this time on fresh water. He traversed the Lakes and sailed down the Mississippi, only to suffer shipwreck on the Florida coast.

Returning to Gloucester Blackburn was seized with the idea of repeating Johnson's exploit. He acquired a dory, half-decked and rigged with mainsail and jib, and set out again for Europe.

This was in mid-summer and he could reasonably expect fair weather, or at least a moderate sea. Far from it; once off-shore he encountered high seas and violent winds and before he had even reached Cape Sable, the south-western corner of Nova Scotia, the dory was capsized in a squall and laid flat on the water. Undismayed, Blackburn managed to get her upright again and went on his way but before long, between Nova Scotia and Newfoundland, he had capsized again twice. Deciding that luck was against him he wisely returned to Gloucester – and nobody can blame him!

He lived on quietly at Gloucester and in 1930 still kept his little shop in High Street, where sailors would come to talk as ever of boats, fishing and the sea. On the walls there hung the simple paintings done by an old shipmate which portrayed the episodes of that terrible adventure, from which at the outset of his career their host had miraculously escaped with his life.

Blackburn lived to the age of seventy, but although his exploits won him well-earned praise, another man of those times impressed his contemporaries even more.

Joshua Slocum (left) on board Libertade, *the boat he built to bring his family home after they were shipwrecked in Brazil*

Four

1895-1898: Joshua Slocum Round the world single-handed

Joshua Slocum in 1906

At the close of the nineteenth century no one could have expected that Joshua Slocum was soon to accomplish a feat that no other sailor had ever attempted – to sail a boat round the world alone. He was a little-known Nova Scotia fisherman (but, like Blackburn, a naturalized American), and a captain without a ship. The remarkable circumnavigation that he was eventually to make began with a wide detour, over and back across the Atlantic single-handed, and took in 46,000 miles overall, a memorable odyssey in itself but hardly more than a postscript to the romantic chapter of accidents that had befallen him in the preceding years. Nevertheless, in 1895 everything seemed to have turned out well in the end for this man over whom the caprice of the sea seemed to gain no mastery.

Joshua Slocum should have been a farmer and no doubt he should have called himself Slocombe. He should have been a farmer because that was his father's modest livelihood, and Slocombe because that was the way they spelt their name before it changed over the years and the little Joshua came into the world under the name of Slocum. But when Joshua was born on 20 February 1844 he was still a Slocombe by descent, a family which had come to America at the time of the War of Independence. Some say that the Slocombes were Quakers, others that they were descended from the great Captain Slocombe. One thing is certain: Joshua was the son of John Slocum and Sarah Sothern, the daughter of the lighthouse keeper at Westport. The Slocums came to live there when Sarah, feeling her health failing, begged her husband to return to the place of her birth. She had indeed borne eleven children in twenty-five years and the hard life on the upland farm where John Slocum laboured his often frozen soil did her no good.

Sarah Slocum died not far from her father's lighthouse at the mouth of the Bay of Fundy. Six years later Joshua left school. At first he was delighted for he was weary of the four walls of his classroom in the cloister of Westport. In a land where nobody talked about anything except boats and where babes paddled on the ocean shore, he often dreamed of the exploits of that famous Captain Simon Slocombe. But alas, the work for which his father had set him free from his lessons was even worse than his desk at school. It was no longer a question of looking dreamily out of the window but just of making as many leather boots for sailors as possible in order to help feed the hungry mouths of their large family. Life with a father bent over his work for six days of the week and a deacon of the church on Sundays had little attraction for a growing boy, and Joshua still dreamt of the ocean and of wide open spaces in the little house swarming with brothers and sisters. He ran away for the first time when he was fourteen and at sixteen parted forever from a father with whom he got on worse and worse.

On his first voyage he managed to get as far as Dublin, and then to Hong Kong and Batavia (Djakarta). It was the inauguration of a notable career that was to take him several times round Cape Horn before he rose from ship's boy to mate and, at the age of twenty-eight, to captain, the first steps in a life-long devotion to the sea. He took out American citizenship at San Francisco and married in Sydney a pretty American girl with some Indian blood. He ran his ship aground in Alaska and then built his first boat to salvage the cargo. His first child was conceived at Honolulu and named Victor somewhere off San Francisco. He set up as a naval architect in Manila, fished for cod along the Russian coast and became the father of twins somewhere at sea. His ports of call bore such romantic names as Shanghai, Nagasaki and Vladivostok – but never Westport. When he next saw his father it was twenty-two years since he had left home. He wished him to see in his old age that his son had made a success of life and invited him on board the new sailing ship *Northern Light* of which he had just been given command.

Joshua was no longer a nobody; he was one of the leading American sea captains and from time to time in the news, as Walter Teller has shown in his biography, *The Search for Captain Slocum* (André Deutsch and Charles Scribner's Sons). His reputation grew with his adventures. On one occasion he is reported as having quelled a mutiny on board that had cost the life of his second-in-command, on another as saving the lives of several shipwrecked mariners in storm-tossed seas. All the same, Slocum often found it difficult to recruit good men; the scapegraces he sometimes signed on a little too readily led him a weary dance and often had to be put in irons. He was not sorry to take command of a smaller ship at a time when steam was beginning to dominate in the major ports. *Aquidneck* was as comfortable as one could wish, and ideal for his wife Virginia who went with him everywhere and never complained of the adventurous life she led with Captain Joshua. Far from it; she shared that life with enthusiasm, a help to him over and above the sufficiently difficult task of bringing up their children and keeping house on board.

With *Aquidneck*, Slocum entered upon a long series of misfortunes. Virginia died on the first voyage. Joshua was then forty and his biographers all agree that he never got over the loss. However, a year and a half later he married Henrietta, a young woman eighteen years his junior; their honeymoon voyage turned into a terrifying series of misadventures that went on for three years. First of all she saved her husband's life, and no doubt her own too, by alerting him to a noise she had heard behind their cabin door in the middle of the night. Some of the crew he had recruited were about to mutiny and he had to fire a shot at one of them to escape with a whole skin.

Then there were the epidemic diseases that raged in South America; there some of his crew fell victim to small pox and he was unable to unload his cargo. Finally, *Aquidneck*, by no means the seaworthy vessel that he thought when he bought her, ran aground on a dangerous bar and broke up in the heavy swell. Slocum was a ruined man.

Captain without a ship, the father of a family without a roof, he was still undismayed. He sold the wreck and, as he had done in Alaska and at Manila, he again turned boat builder. This time he was his own carpenter, caulker and labourer, for his crew, paid off out of the proceeds of the sale, had left him to sign on with less unfortunate captains. He took on his family instead, his wife Henrietta sewed sails with anything they could salvage from *Aquidneck* and his eldest son Victor became his invaluable assistant.

Although he lacked the tools necessary for building a boat he managed to complete the task – a strange craft, the *Libertade*, a cross between a Newfoundland fishing dory and a Japanese sampan.

In the early summer of 1888, with his wife and his two sons for crew, Slocum sailed away from Brazil in this odd little boat less than 36 feet in length. Their voyage was a long chapter of exciting adventures that took them to Rio, Pernambuco and Barbados before they reached Washington on the day after Christmas. They were the delight of the newspaper reporters and the dark and bearded profile of the man, seldom seen without his hat and coat, was to become the archetypal image of the proud and undaunted Yankee captain.

Yet at the age of forty-eight he was a captain without command, and down to his last penny, so he was very glad indeed to accept, as a present from an old friend of the family, Captain Eben Pierce, a sloop that had been built nearly a hundred years before. All the same he was somewhat taken aback when he first set eyes on her passing the days of her well-earned retirement in an apple orchard. Then the happy thought occurred to him. The *Spray* might not be fit to put to sea but he could, at least, use her as a full-scale model and make a copy. His experience in building *Libertade* was to serve him well, and this time he selected the best local oak for her keel and applied himself to the first phase of that wonderful epic – the bringing of *Spray* to life again.

The task took him thirteen months to complete and meanwhile the old whaling men of those parts would come to cast an eye over the rehabilitation of *Spray*, sometimes with bits of advice and sometimes to help, for these old hands appreciated the stout little craft, of a kind no longer built, and did not fail to say something encouraging. 'A boat fit to sail round the world,' one would remark; or, 'You know her so well by now that you could manage her single-handed to the ends of the earth.' Such comments, taken together, set Slocum thinking as he leaned on his axe for a moment's respite from toil.

When he had finished the caulking, about which he had some misgivings owing to some caustic remarks of passersby who expressed doubts about his competence in that delicate art, he set about painting her – two coats of copper paint on her bottom and two of white on the top sides. It only remained to ship the rudder, and on the very next day *Spray* was afloat again. He was now the master of a fine 36½- foot sloop at the modest cost of $553.63 – not counting the value of his own time of course. But he still had one financial difficulty to overcome. To navigate he needed a chronometer; his own had got rusty after the wreck of the *Aquidneck* and he had not enough money left to put it right.

In March 1894 Joshua Slocum had just celebrated his fiftieth birthday. He had other plans for the boat he had built with his own hands than to hug the shores of Delaware and catch lobsters, which was what she had originally been built for. He never said when exactly he took the decision to set out alone and sail round the world. But when a year later, on 7 May 1895, he fitted out again, it would seem that all his friends in Gloucester were aware of his intentions, as the following account from his book *Sailing Alone Around the World* suggests:

The weather was mild on the day of my departure from Gloucester. On the point ahead, as the *Spray* stood out of the

not only did he spend several pleasant days there and complete his stores, but he was able to get hold of the timepiece he so badly needed. It was a tin clock and kept reasonably good time; the man wanted a dollar and a half for it but that was more than Slocum could afford, and because the face was smashed he was able to beat him down to a dollar.

On 2 July Joshua Slocum finally took his departure from the American continent and in the fascinating log that he kept he faithfully records all that happened on the voyage. Above all he knew how to express what many others have felt since – the feeling of total solitude that overcame him in thick fog.

During these days a feeling of awe crept over me. My memory worked with startling power. The ominous, the insignificant, the great, the small, the wonderful, the commonplace – all appeared before my mental vision in magical succession. Pages of my history were recalled which had been so long forgotten that they seemed to belong to a previous existence. I heard all the voices of the past laughing, crying, telling me what I had heard them tell in many corners of the earth.

The loneliness of my state wore off when the gale was high and I found much work to do. When fine weather returned, then came the sense of solitude, which I could not shake off. I used my voice often, at first giving some order about the affairs of a ship, for I had been told that from disuse I should lose my speech. At the meridian altitude of the sun I called aloud, 'Eight bells,' after the custom on a ship at sea. Again from my cabin I cried to an

cove, was a lively picture, for the front of a tall factory was a flutter of handkerchiefs and caps. Pretty faces peered out of the windows from the top to the bottom of the building, all smiling *bon voyage*. Some hailed me to know where away and why alone. Why? When I made as if to stand in, a hundred pairs of arms reached out, and said come, but the shore was dangerous! The sloop worked out of the bay against a light south-west wind, and about noon squared away off Eastern Point, receiving at the same time a hearty salute – the last of many kindnesses to her at Gloucester.

The dense fog off the northern shores of the United States which those taking part in the Transatlantic Races seventy years later were to encounter at this time of year forced Slocum to put into Yarmouth, not far from Brier Island in Nova Scotia where he had lived as a boy. It was a fruitful visit for him in at least one respect:

After sailing round the world Spray *comes back to her mooring at Providence, Rhode Island, where Slocum is reunited with his wife*

imaginary man at the helm, 'How does she head there?' and again, 'Is she on her course?'

On the morning of 19 July Slocum saw land again for the first time, off the island of Flores in the Azores, and on 4 August he was only a few hours' sail from the little port of Tarifa and the southernmost headland of Spain. The British sailors at their base in Gibraltar, who were to give him a warmer welcome than he had ever met with elsewhere, entertained him as he had never dared to expect. But unfortunately all their kindness could not make up for the unwelcome news that they had to give him. Whereas he thought that he had already completed a good part of his voyage he was soon persuaded that he would have to turn back. His original plan of sailing through the Mediterranean, the Suez Canal and the

Red Sea was upset by a factor which he had too readily overlooked. In North African waters man might prove a more formidable opponent than the weather and nothing escaped the attentions of the pirates, not even a dollar clock, still less a fine little sloop.

On 25 August he sailed again from Gibraltar and set a course for the New World. He wasn't turning back, only going the other way round. The pirates were not long in making him see that he had been wise to change his mind, and that he would do better still not to dally off the coasts of their domain:

Above: Slocum demonstrating how he distilled sea water; there would have been a fire under the bucket

Right: Slocum at sixty-three. He is about to go for a sail on the Potomac near Washington

My plan was, in going down this coast, to haul off-shore, well clear of the land, which hereabouts is the home of pirates; but I had hardly accomplished this when I perceived a felucca making out of the nearest port, and finally following in the wake of the *Spray*. Here I was in the midst of pirates and thieves! I changed my course; the felucca did the same, both vessels sailing very fast, but the distance growing less and less between us. The *Spray* was doing nobly; she was even more than at her best; but, in spite of all I could do, she would broach now and then. She was carrying too much sail for safety. I must reef or be dismasted and lose all, pirate or no pirate. I must reef, even if I had to grapple with him for my life.

I was not long in reefing the mainsail and sweating it up – probably not more than fifteen minutes; but the felucca had in the meantime so shortened the distance between us that I now saw the tufts of hair on the heads of the crew – by which, it is said, Mohammed will pull the villains up into heaven – and they were coming on like the wind. From what I could clearly make out now, I felt them to be the sons of generations of pirates, and I saw by their movements that they were now preparing to strike a blow. The exultation on their faces, however, was changed in an instant to a look of fear and rage. Their craft, with too much sail on, broached to on the crest of a great wave. This one great sea changed the aspect of affairs suddenly as the flash of a gun.

Three minutes later the same wave overtook the *Spray* and shook her in every timber. At the same moment the sheet-strop parted, and away went the main-boom, broken short at the rigging. Impulsively I sprang to the jib-halyards and down-haul, and instantly downed the jib. The head-sail being off, and the helm put hard down, the sloop came up in the wind with a bound. While shivering there, but a moment though it was, I got the mainsail down and secured inboard, broken boom and all. How I got the boom in before the sail was torn I hardly know; but not a stitch of it was broken. The mainsail being secured, I hoisted the jib, and, without looking round, stepped quickly to the cabin and snatched down my loaded rifle and cartridges at hand; for I made mental calculations that the pirate would by this time have recovered his course and be close aboard, and that when I saw him it would be better for me to be looking at him along the barrel of a gun. The piece was at my shoulder when I peered into the mist, but there was no pirate within a mile. The wave and squall that carried away my boom dismasted the felucca outright. I perceived his thieving crew, some dozen or more of them, struggling to recover their rigging from the sea. Allah blacken their faces!

I do not remember to have been more tired before or since in all my life than I was at the finish of that day. Too fatigued to sleep, I rolled about with the motion of the vessel till near

midnight, when I made a shift to dress my fish and prepare a dish of tea. I fully realized now, if I had not before, that the voyage ahead would call for exertions ardent and lasting.

Slocum put in only at Fuerteventura in the Canaries before making the coast of South America. Here began the second part of the most extraordinary sea story of the late nineteenth century, in which Slocum showed that he was not only a great navigator but a marvellous storyteller too, his tales enriched by the bizarre cast of characters and remarkable series of adventures that he encountered along the way.

After sailing alone for three years Joshua Slocum came back to Boston, his point of departure, on 27 June 1898, after a voyage of 46,000 miles that took in every ocean. For all sailors he became one of the heroes of the Atlantic, but above all the first single-handed circumnavigator in history. But although he earned both these distinctions there was still one that the history of sail will never accord to him, that of being the first to sail single-handed across the North Atlantic from east to west. Sailing from Gibraltar to Pernambuco he was 'content' to follow the course of the dominant winds between Europe and America. It was a Frenchman who later opened up the more challenging east – west route.

Five

1923: Alain Gerbault Across the Atlantic east to west

At ten o'clock the wind rose to hurricane force, the waves were blown to pieces, short and vicious, their crests torn away in little whirlpools that unwound into white streaks of foam; they hurled themselves at my little ship as if they would destroy her. But ever she fought her way through the waves, so bravely that I wanted to sing . . .

Then suddenly I saw an enormous wave loom over the horizon . . . It was a thing of beauty, yet of terror, and rolled towards me with the sound of thunder . . .

I had just time to spring into the rigging and was about halfway up the mast when the wave swept wildly over *Firecrest*, which disappeared under tons of water and a welter of spray. The ship staggered and heeled under the shock and I wondered if she would ever come up again. Slowly she emerged from the white water and the great wave swept past . . .

The storm suddenly abated, as if it knew it was beaten and could do nothing to my brave ship.

These were fine and stirring phrases, but the literary style of the man who ventured into the Atlantic in an 11-metre yacht that he called a 'ship' only irritated seasoned mariners. For them Alain Gerbault was (as yet) no sailor but just a romantic adventurer. He had set out to accomplish an unprecedented feat at sea as one might try to beat the 100-yards track record without ever training as an athlete – except that on the race track you would only risk a strained heart, whereas in attempting a first single-handed crossing of the Atlantic from east to west your chances of survival would be infinitely smaller. For if Johnson or Blackburn had found that to sail across the Atlantic alone, even with the prevailing winds, was no small matter, then to choose the same route in reverse and sail against those winds was a challenge indeed. But that was just like Alain Gerbault, a man out of the ordinary who lived with a certain swagger, gleaning laurels in the pursuits that generally attracted the bright young people of the twenties.

From the start he enjoyed several advantages: good looks, a family that could afford to give him a good education and enough intelligence to make use of it. He passed all his examinations and went on to the Polytechnique where, as he says, 'I spent the most wretched years of my life shut up within its high walls.' But his studies at least made it possible for him to go through the war with less hardship; as a pilot he flew above the trenches, and survived.

Above: Alain Gerbault, the first single-hander to sail windward across the Atlantic

Opposite above: Gerbault on board Firecrest

Opposite below: Gerbault's return to Le Havre, France, after his six-year round the world trip.

Alain Gerbault's Firecrest *was a 36-foot cutter with a 3½-ton keel. Leaving Cannes on 25 April 1923 he put in at Gibraltar to refit and left again on 7 June to sail across the North Atlantic from east to west*

The young man from Laval was twenty-one in 1914 and therefore one of the 'lost generation'. The four years that followed spelt danger and disgust for many of his classmates, but for Gerbault they meant aviation and its wartime jargon. As for navigation at sea, he had already tried it when as a child on holiday he had spent a few days with the fishermen of Dinard or

Saint-Malo; Alain the intellectual had 'trembled at their tales of bravery and endurance'.

He came out of the war wearing that most attractive of uniforms, an Air Force pilot officer's, but he soon changed to the wide white ducks fancied by French tennis players of that day. At the best clubs his elegant figure might be seen on the court, or in the stands arm in arm with Suzanne Lenglen the tennis queen; some even thought they were married. Gerbault's star was clearly in the ascendant.

In the bridge clubs too, people remarked on a player who had for his partner a master of the game like Albarran. Gerbault could do anything, or rather anything that was in fashion. But since he was a man of action he longed for something more worthwhile than this limited round – alone over the Atlantic perhaps, in an aeroplane of course since he was a pilot. Then he discovered that the sea held its romance too, a more subtle enchantment. And so the Polytechnique graduate decided to leave the card tables and pseudo-intellectual connections that bored him and set out from Europe for America by a course that none had yet followed alone.

Gerbault the Parisian, Gerbault the engineer, acquired a real yacht, the *Firecrest,* a snug and stoutly built English boat, not indeed a 'ship' but a cleanly built 11-metre cutter of teak on oak frames. With her beam of 2.6 metres, Gerbault thought it was 'the narrowest boat that had ever faced the Atlantic'. He was quite wrong there. Johnson's *Centennial* had a beam of 1.80 metres and Lawlor's *Sea Serpent* only 1.5; but Gerbault was a man for ideas rather than details.

His *Firecrest* was not a new boat, in fact she was a year older than he was; in 1921 she was exactly twenty-nine years old. Her hull was in good shape, but though she had a complete set of sails, including three jibs, topsail and shoulder of mutton sail, they were all old and Gerbault's first mistake was to set out with sails that, as those who saw them remarked, had less than a fifty-fifty chance of getting across the Atlantic in one piece. In the eyes of experienced seamen he made mistake after mistake.

The man who was going to tackle the Atlantic had *Firecrest* brought through the French canals instead of venturing across the Bay of Biscay. He had decided to do a two years' apprenticeship in the Mediterranean. Although the stoutness of her hull and the weight of her keel made her more suitable than any other small boat that had yet crossed the Atlantic, particularly against the possibility of a capsize, in his account of the voyage he harps continually on that possibility. He did not realize either that the boat would require particularly stout gear. He bought his salt meat at Gibraltar, 'so that it would be fresher'; it went bad. He acquired brand new oak barrels for his fresh water; the tannic acid tainted the water and made it undrinkable within a few days.

His troubles began even before he reached the Atlantic. He left Cannes on 25 April 1923, quietly and without public notice. On the second day out the boom gooseneck broke; on the fourth day it was a halyard that parted; it took him eight days to get to Gibraltar. There, instead of replacing defective items he just patched them up and by 6 June 1923 considered that everything was in order for a non-stop crossing to New York. He left Gibraltar on 7 June.

Cautiously, he chose the milder trade-wind route with its sunshine and infrequent gales, the 'southern route' of future

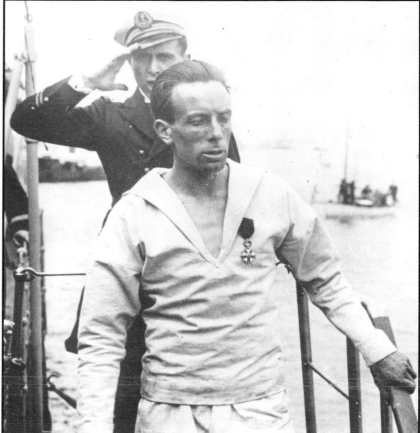

Left: Gerbault's arrival in New York on 5 September 1923 after his east to west Atlantic crossing

Above: After receiving the Légion d'Honneur on his return from sailing round the world

Transatlantic Races. All the same he encountered squalls and variable winds. Off Madeira he resisted the temptation to put in there; by then his sails were already showing signs of weakness and he had only been a fortnight at sea. In July one of the jibs was torn to ribbons, the sheets parted one after the other and so did the topping lift. Even the trysail, which is supposed to be the stoutest, needed some stitches; the graduate had perforce to turn seamstress to keep them in reapir, until by the middle of July he had run short of twine. Worst of all was the water problem, for he had had to throw overboard those new barrels and had only fifty litres for the second half of the voyage, hardly a litre a day if he was to make the same desperately slow progress. And that was an optimistic estimate for next there was a 5-metre split in the mainsail and the jib halyard parted again. Fortunately Gerbault had some luck. He was lucky indeed to survive one mistake that seldom spares those who sail alone – he had ventured far out on the bowsprit without his safety harness and was swept overboard by a wave. By a marvel he managed to grab the bob-stay and haul himself back on board with a strength born of dismay – he was lucky indeed.

He had a lot of bad luck too. The good weather route was not particularly good that summer. Bad weather, high seas, storms and even hurricanes succeeded one another; his stove packed up, he lost his fishing harpoon overboard, he was in danger of being run down by a steamer. He developed a fever and had no drinking water but what he could collect when it rained. That he survived at all was due to the fish he was able to catch with a home made hook. But in spite of all that he refused to put into Bermuda to recoup his strength, still less to refit *Firecrest,* which was becoming more and more battered. He had made a bet with himself that he would make the crossing non-stop and he was not going to let himself lose it.

On 14 September he sighted the American coast at last; it had taken him 101 days to cross the Atlantic, and on 15 September he stepped ashore in New York. Once on land Gerbault the sailor was again Gerbault the super star – photos, interviews, receptions and an American decoration: he was awarded the new Blue Water Medal just established to honour the most deserving yachtsman of the year.

He says that he soon tired of these festivities but all the same he found the American way of life pleasant enough for a while. France acclaimed her hero and his book, *Seul à travers l'Atlantique,* became a bestseller, although it offended captiously critical sailors.

Criticized, admired, and most of all envied, Gerbault grew weary of the noisy world around him and decided on a new project: he would return to France, but this time the other way by making the grand tour, round the world. He took a more cautious approach this time, but still made many of the same mistakes. He made some sensible modifications to *Firecrest,* fitted her out for a long voyage and took stacks of books on board; but he thought he knew his boat well enough to dispense with trying out her new sails. Gerbault left New York on 1 November 1924. More than three months had gone by since his arrival but *Firecrest* was still not really ready for fresh adventures. The first squall stretched his new mainsail, for the cloth should have been allowed to settle into shape. It was spoilt now, and that was only the first of a long chapter of accidents.

But he no longer had the same objective. He had already accomplished one feat, and that achievement had no doubt changed the man. From now on he was under the spell of the open sea and could hope to discover a world very different from the one he had known in Paris and New York. He put in to Bermuda for repairs, and this time without any regrets. Far from it; he spent three months there. 'I am in no hurry,' he said, 'for I take my home with me and I hope I always shall. Every man needs some goal, some mountain-top or distant isle of his own choosing that he must attain by his own efforts, alone and in his own good time.'

He spent three months in Panama. In the Pacific he tarried in the Galapagos, the Gambier Islands and the Marquesas. Then he discovered Polynesia, a world of enchantment in spite of the French administration which attempted to fix on it a straitjacket that he detested. He mixed with the Polynesians and avoided the French officials, who were curious to see this fellow Gerbault. 'I could have nothing in common with them', he said, 'and I was almost as much alone on board *Firecrest* in Papeete as I was in mid-ocean.'

He put in at the Willis Islands, where the natives wanted to make him their chief. It took him six years to sail round the world, a pilgrimage of understanding in which he sought above all to discover the real lives of the native peoples. His was a quest for the deepest truths, leaving the well-beaten paths and scenes already spoilt by a Western civilization that he discounted more and more as he drew nearer home. 'As my journey neared its end I felt a growing sense of dejection. My voyage was almost done and the happiest years of my life were almost over.'

Firecrest reached Cherbourg late in July 1929 after 40,000 miles at sea. He became a national idol, but all the same Gerbault again thought only of getting away. He built a new boat of 10.40 metres' length and called her *Alain Gerbault* because up to the day she was launched he had found no suitable name. He headed for the Pacific once more, where he was to be seen less and less often in the more frequented havens; he was looking for calm and solitude and the companionship of the Polynesians. He thought only of a way to preserve their customs and traditions; like Gauguin and Stevenson he became the champion of their national entity against the invasion of French colonialism. To show his opposition to the law against the wearing of the grass skirt in town, he went about Papeete barefoot in a red *pareo* with white flowers, to which he had

Sourtrouville, 1931. For his last voyage Gerbault built a new yacht which he called Alain Gerbault. *He presented* Firecrest *to the Naval Academy but unfortunately she sank before she reached it. Ten years later Gerbault was found dangerously ill on board the yacht that bore his name and died on 16 December 1941 on the shore of the Banda Sea in the East Indies*

pinned his *Legion d'honneur*. He wandered ever further afield in search of that ideal atoll where he hoped to establish a settlement with his Polynesian friends.

After twenty years of travel and 100,000 miles at sea Gerbault suffered an attack of malaria and was given shelter at Dili on the Portuguese island of Timor. He died there on 16 December 1941. In 1947 the French navy brought his body back to Bora-Bora where he was buried with military honours within sight of his best loved lagoon. He left no descendant in Polynesia in order 'not to adulterate so fine a race', as he himself said. But Gerbault the romantic had set his name on the North Atlantic, by pioneering one of the routes in future Transatlantic Races.

Six

1876-1976: Some Reckless and Wonderful Voyages

Alain Bombard, voluntary castaway, cardiologist and a keen cellist

Gerbault's pioneering journey was not to be the last of the great single-handed transatlantic ventures. Far from it; by opening up a new route from east to west his voyage had ploughed a furrow that other single-handed sailors were to follow in attempting no less remarkable record performances. In the fifty years after the Frenchman's lead, a whole fleet of boats of every kind put out from Europe or from America, and the only thing that their skippers had in common was a courage that many called rashness. Their aims were as various as their boats and the stories they had to tell: the need to get away, to excel, to prove something to the world, or to oneself, to test the limits of human endurance, to carry out some scientific experiment, to establish a position within one's society, or beyond it, to get talked about, or simply to make money.

In 1929, when Gerbault came back to Le Havre from his voyage round the world, Blondie Hasler was still a boy. Thirty years later he was to plan a remarkable single-handed race from England to the United States, the Ostar, his Ostar which was in 1976 to become the greatest single-handed race in the world. But it would never have happened if other men and women of the sea had not achieved alone a host of exploits over the years that followed Gerbault's attempt and shown that the North Atlantic could be the finest setting for a race of giants.

Five years after Gerbault, Captain Romer was to lay down the southern limit of that course – but these race tracks are as variable as the ocean currents themselves. The route that Romer pioneered for single-handed sailors was from Lisbon to the Canaries, the West Indies and New York. Some say that his object was to test the performance of his 'Klepperboat', others that it was to show that a singlehander in distress could survive the Atlantic by taking to a boat of this kind. All agree that Romer must have been slightly mad to venture out into the ocean in such a contraption. That is the common denominator for Atlantic adventurers but in Romer's case it is difficult to see his attempt in any other light; his 'Klepperboat' was not even a boat, just a folding kayak, a long wooden frame covered with rubberized cloth from which he was exposed above the waist. If this little skiff that he had proudly named *Deutscher Sport* was not the smallest that had ever faced the Atlantic, it was certainly the narrowest: it was 6 metres long but only 90 centimetres wide in the middle, its most 'spacious' part. This had one great advantage: he could use his paddle when the wind was too light to fill the little sail of five square metres carried on a slender mast. Her fine lines may have been pretty but they made *Deutscher Sport* simply unendurable for a man who expected to spend four or five months on board. It was impossible to sleep lying down, to shelter from the weather or to find any shade when the sun was high, or even to move about and stretch one's legs.

Nevertheless, *Deutscher Sport* was not the first lifeboat to be tried out in the Atlantic; in 1866 a certain William Hudson, in company with Frank Fitch, had crossed the ocean in the *Red, White and Blue,* a vessel whose description was painted in large letters on her side: 'Ingersoll's Improved Metallic Life Boat'. Leaving New York on 19 July, Hudson and Fitch reached Europe on 15 August and the boat was displayed at the Paris Exhibition. But some of the evidence casts a doubt on the authenticity of the crossing. Humphrey Barton, in his book *Atlantic Adventures* (Adlard Coles) suggests that for part of the voyage the Ingersoll reverted to its proper status, as lifeboat on another ship, or at least that it was taken in tow, while Fitch and Hudson took it easy down below.

The crossing by *Non Such* has, however, never been questioned. Consisting of three inflatable indiarubber sausages held together by a wooden plate, it was the forerunner of the modern inflatable lifeboat. An American, John Mikes, accompanied by two German sailors, left New York on 4 June 1868, sighted the English coast fifty days later and landed next day at Southampton.

Non Such, and perhaps *Red, White and Blue*, had proved that it was possible to cross the Atlantic in a lifeboat, provided of course that it carried enough sail, was manned by two or three experienced sailors and followed the route of the prevailing winds. However, in 1928 Captain Romer proposed to sail alone in a collapsible boat with only an auxiliary sail, and to windward rather than from west to east.

He left Lisbon on 28 March sitting up in his *Deutscher Sport* – seated from the first to the last of the paddle strokes that would mark his wake, his legs festering in the close dampness of the hull. For after a few days at sea the kayak, which was supposed to have a certain minimum buoyancy at the price of some added discomfort, was torn by a big wave; the cloth gave and let the sea into the sitting compartment, turning it into a big salt-water bath where his pre-packed provisions floated about in their supposedly watertight wrappings. The leak continued and added dangerously to the weight of the provisions, fresh water and sails, some 1,500 pounds in all. He had to bail without being able to move, bending double to scoop a little water from between his legs. In this state he could not hope to get a night's, or even an hour's sleep, but he managed somehow to come to terms with the sea; he dozed in the troughs of the waves and when he felt that he was on their crests corrected his course with a touch on the helm, bailed, and then dozed again for a few seconds. That did not stop him being overturned by one breaking wave, and once again he was swamped. Still, he kept his health and after four nights and three days without any real sleep he put into the Canaries. In Germany they were relieved, but nobody thought that he would go on with the project.

On 2 June 1928 Romer set out again with three months of sailing ahead of him. As Jean Merrien says in his excellent book on single-handed sailing (*Les navigateurs solitaires,* Denoël): 'three months of sitting, always sitting, and unable to move, unable to stretch out or bend his legs, straighten his back or properly fulfil the simplest human needs'. Three months with the lower half of his body soaked, as bad with the deck cover on as without it, his kayak becoming an unwholesome vapour bath, a hotbed; without the deck cover the rain and sea came in, but no fresh air. The upper half of his body was baked under the fierce tropical sun which burnt his neck, his arms and even his head, for after the first month he had lost the last of his hats. One danger always haunted him, that sunstroke would drive him mad.

Three months without ever really sleeping or lying down, unable to turn round, unable ever to relax completely, for if his kayak were to broach it would capsize even in a moderate sea. Also very

nearly three months without anything hot to eat or drink, for as happened to Harbo and Samuelson and to Gerbault, his paraffin stove gave him trouble and in a kayak that sort of accident could be fatal. For what little cooking he was able to do Romer used to put the stove between his legs, and one day when it had burst into flames he had had to fling it overboard to avoid being burnt alive. Three months of exacting toil, shaken and tossed about by every wave while he tied himself in knots trying to bail out the boat, exasperated by the incessant flapping of canvas.

They were also months of fear, for he was constantly assailed by sharks, swordfish, porpoises and whales that rubbed themselves against the fragile canvas hull or browsed the weed that covered it. A special device had to be fitted to warn the navigator of their presence; it was useless in fact because he could do nothing to defend himself anyway and only became an added torture to his nerves. To keep his enemies at bay he beat on an empty tin, or at night flashed his electric torch, but then the flying fish attracted by the light flew straight into his face.

One day a big shark accompanied by three little ones attacked the boat; Romer fired at them without effect. Enraged, the biggest shark swam towards him and diving at the last moment struck the bottom of the kayak with its back, so hard that he felt the boat lift and saw the thin fabric yield under the impact. It seemed in no mood to forego a promising meal and dived again. Seizing the first thing that came to hand, the jackstaff of his American ensign, he struck the beast with it as it swam past. In the ensuing scuffle the flag unfurled in the sunlight, the shark reared out of the water, dived again and was seen no more. 'The American colours triumph all along the line,' one reporter noted with a straight face.

Romer did not go mad, but the salt ate into his skin and his body was covered with painful sores. The relentless sun of the trade-wind belt hardened the crust of salt and his hair was white with it until the tropical rains washed it away; but he could not even get up to take advantage of that and his legs were always steeped in a brine bath. He had said that he would get to the Antilles by the end of August and in fact he reached St. Thomas, one of the most northerly islands of the group, on 31 August after eighty-eight days at sea like a 'floating mummy' – the most superhuman ordeal, perhaps even more terrible than Alain Bombard's similar journey, that any man has ever voluntarily undergone. His face under a three months' beard like Robinson Crusoe's, he staggered ashore but collapsed on the quay. He was taken to a hotel, and slept like a log for forty-eight hours.

When he woke everybody in the island knew his story. They would have celebrated the occasion but the sores which healed on the upper part of his body got no better on his thighs, which were swollen and inflamed from the salt water, and he had to spend several weeks in hospital. Governor Evans handed him the decoration which had been specially created for Lindbergh, the first pilot to fly the Atlantic alone.

After some delay before the American authorities could get his papers in order Romer left St. Thomas for New York early in October, which is already dangerously late in the season. Days went by. It is 1,500 miles from St. Thomas to New York and 1,200 to Cape Hatteras, which he would have to pass close in and where he should have been sighted within a month at the latest. By mid-November there was still no news. Early in December a severe hurricane swept from south to north, precisely along his route. If by any chance Romer was still alive this must without doubt have sealed his fate, and in fact he was never seen again.

Thus Romer had failed, or had only partially succeeded, in a demonstration that had cost him his life. In 1952 it was a Frenchman who was to attempt to prove what Romer, for all his bravery, had not been able to prove.

Doctor Alain Bombard's purpose was almost the same as Romer's: to show that a ship-wrecked mariner could survive in the Atlantic if he had the right sort of boat and above all if he knew how to live off the sea itself. The conception was even wilder than Romer's for he meant to put to sea for three months without any supplies, not even fresh water; he claimed that enough fluid could be pressed from fish to make up for a lack of both water and sugars. He even found two companions to fall in with his idea, but one of them soon changed his mind.

That was van Hesbergen, a Dutchman, who was to be in charge of the radio, but he was put off by the mere sight of l'Hérétique in which he was to cross the ocean. With a beam of 1.9 metres she was wider than Romer's Deutscher Sport, but most of the width was taken up by the two cylindrical floats joined together in a V, and she was shorter than Deutscher Sport, less than 5 metres overall. There was no real shelter for the crew and her only sail was a bit of stuff carried on what could hardly be called a mast.

Bombard put to sea on 25 May 1952 with only one other companion for the voyage. This may have made l'Hérétique a little less uncomfortable but the absence of the Dutchman left them with only the bare minimum of contact with the rest of the world; neither Bombard nor Jack Palmer knew the Morse code and could only transmit 'Yes', 'No' and 'S.O.S.'. At twenty-seven Bombard was the younger of the two; he was training to be a cardiologist and his ruling passion was the cello. In the eyes of sailors he was no sailor, although already a man of some note; he had swum the Channel and later crossed it in so frail a craft that it got him a disqualification. At thirty-seven, Jack Palmer, a Scot naturalized in Panama, had already one survival experience – adrift in the Aegean for three weeks and living on the fish he was able to catch.

When they left Monaco early that morning the press was well represented, sure or almost sure that they were taking the last ever photographs of the two 'voluntary castaways'. André Lacaze and Jean-Pierre Pedrazzini, the two special correspondents for Paris-Match, followed them furthest out to sea and wrote:

Since this Sunday morning of 25 May the 200,000 wireless amateurs of the world are on watch, in the hope of picking up a message from the two men lost at sea by their own wish. Leaving Monaco at 5 o'clock this morning Alain Bombard and Jack Palmer, more daring even than the heroes of the Kon-Tiki, have decided to cross the Mediterranean and the Atlantic in a simple inflatable boat in order to prove that it is possible to survive relying only on the resources of the sea. The two voluntary castaways hope to reach Florida in three months. If they succeed it is almost certain that every ship and every aircraft flying over the sea will be equipped with 'Bombard boats'. For their sustenance the castaways are relying on what fish they can catch

and on the plankton they can scoop from the sea surface with a net. The plankton, which is the only diet of whales, is made up of microscopic animals and algae very rich in calories and vitamins. Dr. Bombard, after months of experiment in the laboratory, is convinced that sea water is drinkable if mixed with the juices that can be extracted from fish with an orange squeezer. In fact l'Hérétique does carry one small case of concentrated food and a container of fresh water, but these are sealed and they have sworn not to touch them except in an extreme emergency. Dr. Bombard considers the first leg, from Monaco to Gibraltar, the most dangerous as the Mediterranean, being a land-locked sea, is poorer in fish life than the Atlantic.

In fact the first stage did not bring them to Gibraltar but to Minorca in the Balearic Islands, and it took Bombard and Palmer seventeen days to get there. For Palmer that experience was enough and he too gave up, leaving Bombard with nobody to play chess with after all, although he had provided chessmen on board. He reached the Atlantic a few days later and soon afterwards, when he was thought to be lost somewhere off the coast of Morocco, put quietly into Casablanca. After recuperating there he set off again and reached the Canaries on 3 September, four months after he had left Monaco. Except when ashore he had lived entirely on what he could get from the sea, but it was not until 20 October that he left on the longest stage of the voyage, intending to let himself drift as far as the Antilles; with l'Hérétique there could be no question of deliberate navigation.

Bombard grew gradually weaker during the voyage. His weight at the start had been 69 kilos, and he had soon lost 10 kilos and then another 5; as the days went by this well-built man was down to only 50 kilos. The 30-foot waves did not worry him so much as did Amelia, the affectionate whale who repeatedly failed to overturn the boat. But what worried him most was the risk of a puncture, for although the inflatable had watertight compartments he was always afraid of them getting torn, every shark was a menace and he had only a whistle to keep them away. He found this less effective than good smacks with an oar and these he applied liberally when there were many sharks about. He even allowed himself the pleasure of photographing them if they were around 30 feet in length.

All the same Bombard reached Barbados, on the verge of exhaustion, on 23 December, having covered a distance of almost 7,000 kilometres without breaking into his emergency rations. He weighed only 48 kilos and for sixty-five days he had kept alive, as he had said he would, entirely on fish, plankton and fish juices extracted with a contrivance of his own invention. Before he set out, the possibility of a castaway surviving at sea without food had always been considered a fantasy. After this astonishing seven months' voyage he had proved his point.

On his return Bombard became a well-known figure in France. His name, henceforth associated with the subject of survival, ensured the success of the inflatable boat in which he had made the voyage, although the makers gave him no commensurate reward. It was only much later (after several other spectacular though sometimes less fortunate trials) that Bombard found himself associated with another make of inflatable lifeboat that was to bear

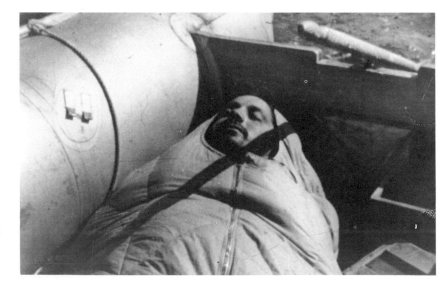

Leaving Casablanca in a small inflatable boat, without provisions or fresh water, Bombard set out alone to cross 3,800 miles of the Atlantic. The fish he caught were his only food and he drank the juice pressed from them mixed with sea water. He took photographs on the way. The one above shows the natives of Barbados inspecting his curious craft

his name, and, as the special correspondents of *Paris-Match* had predicted, the 'Bombard' lifeboat was adopted by several navies.

Four years after this amazing exploit another German was to profit from the lessons of the Bombard technique in an attempt to finalize Romer's experiment. In 1956 Hans Lindemann set out again in a *klepper kayak*. In the intervening thirty years the German firm had made improvements in the design: it was shorter, the sail plan was better and Lindemann had added a small lateral float to reduce the risk of capsize. He carried a supply of food, but definitely less than Romer, and relied on Bombard's method of allaying thirst; but that did not save him from a terrible journey. Taking seventy-six days he was the first to succeed in this exploit, crossing the Atlantic from Las Palmas to the island of St. Martin in the West Indies in a kayak, carrying one small sail but propelled for most of the time by the strength of his own arms. Remarkable as this may seem, there are others who have attempted the crossing without a sail of any kind.

It is sometimes said that an American, John Naylor, leaving Boston in 1911, succeeded in rowing alone to Spain. But unfortunately the evidence for this feat, unique of its kind, is insufficient to corroborate John Naylor's story. On the other hand there is no doubt about that of Frank Harbo and George Samuelson.

Harbo and Samuelson, oyster fishers from New Jersey, claimed no complex motive for their astonishing project. They were convinced that an Atlantic crossing would bring them fame and, still better, the means to support an easy life by exhibiting their boat in the capitals of Europe. This was quite an original idea in

1897 and we shall refer later to how they won the approval and support of the *Illustrated Police Gazette*. If their motive was not of the highest their crossing remains a masterpiece of its kind.

On 1 August, Harbo and Samuelson reached the Scillies, went on to Le Havre and there disembarked after rowing some three million strokes to cross the Atlantic in sixty-two interminable days. The exhibition of their boat in Paris failed to bring in anything like the return they expected, hardly enough to pay for their return passages by steamer, and that was the end of a triumphal progress through Europe that they were never to make.

It was seventy years before two men again rowed across the Atlantic, two British soldiers of the Parachute Regiment who also sought to add their names to the Atlantic legend. On 26 May 1967 Frank Ridgway and Chay Blyth launched their boat *English Rose III* from the beach below a small town in Massachusetts and had not long to wait before their strong constitutions were put to the test; they were crossing the area swept by hurricane Alma, a romantic enough name but of unhappy memory. They survived that ordeal and reached Ireland after rowing for ninety-two days, landing at Kilronan in the Aran Islands. Both of them were destined to experience less happy moments in the single-handed Transatlantic Races.

First, Frank Ridgway competed in the 1972 race in *English Rose IV*, but his crossing was less distinguished than in the famous *English Rose III* and he failed to cross the finishing line at Newport. Chay Blyth had even less luck in 1976. After winning many hard races and a memorable round-the-world voyage single-handed, he had entered *Great Britain III* for the race and was almost the sole hope of the British. But he was swamped in a collision with a freighter during a qualifying trial, narrowly escaping death, and was only just able to save his crippled trimaran. He was unable to get her ready again in time for the start.

The unbeatable now beaten, and the southern limit of the arena for the future Ostar established by Romer, one question still remained to be answered – how far north could a single-hander venture? It was resolved by Commander R. D. Graham in the spring of 1933. His motive was rather different from those of earlier Atlantic adventurers, except perhaps Slocum. It is said that what prompted Graham to set out across the ocean was the steady worsening of his circumstances; it was not a question of running away but of legitimate avoidance, to get away from a situation that was becoming intolerable. He had heard tell of the magnificent austerity of the Newfoundland scene and felt the need to go there and breathe a cleaner air; after several reverses of fortune his only means of getting away was his boat *Emanuel,* a fine little 30-foot cutter. He left Falmouth for Newfoundland on 19 May. He reasoned that the most direct route to St. John's was a northerly one, where at that time of year the winds also promised to be favourable. On the other hand the pack ice breaks up then and the icebergs that drift south are a constant danger, requiring the single-hander to be almost continually on watch. To husband his strength Graham made a final call at Bantry in Ireland before setting out, at 9 o'clock in the morning on 26 May, to face the cold and fog that shroud the margins of the Arctic.

In two weeks *Emanuel* covered 1,000 miles, or nearly seventy miles a day; not a record but very nearly. On 16 June he found an intruder within what he called his 'lonely universe four hundred yards across'; it was his first iceberg. The danger increased with the fogs of the Labrador Current. The watches grew longer, but fortunately the days grew longer too in those latitudes at that time of the year. Twenty-five days after he had put to sea in his little yacht he rounded Cape St. Francis and landed in Newfoundland. He had covered 1,760 miles in all and had shown that the route was possible for a single-handed sailor.

It was almost the same route that Colonel Hasler chose thirty years later when he sought to win the first Transatlantic Race in his folkboat *Jester.* Hasler had gone even a little further north, touching Latitude 57 degrees before turning southwards for New York, a distance of 3,130 miles in forty-eight and a half days.

With the principal routes established, every sort of boat now sailed the Atlantic and solitary mariners embarked on new odysseys. Some of these were admirable, like the first crossing in a motor vessel by Marin Marie in 1936, or the voyage of Vito Dumas from Arcachon to Buenos Aires in mid-winter in 1932. But 'first ever' exploits became increasingly difficult to invent and single-handed sailors bent on distinguishing themselves turned to breaking any sort of record.

First of all there were the speed records: between the U.S.A. and Europe the shortest times usually quoted were those of Lawlor, forty-five days for his 1891 race, and Blackburn, thirty-eight days in 1901. In the opposite direction and against the prevailing winds, Gerbault had taken 101 days; for part of the course and by a distinctly shorter route, Graham had got across in twenty-five days. In 1937 a man in his fifties, Ludwig Schlimbach, made a good passage from Lisbon to New York in fifty-seven days. But all these records were to be shattered in the future Transatlantic Races.

However, there were always good sailors who saw very little in records of this kind. Tabarly said so several times, even on the day after establishing a new record himself in 1964: 'Under sail, wind and calm are factors too imponderable for the worth of a performance to be judged on time alone.' Perhaps that is why other brave men preferred to challenge another and perhaps more astonishing kind of record, that of the size of boat chosen for the Atlantic crossing.

For nearly 100 years William Andrews, the less fortunate competitor in the first race from America to Europe, held the record for the smallest boat. He certainly deserved it for he had come near to losing his life on several occasions in trying to beat his old rival Lawlor. In 1892, hardly a year after the race in which he had been given up as lost, he set out again in *Sapolio,* the 'floating cradle', and leaving Atlantic City, New Jersey, on 2 July reached Palos in Spain on 27 September. *Sapolio* measured only 4.40 metres in length, 15 centimetres shorter than Lawlor's *Sea Serpent.*

Just before the war another American, Harry Young, partly succeeded in breaking this curious record, setting out from New York in an open 4.20-metre sloop but getting no further than the Azores after forty days at sea.

Then in 1965 Robert Manry tried to beat even this impossible record; his *Tinkerbelle* was just ten centimetres shorter than Harry Young's boat, 4.10 metres to be exact, and therefore 30 centimetres shorter than *Sapolio.* As soon as he stepped on board one felt that there was something that would not do about this

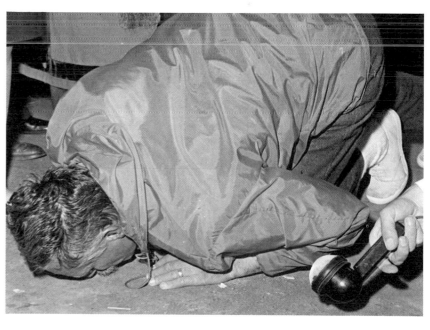

In 1965 the 48-year-old American journalist Robert Manry beat the transatlantic record set by William Andrews with an even smaller boat. Manry's Tinkerbelle measured only 13 feet, and she made the crossing in seventy-seven days, reaching Falmouth on 17 August 1965. The picture above shows Manry kissing the ground at Falmouth

attempt. The contrast in size between the little launch *Queen of Helford,* in which some of his friends kept him company for the first few miles, and the tiny yacht emphasized the disproportion between man and boat. Her skipper towered above her like a child in one of those model boats you see on roundabouts or on ponds in amusement parks – but Manry was no child and the pond was the Atlantic.

Robert Manry had managed to fit out *Tinkerbelle* with a reasonable degree of comfort and had on board all the food he needed for the long weeks of navigation ahead. He even had a spare rudder, which came in useful when *Tinkerbelle*'s own rudder came adrift in the first heavy seas. This called for a first difficult change-over, soon followed by a second when the spare rudder gave way too and Manry had to patch up the first one to take its place. In spite of that, and in spite of suffering hallucinations after the long nights on watch, he reached the British Isles after seventy-seven days at sea; in the 4.10-metre *Tinkerbelle* he had beaten the Andrews record.

But, alas, he only held that record for a few hours for at the same time, but sailing the other way, a strapping young Englishman, John Riding, had reached Newport from Vigo in Spain. Taking his time and relaxing for a while in the Azores and Bermuda, Riding had nevertheless managed to cross the Atlantic in an oddly rounded and egg-shaped craft, 3.60 metres in length and appropriately named *Sjö Ag,* the 'sea egg'. It had been specially designed on a principle which made the fortunes of the motor manufacturers of the sixties – a minimum of external clutter for a maximum of interior volume. His *Sjö Ag* was hardly bigger than an Austin Mini and about the same length as a Renault 5 or a Volkswagen Polo, smaller than a Ford Fiesta or a Chevrolet Chevelle. But Riding's 'egg' was not meant for town traffic; it served him as a floating home for three months. He was greeted with much acclaim in Newport and settled down there to enjoy his new-won fame. He left again after a few weeks, and nobody has heard of him since.

Six years later Jean-Yves Terlain set a record for the biggest vessel ever to be sailed from one side of the ocean to the other by one man alone. But it was a record that did not survive longer than the next Ostar, for in 1976 Alain Colas sailed something even bigger. The organizers of the race, to avoid finding themselves confronted with floating bath tubs or sailing air mattresses, had even gone so far as to write into the 1976 rules: 'Yachts of any size or type may enter, subject to the decision of the organizers . . . It is unlikely that the committee will admit a yacht of less than 25 feet overall on deck.'

Before Colonel Hasler originated the Ostar there was a woman who in 1952, following upon the most poignant crisis in her life, had added a significant chapter to the romance of the Atlantic. Ann Davison had set out with her husband in 1952 to cross the Atlantic in a yacht which bore the reassuring name *Reliance.* It was to have been a second honeymoon, but hardly five days after they left Plymouth it had become a voyage of tears. They encountered one of the severe gales that are sometimes experienced in the Channel and the yacht was wrecked. The rescuers found only one survivor, Ann Davison, a widow at thirty-five.

When late in the following year she announced that she intended to sail across the Atlantic alone, some people already began to talk about suicide, but there were others who said that in this tragedy she had discovered a more profound purpose. Ann Davison herself simply said that she was a journalist in search of something worth writing about. Yet when the small figure of this brunette with the square and determined jaw faded into the distance on board her little 22-foot yacht to face an east to west crossing of the Atlantic in mid-winter, most people felt that they would never see her again. A year later, on 25 November 1953, the *Felicity Ann* lay at her moorings in New York. Ann Davison had taken her time, calling at the Canaries, the Windward Islands and Antigua. She was the first woman to sail across the Atlantic and so paved the way for other 'sailors in petticoats' in the great ocean races of the future.

The first participation by a woman in a Transatlantic Race, in 1968, was to say the least a wretched experience; the photographs of Edith Baumann speak for themselves. In the 1972 Ostar women took their place among the élite of sail, with Marie-Claude Fauroux and Ann Michailoff, and showed up well at the finish. In 1976 Clare Francis won the admiration of her male rivals in a most gruelling race, and was for a long while among the first five before finishing thirteenth.

In that same year sailing people often called to mind the example of Ann Davison and found a parallel in Mike McMullen, a starter in the race three days after his wife's death. They remembered too that fine remark of Ann Davison's:

Most people are intuitively aware of it, but I had to cover miles and miles of sea to discover that courage is the key to living. For courage is the ability to live through each day that God gives us, with all its little daily events and routines. Courage lies in recognizing our own unimportance and accepting this without losing heart.

1957: Blondie Hasler Cockleshell hero and originator of Ostar

four got through. Hasler's odyssey in the company of Marine W. E. Sparks made the two men the heroes of a war story about Operation Frankton, *Cockleshell Heroes* (Heinemann) by Cecil Lucas-Phillips, which recounts:

In spite of all the refusals that constantly met his efforts, Lieutenant-Colonel Hasler would not give up his idea for a race from one side of the Atlantic to the other to which he could challenge his friends. To his mind it was the finest sporting event that one could imagine at the end of the Second World War. And yet nobody fell in with the proposal except the Joshua Slocum Society of New York, which agreed to sponsor the project. Perhaps that was enough from the American side, but an organizer in Britain was essential and none could be found, although Hasler was not unknown in the English sailing world and his name was associated with one of the finest commando operations of the war.

In 1942 Blondie Hasler, a young lieutenant-colonel in the Royal Marines, had been chosen to lead a most delicate operation of marine sabotage. The German ships that maintained the Atlantic blockade from the port of Bordeaux in occupied France were a thorn in the flesh of the British Admiralty and it was resolved to destroy them. It would be necessary to train a commando team for this perilous mission and Hasler was selected by Admiral Mountbatten to recruit volunteers. He established contact with Mary Lindell, a woman who, under the name of Marie-Claire, was to be their liaison in France. He chose eleven men to form the commando team for 'Operation Frankton', charged with the sinking of German vessels in the estuary and equipped only with six kayaks and a handful of explosives.

At nightfall they cast off from a submarine at sea off the Bordeaux estuary. The Germans intercepted eight of them but

After about ninety minutes' paddling, round a long bend of the Garonne the hunters saw at last their prey. In the distance, moored to the quays on the west bank, some of them brightly illuminated, was a long line of ships. How many, they could not yet count. Hasler and Sparks were filled with elation . . . From now on they must keep to the deep shadows within a yard of the quay wall or cling close to the water-line of each ship they came upon. They were in single paddles and must use all that they knew of the hunter's wit and cunning.

The first ship was a tanker. She was not their meat and they ignored her, creeping along her hull. Next to her was a liner or cargo-liner. They passed her too, but noted her for a kill on the way back if they still had any limpets to spare. Next in the flock was a good cargo ship, but a tanker that was moored alongside made it extremely difficult to get at her. The next ship was a perfect target – a large cargo ship with nothing moored alongside her – and Hasler eagerly prepared to begin putting in his claws. The tide was already beginning to ebb. Just past the bows of the ship he stowed his paddle. Behind him, Sparks, taking up the signal, clung to the ship's side with his magnetic holder, while Hasler reached under his cockpit cover for the first limpet. He attached it to the placing rod. Then he lowered the mine into the water as far as the rod would go, gently brought it up to the ship's side and felt the mine cling. The first blow had been struck.

A few yards on and they were amidships. No alarm yet. No

Blondie Hasler, Lieutenant-Colonel, Royal Marines

one had heard or seen them. But already Hasler had felt the thrust of the tide against him. He knew he must hand over to Sparks, or the tide would swing the bows of the canoe out and away from the ship's side. Stopping amidships he therefore passed the placing rod back to his No. 2. Sparks understood at once and gave him the magnetic holder. The roles were reversed and it was now Sparks who dug in the claws. He did so again when Hasler stopped a third time near the ship's stern. That would be enough for this ship.

As they moved along each ship in turn, there was little that they could see except the towering rusty cliff of her side. From the hum of the auxiliary engines they could locate the engine rooms, and from men's voices or a fragment of music the crew's quarters.

They came to the last ship in the group. They could not identify her nor get at her properly, for, moored alongside her, was a small German naval craft of the type known as a sperrbrecher, about the size of a frigate. He had five limpets left. As a German naval vessel, the sperrbrecher was anyhow fair game and a justifiable target, so he decided that she should have two limpets. With a few hard strokes *Catfish* was under her bows.

He stopped alongside the German's engine room and there Sparks fixed two limpets spaced several yards apart. Now they must turn to go back downstream, which meant that they must swing out and away into the stream from the ship's side in a wide loop. As they were in the middle of this risky movement they heard a clang on the ship's deck and a torch shone down on them. A sentry had seen them. His shape was clearly outlined against the night sky as he looked over the rail.

There was only one thing to do. With a cautious drive of the paddles, they slid in right up to the ship's side and froze in the forward low position, hooded heads in their laps. 'I felt,' said Hasler, 'as though my back had been stripped naked.'

No shot, no clamour, but the torch still shining down on them from fifteen feet above. Bodies and paddles motionless, they allowed the canoe to drift gently with the tide along the water-line. The sentry, torch in hand, followed them down, iron-shod boots clanging on iron deck.

As *Catfish*, like an idle log, drifted down, the sperrbrecher seemed to the two marines to have the length of a battleship and that each clang of the sentry's boots was like the toll of a cracked bell. After an eternity of time, they reached the end of the ship's water-line, drifting in under the flare of her bows, where they were at least invisible from the deck. What now? Go on drifting into the open water beyond and under the glare of the lights? Quietly Hasler handed the magnetic hold-fast back to Sparks and made the hold-on signal. With infinite care, Sparks 'rolled' the magnet on the ship's side with a barely audible 'click' and the canoe clung motionless, moored by the stern with the ebb tide running past them to freedom.

When they stopped, the sentry above them stopped too. Presently his torch wandered over the surrounding water, then went out, but he was still there, shifting his feet occasionally. An age passed. No sound of the boots moving away. What was he doing? Waiting for them to show themselves again? Or had he decided they were a piece of driftwood and was taking a rest?

COLUMBIA PICTURES presents A WARWICK PRODUCTION, **JOSE FERRER** and **TREVOR HOWARD** in **COCKLESHELL HEROES** (Canoe Commandos), in CinemaScope and Color by TECHNICOLOR. Directed by JOSE FERRER

During the Second World War Hasler organized an expedition to the Gironde to destroy German shipping. Out of twelve men only two survived 'Operation Frankton'. The story was made into the film Cockleshell Heroes, *with Trevor Howard and José Ferrer in the leading roles*

Well, they could not wait for ever. There was another fish to fry. Hasler signalled 'let go' and Sparks removed the hold-fast. Without paddling, crouched in the lowest position, they drifted quietly out from under the bows, letting the tide carry them downstream. Once again the agony of waiting for a shot in the back. One minute, two minutes – at last they began to breathe again. They were out of the range of vision and no alarm had been raised. The whole incident was a triumph for those at SOE who had devised this camouflage technique and for the men who had now practised it so convincingly.

Moving quietly on downstream, they passed the ship they had already attacked and came to the awkwardly placed cargo ship, with the tanker moored alongside. Hasler wanted, of course, to distribute his limpets along the length of the merchantman, but the presence of the tanker prevented him from getting at her amidships, so he decided to attack stem and stern. They laid *Catfish* accordingly between the bows of merchantman and tanker and let her glide ahead until she was almost wedged in between them, with the tide now running strongly. Sparks, about to ship his paddle and get out the holder, saw Hasler in front of him suddenly spreadeagle his arms, one on the hull of each ship, as if trying to push them apart. Then he realised that the two ships, yawing slightly under the influence of the tide, were closing together and about to crush the Cockle between them. Sparks at once followed suit, and together, pressing with all their strength, they pushed the canoe backwards just in time. 'I felt,' said Hasler, 'like Atlas holding up the World.' Back-paddling hard against the tide, they rounded the bows of the tanker and drifted downstream to the stern.

Here they successfully pushed in between the two ships, planting two limpets on the stern end of the cargo ship, spaced as far apart as possible, and the last one on the stern of the tanker.

Their job was done. All their limpets had been successfully planted. The canoe, relieved of the weight of them, suddenly felt lively and unstable. Her crew also felt as though a great weight had been lifted off them. Hasler twisted round in his seat, gripped Sparks's free hand and shook it warmly. They were both smiling for the first time for many hours. Neither of them felt any worries about the dangers of the withdrawal; indeed a kind of quiet recklessness gripped them.

'I felt,' says Hasler, 'as though I owned the river and my respect for the enemy gave way to contempt. I took *Catfish* straight out into the middle of the river, where the tide was strongest, and we shot off downstream, paddling strongly in single paddles. We must have been visible and audible to both banks, if anyone had been looking, but we just didn't seem to care.' . . .

Presently they heard a faint but familiar noise astern of them, rapidly getting louder. 'It sounded,' says Hasler, 'like a Mississippi stern-wheeler at full speed, but we knew what it was and we laughed aloud.' Turning *Catfish* round, they soon saw the shape of a canoe materialize out of the darkness, travelling fast in double paddles 'with a bone in her teeth'. Suddenly the paddling stopped, and the oncoming canoe 'froze'. They had just spotted the stationary *Catfish*, but were not close enough to identify her. 'Good work, Laver,' thought Hasler.

Instantaneously, the other canoe 'unfroze' and paddled swiftly up. It was Corporal Laver. They rafted up together joyfully, Laver and Mills in great spirits.

'We went right down the east bank as far as we could, sir, like you said,' Laver whispered to Hasler, 'until the tide turned against us, and we found no targets at all. So we came back and attacked the two ships at Bassens South.'

'Well done. What did you give them?'

'Five limpets on the first ship, sir, and three on the second.'

'Meet any trouble?'

'None at all, sir.'

'Just as well for both of us. Anyhow, well done indeed you two. And' – turning round to his own No. 2 – 'well done, Sparks. You've all done wonderfully, and I'm really proud of you.' . . .

It was now six o'clock in the morning, only an hour and a half before dawn, and the flood tide had already begun to turn against them. But they had got far enough to be able to land in open country to the north of Blaye, with a clear escape route to the north-east. For five successive nights the two canoes had been at large in enemy waters, covering a total of 91 sea miles, or

105 land miles, by canoe alone. Their Cockles had proved themselves.

For the last time, Hasler made the 'raft-up' signal. As Laver and Mills came alongside he said:

'Well, Corporal, this is where we have to separate. You are about a mile north of Blaye. Go straight ashore here and carry out your escape instructions. I shall land about a quarter of a mile further north.'

Laver looked at him steadily and said:

'Very good, sir. Best of luck to you.'

For him it was perhaps an even harder moment than the time, nine hours before, when they had separated for the attack. Now, a young fellow of twenty-two, without superior schooling, he would have to land in a completely strange and semi-hostile country, knowing nothing of the language, and use his own wits to get through, venturing into the unknown without guide or leader. It would have been a lot to ask of an officer, but Corporal Laver did not shrink from it.

'Good-bye, both of you,' said Hasler, 'and thank you for everything you've done. Keep on as you've been doing and we'll be meeting again in Pompey in a few weeks' time.'

Reaching across the gunwales, they shook hands all round, each with a 'Good luck!' for the other. But it was Sparks who struck the right note at the final moment.

'See you in the "Granada",' he said with his infectious smile. 'We'll keep a couple of pints for you!'

So it was with a quiet laugh that they pushed the canoes away from each other and paddled away on their separate courses. Just once Hasler looked back over his right shoulder at *Crayfish*, paddling strongly for the shore. She looked to him suddenly very small, very helpless, and he quickly looked away again. For a moment his heart was heavy . . . and it was with an effort that he forced himself to concentrate on the problem of landing.

It was the last they ever saw of the gallant Laver and Mills.

Back in London Lord Mountbatten himself did not expect anyone to return from the Frankton expedition. It was asking a lot of anyone to penetrate 60 miles into the heart of enemy country along a well-used waterway, blow up enemy ships and make good one's escape by one's own wits. Yet when he asked a month or so later whether there were any survivors from 'Frankton' and was told 'None,' Mountbatten glowered at Neville and said: 'I was persuaded, against my better judgment, to let Major Hasler go on the raid and now we have lost him.'

Nevertheless, in the report that he sent to the Prime Minister Mountbatten had not given up hope.

'It seems possible,' he wrote, 'that the Germans may have only intercepted one section of the raiding party. The Commander of the party was Major H. G. Hasler, R.M., who would probably have been with the leading section.

'The capture by the Germans of one section would not necessarily have compromised the other section, since no papers were carried other than charts.' . . . When photographs were at length taken, they showed one good piece of news – that several ships had in fact been sunk or severely damaged. Some, at least, of Hasler's party had therefore reached their objective and achieved their purpose. But of the men themselves all was still

coldly silent, and on 25 January 1943, all were officially reported by Jock Stewart, on instructions, as 'Missing'.

The mothers of all the men who had set out on the expedition accordingly received immediate telegrams to this effect, and although this was to some extent a routine process, it caused acute distress to them all. Mrs. Hasler, in particular, remembered that it was an exactly similar 'Missing' telegram that had presaged the news of the death of her husband in 1917.

It was not until towards the end of February that the sky lightened somewhat. At that time a coded message, sent from Switzerland by the Englishwoman known in the French escape circles as 'Marie-Claire', arrived at a secret office. It consisted of a continuous string of letters and the Intelligence staff were quite unable to decipher it, the only fact known being that it was from Hasler. . . . At Hitler's headquarters . . . the news of the 'heavy damage' was received with consternation.

Long after the war, in 1955, this action was re-enacted in the film *Cockleshell Heroes* and Admiral Mountbatten wrote this foreword to Lucas-Phillips' book of the same title:

Of the many brave and dashing raids carried out by the men of Combined Operations Command, none was more courageous or imaginative than 'Operation Frankton'.

An immense amount of trouble was taken over the training of the small handful of picked Royal Marines who took part under the indomitable leadership of Lieutenant-Colonel Hasler. They maintained their object in spite of the frightening losses of the first night and the subsequent ever-increasing difficulties encountered. Although the force had been reduced to four men, the object was finally achieved.

The account of this operation brings out the spirit of adventure always present in peace and war among Royal Marines. It emphasizes the tremendous importance of morale – pride in oneself and one's unit – and what a big part physical fitness plays in creating this morale. . . .

Invalided from the Royal Marines with spinal injuries, Hasler had one major hobby, the yacht in which he lived during the winter and sailed in summer. He happened to make the acquaintance of a young journalist, Christopher Brasher, who was amused by his new friend's enthusiasm; he says:

Since 1953 Blondie has been building himself a Scandinavian folkboat, which he calls *Jester* because with his unfailing sense of humour he considers her just a big joke. But that has not stopped him from persevering in his attempt to perfect a very simple sail plan on the lines of the Chinese junks. In principle it requires only two lines to hoist and trim the sail. There is no cockpit, just a round hatch covered by a nice little hood, from which position he can do all that is needed to handle the ship. From 1953 to 1959 it has taken him no less than six years to perfect the rig.

Left: Hasler's Jester *is completely decked in, with a central control hatch in the cabin roof through which it is possible to handle the sail*

Right: Another man who dreamed of racing across the Atlantic – Francis Chichester

Meanwhile Hasler was seeking support for the enterprise which he considered the ideal testing ground for *Jester* – a single-handed transatlantic race. Even his wartime companion David Astor, in later years the editor of the *Observer,* tried in vain to persuade him that it would be impossible to assure the safety of such a trial. Hasler was unconvinced and approached every newspaper and society that he thought might be able to help, but everywhere he was met with a polite but firm refusal. Another thing that was lacking was any opponent as mad as himself to take part in the venture. In spite of the moral support of the Slocum Society, nobody had yet taken up the challenge that he had posted on the notice board of that eminent London sailing club, the Royal Ocean Racing Club, on 21 September 1957, announcing that he was prepared to race any one who might come forward across the North Atlantic. The rules for the contest were as simple as possible and might be summed up in three words: a man, a yacht and the ocean. There were no other limitations, except of course against the use of an engine, unless it was to provide electricity on board or only to work a wireless transmitter, and he did not even think that necessary.

When in 1957 Francis Chichester first saw the notice through his little round spectacles it cut him to the quick. Ever since he had succumbed to the lure of sail, this race in which Hasler now invited

any sailing man to participate was exactly the contest of which he had dreamed. But at fifty-six he was a victim to violent attacks of asthma, and perhaps to a wasting disease that none could speak of lightly. As Christopher Brasher wrote in the *Observer* of 11 June 1972:

Francis at this time was extremely ill. Five different doctors had given the same verdict: 'cancer of the lung'. His office in St. James's is just around the corner from the club's headquarters, and Francis called in there on his way to hospital, for what he believed was a farewell drink with friends. As he left, he saw Blondie's notice, and thought: 'That would be a terrific race.'

Chichester knew that the hospital treatment which he was to

Above: Chichester shortly before his solo flight from England to Australia

Opposite: His triumphal arrival in Sydney

undergo within a few weeks would put him out of action for a long while and make it impossible for him to participate in another dangerous sport in which he had excelled: aviation.

However, his first press notice had been in connection with a remarkable feat on a bicycle. Although he was given a good education his father, a parson, had omitted to warn young Francis that you must never pick up a snake by the tail and a boy of eleven roaming the woods was always tempted to do just that. Young Francis did, and came home with a swollen arm after he had been bitten. His father ordered him to get on his bicycle at once and go to the nearest hospital, five miles away, for treatment. 'By the time I got there,' Chichester remembered, 'I was beginning to feel dizzy. I was told later that I nearly died; but my misfortunes were reported in the local paper and I made a lot of friends.' Another story that also drew the attention of the press was about the rugby match, never to be forgotten by him, when, as captain of the team, he had scored a try – against his own side! He had lost his spectacles in the scrum. Francis Chichester was extremely short-sighted and at that age such short-sightedness was no laughing matter. He felt it keenly as a handicap and, perhaps on that account, and certainly after a quarrel with his parents, he went off to Australia to forget his troubles.

As a sheep farmer in the Antipodes he was away from unkind criticism, but he found it a dull life and went on to New Zealand where, he was told, there was gold. He did find a few nuggets, but the rich vein that he struck was green gold. He operated a big forestry concern, and in doing so soon discovered that an aeroplane provided by far the most effective means of transport. He also set up a small aviation company, a new idea in the twenties but by now Chichester was not averse to some degree of unconventionality – or publicity for that matter.

When he came back to England Chichester had a comfortable bank balance and devoted himself to his new hobby, flying. But short sight made his progress painfully slow; he was only passed after twenty hours of dual control whereas others seldom required more than half that time. Hardly was he licenced before he amazed and alarmed his friends by buying a biplane to fly back to Australia. He flew solo in a plane with the intriguing name *Gipsy Moth*, intending to break the Croydon-Sydney record. The record stood, but the arrival in Sydney of this fragile biplane, piloted by a man as short-sighted as he was inexperienced, won him a triumphal reception. It was only the second occasion on which such a flight had been accomplished.

Not long after, he did establish a new record by flying solo from New Zealand to Australia. On the other hand he crashed in an attempt to fly to Japan in a seaplane and narrowly escaped death. The plane was shattered and, with six fractures, her pilot did not come off much better.

Now an experienced solo pilot, he was also a past master in the art of navigation. During the early years of the war he was employed in writing navigation manuals for the Air Ministry. In 1942 Coastal Command even included in its manual the navigational procedure by which he had been able to locate an island in the Tasman Sea. He became chief navigation instructor at the famous Empire Flying School, where he developed new training methods for the pilots of low flying pursuit planes.

THE END OF CHICHESTER'S LONE FLIGHT FROM ENGLAND

"THE END OF "ONE OF THE MOST AUDACIOUS FLIGHTS EVER ATTEMPTED"—That was how an English paper described Mr. F. C. Chichester's departure from Croydon at 3 a.m. on December 20 last. Chichester said "Thanks, cheerio," to a mechanic who helped prepare his machine—and away he flew towards Australia. Despite a forced stay of 16 days in Tripoli, the New Zealand airman reached Darwin on Saturday last, beating Sir Alan Cobham's time by a day. He landed at Mascot yesterday afternoon, and was enthusiastically received by a large crowd. Picture shows the 'plane passing near Botany Bay.

The Daily Pictorial's *coverage of the end of 'one of the most audacious flights ever attempted'*

When the war was over it was only natural that he should open a map publishing business, and he made it pay by producing pocket maps. He set up shop in the fashionable St. James's Square area, only a stone's throw from the famous R.O.R.C. In time he turned his attention to navigation at sea, and began to enter races. But in spite of a dozen such contests since 1954 in his little yacht, named

Gipsy Moth II, he had not yet shown his true stature as a sailor – in an ocean race for example.

After the hospital treatment he underwent in 1957 and a long convalescence at Vence above the blue waters of the Mediterranean, Chichester came back once more to the Royal Ocean Racing Club. He could hardly believe that nothing had changed and that Hasler's little note was still on the board, just a little yellower with the years. He began to dream again, and this time it seemed that the dream might come true.

Chichester had a third *Gipsy Moth* built for the race, a very fine boat which he describes as follows:

My boat is nearly 40 feet long (39' 7") overall with a waterline length of 28', beam 10' 1¾", draught of 6' 5" and Thames measurement of 13 tons. Normally I would race it in the Royal Ocean Racing Club races in British waters with a crew of six. It has berths for six. The mast is 55' high from stem to truck, the same height as my bedroom window at the top floor of my five-storied London house.

To say the least, it was a monster for single-handed sailing. The iron keel weighed 4½ tons. The mainsail and genoa each had an area of about 270 square feet; there was a trysail of about 90 square feet and a small jib.

But he was proudest of all of 'Miranda'. Miranda was the self-steering gear that he had designed to take his place at the tiller when he was resting or attending to the navigation. To a layman's eye it looked like an enormous fan, half opened as if to ventilate the after part of *Gipsy Moth*. In fact it was an ingenious contrivance comprising a mizzen sail that weather cocked with the wind; with collars, arms and clamps it provided Chichester the skilled helmsman with an automatic pilot that took him several weeks of trials to perfect.

Hasler and Brasher had at last persuaded their friend David Astor to have the project sponsored by the *Observer*. It only remained to find a yacht club willing to organize the start, and the Royal Western Yacht Club of England seemed to be the most favourably situated geographically. Situated on the Hoe at Plymouth, its rooms opening on to a little private harbour would make an excellent headquarters for the start of the first Ostar in history.

When Chichester called on Hasler and put down a half-crown as a symbolic wager, Blondie knew that he had at last found the worthy adversary he needed. He knew too that his life-long dream had come true.

Eight

1960: Francis Chichester Alone across the Atlantic

Francis Chichester

On the day before the start of Blondie Hasler's race there was no crowd gathered at Plymouth; in fact there was hardly anybody there. As for the foreign press *Figaro* was practically the only European paper to notice the event, and that was because a young sailing enthusiast, Alain Gliksman, was able to get a few lines in at the foot of the sporting pages. He had already guessed that this was going to prove a big event. Four years later he was to come again to write a second chapter, but this time as a competitor in the race. Gliksman was somewhat mystified by what he saw. He was fully aware of the magnitude of the challenge these men were about to face and yet there was hardly anyone of importance to be seen on the quayside at Millbay Dock. A signals officer went quietly from boat to boat checking the transmitters. The scene slowly came to life in the pale sunlight of that day, 10 June. According to Gliksman:

On this unsheltered dockside it would have been a fatal error to embark foodstuffs in the rain. Chichester arrived late in the morning. He was wearing the traditional yachtsman's high buttoned reefer jacket with, as a finishing touch, old black buttons with embossed anchors – just the thing – but he had not yet acquired the American cap with the long peak which is now sold under his name in England; he was still wearing the flat British type with a patent leather peak. A few newspapermen were at work with their usual apparent indifference, asking each contestant a few polite questions while two or three photographers went around getting them to hold some seaman-like object or bit of rope while they immortalized that now historic scene.

There are very few French reports. *Paris-Match* and *France-Soir* thought it unnecessary to send anybody for the editors of the Paris newspapers and magazines did not think much of the chances of the only French competitor. And they were right. It was almost dark when Lacombe reached Plymouth on the eve of the race. A stocky, thick-set little man, he meant to show that it was possible to cross the Atlantic in a standard run-of-the-mill boat; his light, centre-board 6½-metre *Cap Horn*, as she was proudly named, was capable of entering shallow harbours or of being trailed by an average sized car and seemed best suited to an inland regatta or inshore cruising. Lacombe had no illusions about her; *Cap Horn* was far from being the ideal boat but she had made it possible for him to save a good deal of expense. Living in New York, he had got her through the good offices of an importer who was to take her over after the race; she was in fact being delivered. As it was almost dark when he put into Plymouth it was too late for him to be included in the group photograph of the contestants.

The little Frenchman was the only one of them who had not been born an 'islander'; before taking to the sea the only fresh air that he had breathed had been over the nearby Seine, on whose bank stood his fancy leather workshop. He was looked on by some as a Parisian street urchin who had run away to sea, even though he had later gained valuable experience in single-handed sailing. He had

crossed the Mediterranean and the Atlantic alone and recorded his impressions in a book which, in spite of its almost British sense of humour, had made a negative impression on Colonel Hasler and the other organizers of the race. From the pages of Lacombe's *A moi l'Atlantique* Hasler came to the conclusion that his ocean voyage had been a compendium of mistakes to avoid!

Valentine Howells was the most impressive of the starters. He was a giant of a man with a black beard, a reputation for being able to do without sleep and a nickname 'the bearded lady' that arose from some English journalist speaking of a 'Miss Valentine Howells' in the race. On the eve of the race he seemed the most relaxed of the five; with his humorous eyes and mocking smile and wearing only a simple shirt and cotton trousers, he seemed at the comparatively youthful age of thirty-four to be the most likely winner. He also had a sound knowledge of the sea, gained from his experience as a fisherman and in the merchant navy. But his boat was hardly in the same class; *Eira* seemed even smaller when he stepped on board although she was a popular 26-foot type with almost the same sail area as Hasler's. He had made no changes for the race. He moved easily about the deck and took a few photographs, or posed obligingly when asked to do so. Chichester saw him as likely to steal the victory and throughout the race was worried about him.

David Lewis, the last of the five, was not as well known as the others. He was an affable fellow but all that was known about him was that he was a doctor and had spent most of the forty-three

years of his life in New Zealand, where he had acquired a taste for the sea. He was also a family man, with a blonde wife and two children who stayed on board *Cardinal Vertue* (sic) till the last minute. Lewis was to become the first casualty in the race.

Next day, for the start of the race, Alain Gliksman was in one of the only two launches that had been provided for the press and spectators and wrote:

11 June 1960. At the starting line in front of the Royal Western Yacht Club the weather is grey and cheerless; beyond the lee of the great mole that protects the Sound the waves are beginning to show their white crests. Several yachts and motor boats and one or two naval launches are moving across near the line. The sound of the starting gun is carried away on the wind and both the warning and starting shots are only seen as puffs of white smoke.

Chichester set his genoa just before the gun, his boat powerful enough to carry all sail; tossing heavily in the seaway he soon took the lead. His neat figure and cautious movements on deck were strangely in contrast to the sense of power in the boat. On the other hand Howells, the black-bearded giant, dwarfed his

Above: The almost unnoticed start to the first Ostar on 11 June 1960

Right: Four of the five competitors. Left to right: Francis Chichester, Blondie Hasler, Valentine Howells, David Lewis. The fifth participant was Jean Lacombe

little folkboat by his very size. You could not help thinking that, like some parody in a comic film, the two men had swapped boats. Tacking against the westerly wind, Lewis in *Cardinal Vertue* missed stays and had to wait for his sails to fill before he gradually got some way on her. The rough sea soon discouraged the attendant motor boats and they turned for home leaving the five yachts to fade into the grey distance.

At 1109 hours Chichester got out his blue book and red pen for the first time; during the race he was to commit 50,500 words to writing in this diary. In the book he wrote about his experiences (*Alone Across the Atlantic,* George Allen and Unwin) he writes:

Daily after breakfast when I had come through the night and was feeling rather pleased and optimistic with the next night some way off, I used to settle down, get out my blue book and imagine I was talking to my wife or some friend. I used to look forward to starting my little prattle. And again later in the day with a glass of whisky in my hand.

He was to set down with remarkable simplicity the romance of that first victory in the Transatlantic Race. It is the story, written in a low key and free from all overstatement, of how he and his 'crew' (his self-steering gear that he called Miranda and his Tilly lamp; he was as proud of them as if they were a team he had trained himself) were to overcome the elements. Whenever he brings off anything remarkable or takes some decision that is to win him the race he passes over it lightly, with humour and with that understatement so dear to the English – 'by chance . . . it so happened . . . my lucky star'. Yet nothing could be further from the truth; everything he did was carefully thought out. Sometimes he even goes so far as to apologize for letting himself go on about the details of his solitary existence.

Chichester was very soon to realize that the race was anything but a regatta, and that whisky sometimes helped the mariner to forget his woes.

Enjoying a whisky and lime plus biscuits after a strenuous

start. No particular blacks. Must have had race fever because I could not eat my breakfast, but had two Sealegs (anti-seasick pills) instead. Will probably shake out reef after refreshment. Feel better already. Stowed Plymouth charts. . . . Everything is going pretty well, but it obviously takes me longer than the others to set sails and the smaller boats are leaving me astern. Blondie's boat looks very odd. I wave to them. David tacks inshore after rounding the breakwater. He is well to windward of me and not far behind. By Jove that was good whisky! I really must have another.

The crossing was to take forty and a half days, all of them taken up with futile attempts to do something about the dampness below deck while tiresome everyday details assumed the importance of affairs of State. In his battle with the ocean they were like points scored by a boxer against his opponent – 'one direct hit to the plexus', when the toilet door swung open and bruised his right side severely; he was knocked down for several seconds. Later when in the cockpit, it was the cabin door that bruised his left side. 'Never a dull moment,' he says, unable to sleep at night from the pain. Six days later, when he had recovered from being pitched forward while trying to light the lamp, another injury on the same side – 'a fine double'. Then, having to brace himself against the rolling of the boat to avoid being thrown off the cabin seat he ended up with a stiff back.

Chichester's log is reticent on each occasion about these little mishaps, but he does admit that one much worse knock injured his foot so badly that he was unable to wear a shoe, making it difficult for him to keep his balance. As for his hands, bruised by the work of the first few days, they were in such a state that it hurt him to do anything.

For example I work the sink pumps with my small fingers to spare the bigger ones. My fingers are so swollen that I cannot close some of them and several finger nails torn into the quick. And last night I had difficulty in sleeping for longer than a few minutes because the muscle or whatever it is in my shoulder behind my neck aches so much.

There was worse to follow, an 'insuperable disaster' as he says:

I made some coffee before going on deck this time, but I had a bad start because I let myself be thrown across the cabin with serious detriment to my coccyx, the first part of my anatomy to hit the other side of the cabin, but that is repairable whereas my Thermos is not. It not only fragmented itself but did it all over the cabin sole, where I had to spend ten minutes trying to sweep it up.

Then there was another disaster:

My hat, the most comfortable of the type, be it Homburg or Stetson, I have ever had, personally selected for me by the

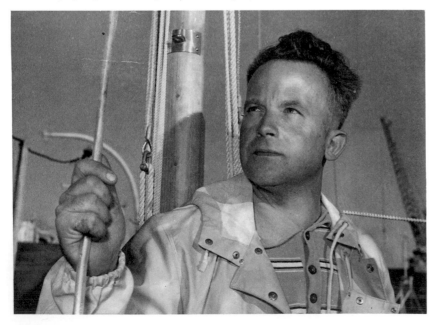

Jean Lacombe (left) raced a series boat that he was delivering to New York. Chichester (right) got off to a good start and was ahead when they reached the Channel

proprietor of one of the world's best hat-shops (Scotts of Piccadilly) . . . words fail me but I have made the tea. Ah, that's better . . . well I specially placed a hook for this hat in the safest snuggest place I could think of: just round behind the bulkhead of the forepeak. I thought it was the one place where nothing could crush it. I looked at it to find it covered with mildew.

And again:

Sad P.S. I dropped my barometer tonight and bust it; an old friend which has been with me on all my flights starting in 1929 and all my sea voyages and races.

As the days and nights went by he was assailed by loneliness and every attempt to establish radio contact failed. It was not that he was at all alarmed, but he was worried at not being able to tell the outside world of his progress. He thought of his wife Sheila whenever he went on deck because he had promised her that he would always wear a safety harness. He had also been given a splendid red and white lifebuoy as a present before the start of the race, but as he says: 'the trouble is that if I fall overboard I shall have to get back on board again to be able to throw it to myself!' He thought of his wife more and more as his difficulties increased, and remembered the secret bet he had made with himself – that he would get to New York before she did. Sheila was in the liner *Flandre* which was due to reach the United States on the 2 July and, having been thirty days at sea, he judged that he would not get there before the tenth. And that was over optimistic – it took no account of the clouds that were gathering on the horizon.

It is by reading between the lines of that little blue book that one begins to realize the measure of the undertaking. In worse physical condition each day after his departure from Plymouth, Chichester was pitted for twenty-four hours a day against the elements. His log gives some indication of his difficult moments.

. . . This time last night I was fast asleep among the blankets. A feeling of urgency, of apprehension, woke me.

Ten minutes later I was standing in two inches of water in the cockpit (in rubber boots); I got up to the mast, clipped my belt to a halliard and wrestled with the mainsail halliard in one hand to slack it away as required, grabbing handfuls of mainsail with the other hand to pull the sail down as I let the halliard go up. The wind, blowing gale force, bound the sail and its slides against anything they touched so that it was hard pulling to get it down.

The bows lifted in the air and smacked down 10 feet to dash a hose of water over my back. Flashes of lightning made the fog brightly luminous. There was no sound of thunder above the sail's own thunderclaps as it flogged in the wind. The rain was a deluge but I didn't notice that or didn't distinguish it from the sea-water hitting me.

The ship lurched, pitched, rolled, trying every trick to throw me from my hold. Standing on top of the dinghy to gather the sail to the boom, the seething white water from the ship's bow-waves rushed past at what seemed a terrific speed in the dark. One moment I was looking down at it from a height and the next it was quite close to me again near my own level.

On 4 July Chichester was nearing the American coast at last. He knew nothing of the positions of the other competitors; one thing he did know and that was that he could not afford to lose any time. He was almost in despair when off the Grand Banks of Newfoundland:

. . . I was not happy last night about charging blindly into the night, in dense fog, visibility 75 yards. I've always understood the Grand Banks are the greatest fishing-grounds of the world and must be stuffed with trawlers. Far more trawlers than even icebergs I would think . . .

All the same I shall be thankful to be off them. What a place! If you come around to the Grand Banks in a year's time you may see me there still tacking against light head-winds and against the current. My position has not changed much in two days. At present I'm doing 1⅓ knots in a direction I don't want to go, with a current of ½ knot against me from the direction in which I do want to go.

Then he found that he was approaching an area where his radio warned him that the U.S. Air Force was about to carry out bombing and rocket firing exercises.

It was only ten miles away when I tacked. I have been shot at or over a number of times by French and English guns while in a yacht and I dislike it. Though really the nearest to a hit was a shell which landed 50 yards away. I often wonder why but will never know I suppose. I don't wish to try out an American gunner's aim!

The nearer he came to land the more the weariness of forty days and nights at sea began to tell.

When I came to plot the night's doings on the chart I found I had made a most stupid blunder the night before in my plotting. There were two charts on the chart table. The top one on which I was plotting had its left-hand margin turned down to make it fit on the chart table. The edge of the chart below was showing on the left and I had measured my distance off the coast from the latitude scale which was less than half the scale on the chart below, thinking it belonged to the chart above. (This was all by candle light.) Therefore instead of being 20 miles from land I must have been only 8 off and when I tacked only 3. Therefore, had I gone into a deep sleep for two hours I might have had a rude awakening.

But he had come to the end; he had surmounted one after another the trials and tribulations of daily life on board, and always they served as an occasion for some jesting remark, as with his oilskins:

I made myself a pair of braces for my oilskin deck-pants with enormous success. These trousers always worked their way down however hard I belted them up. The number of times those damn things have hindered, hampered and harassed me by beginning to slip just as I got into a tizzie on the foredeck in the

Francis Chichester's Gipsy Moth III *was the largest yacht in the race and although 'Miranda' – his self-steering gear – was clumsy it enabled him to stay on course even when he was asleep. 'Thanks to her,' said Chichester, 'Gipsy Moth* can sail herself and her dead straight wake is a fascinating sight'

dark and wet. It is another of those music-hall chestnuts which are based on personal tragedy.

He was still unable to establish contact with the outside world, but on 7 July sent off the ironic message: 'Have reached Cape Race. Pleasant voyage. Still weigh 170 lbs and feel well. Tell my wife that I shall be late for dinner.'

At last on 8 July his signals were picked up and he was able to get in touch with Sheila in New York:

. . . It is quite an odd feeling of excitement to speak to someone after four weeks' silence. I said I would call back at 2100 hours tonight.

I lost my head this morning with all the excitement and fun, and I went in for an absolute orgy of cleanliness. I not only shaved – and really a self-binding harvester would have been more suitable than my Gillette razor – but I had a terrific bath. This is my name for a wash in toto.

Then the continental stations began to ask him about his state of health, the state of *Gipsy Moth* and his date of arrival. His replies were not without humour:

Thanks. Breakage of stanchion fastenings was unimportant but damage to steering vane was serious and inaccessible except to monkey. Took on role of monkey for several hours. Result success and thirsty monkey. For ETA supply accurate weather forecast, but try nineteenth.

British humour had to have its way – on an eighteen-hole golf course the nineteenth is the bar; and it was there that he proposed to meet his friends.

At 1330 hours on 21 July there was another message:

'This is *Edith G* at the Ambrose Light. Your wife is on board and wants to speak to you.' I was surprised at this voice. I knew it but couldn't place it. (No wonder! it was Captain Percy, senior captain of BOAC – a fellow court member of the Guild of Pilots and Air Navigators, who had been sent by the Grand Master, Prince Philip.) He said, 'Your wife wants to speak to you.' I could hear a word or two from her but she was pressing the wrong button. Then Percy came on, strong voiced: 'We will meet you . . . What is your course?' '270 degrees.' 'O.K. Two seven zero,' he said. . .

At 1550 I was met by a fishing boat with my wife aboard, looking very smart in her Mirman hat, and friends waving greetings.

As soon as I could decently do so I called out 'Any news of the others?' The reply was honey-sweet, 'You are first.'

But I was not to cross the finishing line all that easily. The wind veered and freshened. I had to down the ghoster and set old No. 2 jib, the old warrior. Then I had a snappy beat to windward to reach the light-vessel.

I rounded the light-vessel at 1730. The race was over 40 days 11 hours and 30 minutes after the starting gun. Distance sailed 4,004½ miles!

However, his arrival was anything but a triumphal procession. There were no escorting flotillas and the press, which had so far been content to publish such messages as the contestants had been able to transmit during the crossing, did not bother to interview Chichester; the American papers printed practically nothing about the future Sir Francis. Only the U.S. Air Force seemed to be interested in him, and in New York he was questioned by an Air Force captain who wanted to know, as Chichester says:

. . . if I had had any uncanny experiences or felt peculiar or if I had done anything odd during my 40 days of solitude. I did hear voices once. This was off the George's Bank in U.S. waters and I was opening my last bottle of gin. Startled by the voices I popped out to the cockpit and there were the owners – about five people sitting up on the top deck of a big steamer just going by, obviously enjoying their evening cocktails.

I need not have worried about being unable to think of any queer behaviour of mine because in the end he said that he was investigating the effects of solitude with a view to forecasting what it would be like for the astronauts when projected into space. I'm relating this because since then I've come to some conclusions about it. First that the sailing solitude doesn't have a real bearing on what the space travellers are likely to experience. On recalling some of my flights, I think that the sort of desolate loneliness you can experience in the air is quite a different matter. In 1931, nearly thirty years ago, I was making a solo flight in a seaplane from New Zealand to Japan, the first time that a long-distance flight had been made solo in a seaplane. I was crossing from New Zealand to Australia, 1,450 statute miles

of a sea crossing and I was having a rough time between the small island of Lord Howe and the Australian continent. I had motor-trouble, got into a severe small storm, and for hour after hour had been expecting to be dumped into the sea . . . When I reached safety and friendly people I felt cut off from them by a bottomless gulf of loneliness. I wrote then, 'If man ever flies alone out of the earth's atmosphere into space – to the moon – though he return safely, he will not live. The awful emptiness of space will change his soul and isolate it. Never again will he be able to make contact with man, beast, plant, or anything. And across the gulf of unutterable loneliness cutting him off from the world he knows, he will only see distantly through a film of strange, hard air. Perhaps the soul, belonging to space, will have recognised its home, and languish in utter loneliness for it until, loosening its hold on the body, it floats back again.' This was my view nearly thirty years ago. Well, we shall soon know now.

That is what Chichester wrote in 1961, merging the thoughts of a sailor with those of the lone flier. It was characteristic of the man to speak of eternity and solitude, of space and of navigation; but also of death, and that was always close at hand for him. Reading these words again, a dozen years later, there were those who felt that the great Sir Francis had chosen the fourth Ostar for his meeting place with a death that he had resolved not to await in a hospital bed.

Chichester and his wife Sheila enjoying his victory

Nine

1963: Eric Tabarly A resounding victory for France

In the dining-room of the manor house of Chalouère, not five miles from the pretty town of Angers, the Tabarly family was gathered round the big table. In the middle, as if hanging by the wire that led down from the chandelier whose socket was the only available power point in the ancestral home, the old wireless set crackled horribly. Eric's grandmother was holding the earth wire in a vain attempt to increase the feeble volume. It was after 3 o'clock and they were still waiting for the signal that they hardly dared to expect: 'The French sailor Eric Tabarly is about to cross the finishing line and win the second Transatlantic Race.' Yet to Guy and Yvonne Tabarly their son's victory seemed no more than a fitting climax to a lifelong devotion to sail.

It was only by chance that Eric had been born on the Atlantic coast; the summer of 1931 had been particularly oppressive and Mme. Tabarly, who was expecting a baby, had decided to leave the family home at Blois and spend a few days in the fresher air of Nantes. And so Eric first saw the light of day beside the ocean that was to make him famous.

After his son was a year old Guy Tabarly, agent of a textile concern and week-end sailor, lost no opportunity to take him with him in *Annie,* their easily-handled little yacht, and as soon as he was old enough his grandmother Marie gave him a sailor suit to wear. No wonder then that when he was four he spent all his spare time playing with boats on the ponds at Blois.

At twelve he had developed a habit of independence and did not hesitate to sail dinghies by himself at Préfailles in Brittany. But in 1942 it was unwise to go far from land and the occupation forces had prohibited all unauthorized navigation; young Tabarly, deaf to orders and even to the blank cartridges of the coast guard, went on sailing in spite of parental veto. After the war his mother had said: 'I did not think I should be afraid of anything after the experiences of those times.' She little knew what was still in store.

Attaining the years of discretion, so called, he was fonder of (and probably better at) making models than of learning French. His first model was 2 inches long and as he could not find any thread fine enough for the halyards he begged his mother to 'lend' him a lock of her long hair. She agreed with some reluctance, as she remembered long afterwards.

His progress at school made no memorable impression on his teachers, though he did reasonably well in mathematics and geography. What did get him through his earlier examinations was a curious command of English, but in the tongue of Shakespeare it was only the nautical terms that stuck in his memory and these he had learned by devouring the specialist magazines. In spite of these stumbling blocks he duly presented himself for the baccalaureat oral and was well below average until it came to the foreign language exam. The question put to him was a godsend: 'What do you do in the holidays?' Tabarly said a few words about Brittany and then mounted his sailing hobby horse. For a quarter of an hour the examiner got a veritable lesson in navigation and found that he was far from possessing the same mastery of the marine vocabulary as his examinee.

But this miracle didn't happen again. It was mathematics that kept him out of the Naval Academy, for at nineteen he could not hope to take the examination. He had reached the age limit for entry and was paying dearly for the hours spent aboard *Pen Duick,* a boat his father had bought. But he found a way round and

Eric Tabarly, the first to design a yacht specifically for the Ostar

prepared for the naval air-arm instead. This involved a year's service in Indochina and proved to be good preparation; he learned his navigation in Lancaster bombers just as Chichester had done before in light aircraft. As he still wanted to go into the Navy he applied for special permission to go back to France and sit the examination, which as a pilot officer he was entitled to do despite his age. This time he succeeded in getting in.

He still preferred 'practical work' with his father at the week-ends to his desk at the academy, and sailed in *Pen Duick* as often as he could. She was a stout little vessel built in 1898 and therefore of about the same generation as Slocum's *Spray*. Father and son were, however, already bitten with the racing bug and to satisfy their taste for racing Eric's godfather entered an 8-metre in the offshore events in the English Channel racing series. In spite of the meagre accommodation on board *Pen Duick*, she became the floating hotel for the crew of the 8-metre and sailed alongside the thoroughbred. The Tabarlys won their first trophies in boats belonging to friends. Meanwhile, Eric was doing his naval service in a mine sweeper based at Cherbourg and was later in command of a landing craft at Lorient.

In June 1962 Eric Tabarly saw in one of the magazines that the Royal Western Yacht Club of England was about to organize a second single-handed Transatlantic Race. The narratives of participants in the first race had already convinced him that this was an event exactly suited to his own passion for sport and for the sea. It now remained to find the right boat, for it was clearly out of the question for the old *Pen Duick* at sixty-six to attempt such a voyage. Reading about Chichester and Hasler had convinced him of two things; she must be light, and not too big or it would be difficult for one man to manage the sails. He therefore chose a length between Chichester's 12-metre and Hasler's 8-metre; this was *Margilic*, a 10-metre marine-ply boat that his friends the Constantinis built for him under his direction.

After her first trials in the summer of 1963 Tabarly soon realized that he had underestimated; if he wanted to win he would not only have to sell *Margilic* but build another boat within the year. Five months before the starting day he had still not got the money to build her. Tabarly the sailor had found, and not for the last time, that good intentions are not enough to take part in the race.

By scraping the barrel and salvaging the upper works of the old *Pen Duick* that had been given him by his father, and with generous loans he had received when all seemed lost, he set about building *Pen Duick II*. With a length of 13 metres she looked promising, but it still remained to rig her and fit her out. On 5 April, two months before the start, she was still an empty hull when she was launched at Saint-Philibert. He did not see how he could possibly beat the clock and get her ready in time for the race until the Navy came to his help at the last moment and put the dockyard and several men at his disposal. In his book, *Victoire en solitaire* (Arthaud), he wrote:

I sailed from Brittany on 16 May. I rowed my mother ashore in the dinghy; neither of us felt too good as I saw her force a smile in spite of her tears and I could not but feel a certain sense of guilt. I told her again that I would come back and that she need not worry. I could say no more for there was a lump in my throat. For me the Atlantic crossing had already begun as I saw her slight figure dwindle on the quay.

Twenty-four hours later he put into Plymouth where almost all the other contestants in the second Ostar had already arrived. *Pen Duick II* made a good impression there. She had been built for the race on the three basic principles of speed, lightness and strength. She was the biggest boat of them all and particularly noticeable was the perspex dome for shelter. Tabarly now met the heroes he had read about and with whom he was suddenly to share a new world. Chichester even came on board *Pen Duick II*:

When the boat was moored to the dock wall for inspection he seemed particularly interested in my self-steering gear. He had spent a lot of time perfecting his own, which had a big vane festooned in cordage at the stern of his boat that looked like a sail. My own, or rather Gianoli's, for he made it, was new and quite different. So far it had only just been tested in a wind tunnel; would it stand up as I hoped to conditions at sea?

Plymouth Sound was invaded by a whole fleet for the start: luxury yachts, old tubs, dinghies, sailing boats and canoes of every size were made fast alongside the breakwater to hail Francis Chichester and the other ocean racers.

Tabarly was up at dawn. His log had only been delivered the evening before and he and his father had worked like demons to get it fixed, for the start was at 10. At 9.30 he had just finished the job while the other boats were tacking up and down before the starting line in the Sound. The first gun was fired at 9.45; Tabarly didn't even hear it. His father was still on board *Pen Duick II* as she steered towards the line; a launch was to come for him and the two journalists who were aboard taking final photographs.

At thirteen minutes to the hour Tabarly was faced with a totally unforeseen crisis – disqualification – for the launch had not turned up:

I couldn't possibly go up to the starting line with a crowd on deck because the racing rules came into force ten minutes before the start. If the launch didn't come we would have to do without it, we still had the journalists' dinghy in tow. I luffed a bit to take some of the way off *Pen Duick II* and let my father and the two journalists get themselves and their forty pounds of photographic equipment into the little 9-foot dinghy. They sculled away with an oar that I gave them.

By 11.30 it had started to rain and the yachts were already out to sea. The first drops began to discourage the spectators in the boats that followed the race and by midday almost all of them were back in Millbay Dock. By 15.30 the land was no longer in sight astern and Tabarly had seated himself on the Harley Davidson saddle from which he conned ship, when the sound of a motor could be

The 44-foot, hard-chine, laminated plywood ketch Pen Duick II. *Tabarly felt that for the second Transatlantic Race he would need a boat that would sail close-hauled*

in heavy weather

In the calms off the American coast Tabarly hoists his spinnaker

heard through the mist; the missing launch had at last shown up and Eric's father had managed to find *Pen Duick* in spite of the decreasing visibility: 'We exchanged our last farewells and then the launch turned away and made for Plymouth at full speed. She sped into the mist and her wake soon vanished. At last I really felt alone.' So Tabarly found himself with nobody to talk to except his log book and, almost as broad-shouldered as he was tall, he lacked the pen of a ready writer; journalists thought him even churlish and inarticulate. All the same, his modest style is not without a certain appeal.

He explains that cooking took up a good deal of time and why he was not satisfied with bully beef and biscuits, why he thought it necessary to have a hot meal from time to time, why rice played so important a role in his diet and why, although it is easy to prepare it is so difficult to cook. 'At midday I added bits of tunny fish, as long as that lasted, and made it into an hors d'oeuvre. In the evenings, at least one day in three, I had rice with milk and jam. I also made omelettes flambées and spaghetti al pomodoro.' He also tells us that he habitually slept in pyjamas because he did not sleep so well in his clothes, although he had to put everything on again whenever he had to go on deck. But that's the official version; it's true that he undressed but it's equally true that he didn't have any pyjamas on board.

Occasionally he records his feelings in a few simple words, as for example when he found the stowaway:

Going on deck after lunch one day I found an unexpected passenger in the shape of a little bird, and it wasn't a sea bird. I had never seen one like it, it was bluish black with an almost completely round head, the face darker than the rest of the plumage and with a pointed beak surrounded by tawny lores. It was exhausted. We were four hundred miles from Ireland; it must have been carried up by some ascending air stream and lost its way in the rain and wind and mist when it came down again. *Pen Duick II* was too late to save the little stranger who had something in common with her own name, for in Breton 'Pen Duick' means 'coal tit'. In fact it was dying and a few minutes later it was only a little ball of feathers soaked in the incessant rain.

A little while after that he speaks of coming across a school of porpoises and one can imagine the conversation he might have developed with these supposedly highly intelligent creatures. One recalls Slocum's 'conversation' with the sailor from Christopher Columbus's ship who came to see him in his lonely nights.

But on Sunday, 31 May, after eight days at sea, the situation was not conducive to day-dreaming. The automatic pilot showed signs of distress and Tabarly went through what he describes as the most critical moments of the voyage.

This time I am really worried. Without self-steering the race seems to me already lost because to make any progress the boat will have to be steered all the time while the helmsman himself needs at least six hours sleep a day. That means that *Pen Duick* would be stuck, hove to, for a quarter of each day and while I slept the others would be on their way. The situation is disastrous . . .

I may reckon that I have practically no chance of winning. When I left Plymouth I had Chichester astern. I had set the spinnaker to get ahead, while he was content to follow with his twin jib topsails; but that didn't get me very much ahead. Chichester knew his boat from top to bottom whereas I was just beginning to know *Pen Duick* . . . I can imagine him comfortably sitting in his dog-house in friendly conversation with a bottle of gin or a Guinness and writing up his notes on 'how I won the single-handed race' while *Gipsy Moth* holds her course without his having to do anything about it . . . In the circumstances it seems only reasonable to give up the race and make a gentle cruise to Newfoundland where I could repair the automatic pilot and think things over; a reasonable plan but definitely the easy way out. I have every possible excuse . . . But uppermost in my mind is what I would do when I got back to France and how I would explain away my difficulties to all those who had helped and encouraged me. I must therefore at least finish the race; where I come in doesn't matter much. But not to give up and to finish somehow seems to me the most sporting thing to do. To give up a race because one no longer hopes to be first is unsporting. Having made up my mind it only remains to stick to the decision and get on with it.

Tabarly put together a contrivance of shock-cord and two blocks but it needed adjusting every hour and a half, day and night. *Pen Duick*'s alarm never stopped ringing in mid-Atlantic until, one day, it too ceased to function. But nothing daunted Eric. On his transistor he picked up the first unmistakable notes of pop music from Newport and Boston; they seemed to him like a contemporary American version of Odysseus' sirens and they kept him awake to the end of the race.

On 18 June at 10.45 he rounded the Nantucket light-vessel and asked if any other yacht had yet crossed the line. 'You are the first,' shouted one of the crew with a scribbling pad in his hand. Tabarly asked him to say that again, but that did not seem to be what interested the man:

'Where are you from?' he asked.

'What do you mean? I've come from Plymouth.'

'Where are you bound for?'

'Newport.'

'Are you the only man aboard?'

'Yes.'

The man wrote it all down carefully and Tabarly wondered if he had really understood his first question since he evidently knew nothing about the race. It was only several hours later that some reporters in a launch told him that he had indeed won the race.

At 15.45 the telephone rang at Chalouère. Guy Tabarly picked it up; it was a call from Paris, an official call from the R.T.L. radio station. Eric had won the race; already they wanted to have his first reactions. In that old room they were able to control their emotions; Eric's mother simply said, 'I have prayed every day since the race started that he would come back safe and sound. I was afraid that he might risk his life to finish the race – and he has won it.' Guy Tabarly rang off, 'Well the English have patently come off second best this time,' and he added, 'they say Chichester is still a long way off.'

At *The Times* office in London they were looking for references to other French achievements and even found a thirty-five-year-old editorial about Alain Gerbault. The popular press took a different line: The *Daily Mirror* commented sourly that one could not see why a Frenchman must always eat well, even by himself in the middle of the Atlantic, and attributed his success to the spaghetti. In a gentler vein the *Guardian* said that a slight earth tremor had been felt in Trafalgar Square as Tabarly crossed the finishing line. The *Daily Express* even had a headline running across five columns with the single word '*Merveilleux*'.

Tabarly sails past Brenton Reef Tower, marking the end of the race after a passage of twenty-seven days and three hours. Chichester, pictured below with Tabarly, arrived two days and twenty hours later. After congratulating Tabarly, Chichester added: 'His seamanship, his handling of his sails, his determination and his endurance made a formidable combination and he deserved to win'

By crossing the fiishing line between the Brenton Tower and No. 2 Buoy at 10.02 (local time) Tabarly, having taken twenty-seven days, three hours and fifty-six minutes, had completely shattered Chichester's record. The fire tender *Castle Hill* turned on its pumps to salute *Pen Duick II*'s arrival with a triumphal arch of water, and was soon joined by the launch *Malabite*. Tabarly could not hear above the din of welcoming sirens the few words shouted to him: 'I am Jean Savelli, the French consul in Boston. As a special distinction, General de Gaulle has appointed you a Chevalier of the Légion d'Honneur.'

Once on dry land Tabarly was to discover an America that never ceased to astonish him. On the one hand he was jostled by photographers loaded with cameras while on the other he was assailed by customs officers only interested in what foodstuffs he might still have on board, as if *Pen Duick* plied an ordinary trade between Europe and Newport.

And there were stranger things still. The finish of the race was not in New York but at Newport, that stronghold of upper-class, Anglo-Saxon, Protestant America. For some weeks past a society of distinguished linguists had been organizing a big reception for the winner, but no member of the English Speaking Union had imagined for a moment that a Frenchman would beat the redoubtable Francis Chichester. Tabarly's performance had ruined the grand Anglo-American gathering, but that did not stop his hosts from extending a cordial welcome to the French sailor who had now been joined by his mother and father. The *Newport Daily News* had a welcoming headline and Sir Francis Chichester was perfectly fair to the man who had beaten him by almost three days. And then, on the evening of the big reception, which had originally been conceived for his benefit, the cup awarded to the runner-up was given by mistake to a Belgian, who had indeed sailed across single-handed but who was not in the race. Only too pleased to find himself so highly honoured, he declined to hand the cup over to Francis Chichester. The man was Joan de Kat; we shall have more to say of him in the account of the next Transatlantic Race.

French radio and newspapers made Tabarly a star; some even said later that he had set France afloat again and it is certainly thanks to him that that country has become fully aware of the Ostar. It did not change Tabarly – his sole ambition was still to race and to win. But what had been no more than hinted at in 1964 was to become only too clear to all his circle – to win a sailing race you need solid financial backing.

Rehu Moana, the first multi-hull to be raced single-handed across the Atlantic. She was a fine catamaran, built for a three-year cruise, and gave a good performance, finishing seventh. She was the only home of David Lewis, the distinguished sailor who had competed in the first Ostar and had sold all he possessed, his medicine chest and his house, to sail the oceans

Overleaf: President Charles de Gaulle awarding Tabarly the title of Chevalier de la Légion d'Honneur after he had crossed the winning line

Ten

1968: Geoffrey Williams
The 'electronic teapot'

Sitting in the bar of the Royal Western Yacht Club of England at Plymouth, the Commodore, Jack Odling-Smee, scowled over his half pint. He had been involved in the organization of the Transatlantic Races since their inception and he thought that the way things were going Blondie Hasler would give it up sooner or later. 'Blondie is above all a man of ideas,' he remarked, 'and the Ostar has grown to such proportions that Blondie would prefer to leave the arrangements to somebody else.' *Jester* was indeed to set forth again but this time it was not with Blondie at the helm; Michael Richey had taken her over and Blondie had gone to Scotland for the salmon and trout fishing. The Ostar had grown into too vast a concourse for Hasler the ex-commando.

There were several things about it that he very much disliked: the huge financial outlay by some competitors, for example, or Geoffrey Williams' sailing machine that had brought the computer into the field of ocean racing. Thanks to the elasticity of the rules, or rather to the lack of rules, it was impossible to disqualify this vessel although her navigation was directed by a ground-based computer, just like an air liner; nor could they disallow the use of the boat as a sort of advertisement, although he thought that hardly right. It is true that she bore the famous name of Sir Thomas Lipton, the great yachtsman at the beginning of the century who bearded the Americans in their stronghold of Newport and did his best to win back the America's Cup from them. Nevertheless, the hull and canvas of the most beautiful boat in the third Ostar had been paid for out of little packets of tea!

But it was not this man who had done rather too much to win the race, but others who had done too little that worried Odling-Smee. Faced with a flood of would-be entrants, he and his colleagues had found it necessary to impose some sort of qualifying test; each competitor was required to have sailed his boat single-handed in the North Atlantic over a distance of 500 miles. He was well aware that this was no great matter in comparison with the unpredictable emergencies that can arise in mid-ocean, but he hoped it would discourage some of the freak sailors whose applications were always coming in. Yet day by day from the club windows he could see the fleet of boats in Plymouth Sound growing bigger and bigger. The helmsmen in the two previous races had been accomplished men, seasoned sailors who knew their boats from top to bottom and had plenty of experience. This time the thirty-five entries included quite a few lightweights, with boats unsuited to high seas and an experience woefully inadequate for the extreme difficulty of the course.

Immediately after the start on 1 June there was a feeling of anxiety at Plymouth, not unjustified in the light of subsequent events. Never had the weather forecast been so unfavourable, and the Channel had become a veritable thoroughfare for merchantmen and tankers of all sizes, putting even the best helmsman at risk. By 2 June these fears were seen to be well-founded for even the favourite had fallen victim to the

Geoffrey Williams, the planning perfectionist

dangerous traffic. It was dramatic – Eric Tabarly was run down by a cargo ship in the night and had to put back; one of the floats of his trimaran was damaged and he was worried about her rigging.

In *Pen Duick IV*, Tabarly had a vessel of revolutionary design that was the admiration and envy of all the others. 20 metres over all and 10.60 metres in beam, she was the biggest boat in the race, a fast ketch-rigged aluminium multi-hull. Tabarly had long debated whether to enter this boat or his fine *Pen Duick III*, a conventional yacht of an earlier vintage. *Pen Duick IV* had been completed only a few days before the race and he had had little or no experience with her, but the turn of speed of the great boat seemed a decisive argument and he remembered *Pen Duick II*, and how four years ago he had known as little about her.

He was able to start again after a delay of seventy-eight hours, which he hoped he would soon be able to make up, but this time it was his automatic steering that let him down. Within a few hours of his second start he had to put into Newlyn to repair it; it had jammed tight to the rudder and the boat was unmanageable. He made yet another start but found himself back again the same evening.

Tabarly the prime favourite was beaten: within a few hours of the start he had given up. It was partly his own fault, since the lack of preparation and the time taken to make *Pen Duick IV* ready were due to his decision, but the collision and the storm clouds that were gathering on the horizon of the third Ostar could only add to the gloom that already pervaded the race.

These fears were to be further justified by Joan de Kat. Basically, he was not the most unlikely of the contestants; at least he had the merit of having sailed across the Atlantic alone four years before, and even managed to get hold of the cup meant for Chichester although he had not taken part in the race. He was definitely an official entry for this race, but things were hardly to go according to plan. His boat was a 15-metre trimaran bearing the folk name *Yaksha*; the big bearded Belgian of twenty-seven had built her with his own large hands. A light trimaran entirely built of plywood, she did not give the impression of being able to stand up to heavy weather and after two days in rough seas the first news of damage to *Yaksha* came when de Kat was obliged to put into Alderney for repairs. Disgusted, he set out again but did not survive the first gale, losing his mast, his rudder and one of the floats. Little by little the trimaran broke up as she was struck by each succeeding wave. De Kat sent out an S.O.S. and launched his life raft. In London they had to mount an extensive search and rescue operation and the RAF and the French Navy scoured the ocean. After thirty-six hours hope began to fade, but two days later he was sighted by an RAF aircraft and taken on board a cargo ship. A week later the ship put into a small Danish port and the press was there to welcome the survivor of the first major shipwreck in the history of the race. De Kat had not expected that and was delighted; stepping ashore he said: 'I didn't have a chance in bad weather, but with a nice northerly or easterly wind and a calm sea all the way I would have made Newport in twenty days.'

There was one woman in the race, but when she was asked at the Royal Western Yacht Club about her chances her reply was immediate: 'None at all.' The charming Edith Baumann had no open-sea experience and her only qualifications were from instruction courses at several sailing schools. Only Jack Odling-Smee remembered that an Englishwoman, Ann Davison, had sailed alone across the Atlantic sixteen years before. She had indeed taken a year over it but that first feminine odyssey had been a brilliant success. Edith's object was of course quite different from that of her amiable predecessor's: she was not going for a cruise but to race – and what a race!

In *Koala III*, a trimaran exactly 11.70 metres over all, she began by messing up the start; twice she was carried onto the Plymouth breakwater. She came back to her mooring and then, when the wind changed a bit, tried again. This time she managed to get out of the Sound. On 26 June she sent out a distress signal saying that she was in danger of losing her floats. A search was started and on the same day she was taken on board the French warship *Henri Poincaré* and abandoned the race and her yacht.

Commandant Waquet had an even shorter run. His trimaran *Tamouré*, 8 metres overall, with a width of 6 metres, had such a ridiculously low freeboard that the tiny cabin seemed to stand straight out of the water. Nevertheless the safety committee had, after the prescribed inspection, allowed him to enter the race although for once all the experts were unanimous: the arrangements on board were hardly reassuring and his provisions inadequate; furthermore, he had taken on only about five gallons of water on the absurd assumption that he could make the crossing in ten days.

He had hardly crossed the starting line before he set a course for Brittany and so came back to France. His official reason for abandoning the race was the Air France strike; he had counted on being able to get his position each day from the pilots of the transatlantic Boeings and hoped to beat all records without the bother of navigation.

Lionel Paillard, a twenty-three-year-old science student, had already sailed 2,000 miles single-handed and had entered the race to prove that a small boat had a chance on corrected time. He was sailing the 11-metre sloop *La Délirante* but, knocked down by a breaking wave, he was dismasted. He did, however, manage to rig a jury mast, using the jib as mainsail and the storm jib as jib, and made the French coast sixteen days after he was dismasted. That was the end of the race for him.

As the days went by after 1 June the chart of the Western Approaches and then the Atlantic chart bristled with marks to indicate either distress calls or retirements. After 12 June all the boats ran into a deep depression; it very nearly finished the Swiss, Guy Piazzini in *Gunthur III*. Since the start he had sustained damage to his rigging and in spite of his considerable experience he had been unable to cope with problems arising from the stepping of his mainmast. He gave up on 13 June.

Marc Linski, who had not been allowed to compete in the preceding race because he was too young, was now twenty-two and had a good grounding in off-shore sailing. That saved his life, for the Force 10 storm winds literally knocked his little *Ambrima* to pieces and he was left adrift, dismasted and rudderless, and with a leaking hull that was little more than a wreck. He had neither radio nor an emergency transmitter because the rules did not require them, and nobody was worrying about what had become of him. At Plymouth they were only surprised that he had not been sighted from the air. And so he was adrift off the Spanish coast and it was only by a miracle that he was spotted by a fishing trawler before the situation became desperate. Linski was hardly on board before he saw *Ambrima* sink. It was only then that news of him reached London and Plymouth for the first time after the start; but even that didn't persuade the organizers of the race to make the fitting of a radio transmitter compulsory.

The list of retirements continued to grow. The British catamaran *Ocean Highlander* and the mono-hull *Zeevalk* withdrew from the race on 19 June, and on the same day David Pyle in *Atlantis III* put into the Azores for repairs. The Italian, Carozzo, withdrew on 27 June and the German, Heinemann, in *Aye Aye* on 30 June. The Swede, Willy Wallin, in *Wileca*, gave up six days after the start saying it was 'too cold'. Even into July there was still a sense of apprehension at Plymouth; on 1 July Eric Millis in *Coila* had abandoned the race 300 miles from Newport, due to the effects of contaminated drinking water. Pulsford in *White Ghost,* who had made a second start after losing a float early on in the race, retired with a damaged rudder on 4 July.

But the toughest sailors managed to get through – the French sailor André Foëzon for example, an instructor at a school of navigation and father of three children who was well qualified to handle his *Sylvia II,* a one-tonner designed by the great Stephens. He too had been a victim of the early storm and was dismasted. He thought at first of retiring but changed his mind and after putting back for repairs made a fresh start on 12 June. He finished twelfth at Newport and third among the French, after Bertrand de Castelbajac and Jean-Yves Terlain who had also got through the worst storm ever encountered in a Transatlantic Race, but fifteen days behind the winner.

'Geoffrey Williams sailed an electronic teapot,' people said, alluding to the financial backing provided by the firm of Lipton and to the system he had worked out for relying on a computer; purists in sail felt that his capacity as a businessman and applied scientist somewhat overshadowed his talent as a sailor. They challenged his victory to the last but that was hardly fair; if Geoffrey Williams was a late-comer to sail he was nevertheless an enthusiast.

Up to the age of eighteen Geoffrey had shown little interest in sailing; his home town of Redruth in Cornwall, though near the Atlantic, was more famous for its tin and copper mines. Sailing men did not much care to venture along that iron-bound coast pounded by heavy seas, where not a day went by without some tale of drowning and shipwreck. He grew to distrust the sea while developing a passion for meteorology, though the sea did begin to fascinate him. At school he used to sit by a window that opened onto a sea and sky swept by the west winds. After his mother's death he was a lonely boy who had no taste for the company of footballers and tennis players; all the excursions and discoveries of his youth were made by bicycle. It was when he was eighteen and his trips took him along the coast that he first came to admire the yachts with all sail set threading their way among the buoys in the sheltered estuary of the Fal: 'It was there that I experienced love at first sight and decided to become a sailor,' he said later. For the next two years he devoured the sailing magazines and acquired an encyclopaedic knowledge of the subject. He was nineteen when he boarded a yacht for the first time; it was their family doctor's and

that was his last sail before he left home for the United States.

He wanted to see the New World and after arriving soon discovered why so many had emigrated to that land of plenty; working as a jobbing gardener he was amazed to find that he could earn as much in a couple of weeks as one would need to live on comfortably at home in England for three months. But that was not what he wanted; he had dreams of a boat, and thought that he could afford one if he returned to work in America.

When he was twenty-one he had only sailed that one time. His second attempt only added to his enthusiasm and he spent the summer as deck hand in a '420' racing in Carrick Bay. Next year, and now with an honours degree, he went back to America and as a teacher at Saint Bernard College instructed young New Yorkers in the rudiments of sailing at the weekends. With one of his fellow teachers he chartered a 12-metre overall yacht and sailed to the Virgin Islands, taking with him six of his students for a practical course in the trade winds.

He soon found, however, that on land diplomas are not always as useful as some degree of manual skill and that teaching may be less profitable than gardening; he must work harder if his dream were to come true. The need for money led him to take a job in an employment agency. The tempo of American business and its competitive spirit astonished Williams and he was captivated by its efficiency; it took up all his time except when he was reading Tabarly's book on the 1964 Ostar. That was a revelation to him and Tabarly's attitude made a profound impression on him because, as he said in his book *Sir Thomas Lipton Wins* (Peter Davies, London):

It was clear that he had driven the boat in the same devil-take-the-hindmost attitude that is more commonly associated with off-shore racing in crewed yachts. He did not regard the crossing as a long and arduous cruise, but he had a fiercely competitive outlook which helped him to keep the boat going fast . . . his sleeping habits and his constant sail changing all reflected his determination to win the race.

Late in 1966 Williams wrote to Robert Clark, a British naval architect, saying that he wanted a boat for the forthcoming Transatlantic Race, giving his references and adding that he only had £3,000 at his disposal for the purpose. The reply was immediate, a short telegram simply saying 'Come immediately'. Williams hesitated at first but then flew back to London and told Clark all about his own limitations:

I had never sailed at night, never been to sea alone and, with the exception of two weeks in the Caribbean, my experience of ocean-going yachts was limited to about half a dozen short races. Curiously, Clark seemed rather heartened by these admissions. My pleading guilty to total ignorance of celestial navigation and only a theoretical knowledge of coastal navigation brought such a loud laugh that it made his trousers drop a couple of inches off his hips.

His eagerness came as a surprise to Clark who was also impressed by the soundness of many of his conclusions.

Edith Baumann was following in the footsteps of that great English yachtswoman Ann Davison, the first woman to sail across the Atlantic alone. She had a dog on board to keep her company and Tabarly's book to round off the seamanship she learned from her sailing instructor, Commandant Waquet. But she had no time to put it into practice; her trimaran Koala III sank soon after the start and she was picked up by the French frigate Geupratte and returned to France in the warship Henri Poincaré

Geoffrey Williams, an English lecturer, revolutionized the Transatlantic Race by building a superb yacht, the Sir Thomas Lipton, *with the financial support of Li*

Tea. He relied on a land-based computer to indicate his best course. The Lipton's fine lines earned her the name 'toothpick'

Experience, he pointed out, was a matter of intelligence, and the more intelligent a man was the less need would there be to show him what to do in a given situation, and the easier it would be for him to extrapolate from what he already knew.

Williams followed his suggestion to try to raise funds by finding a commercial sponsor, and during the first half of 1967 he wrote 3,000 letters, hoping that someone would come forward and that the boat would be a 60-footer. The last of the letters was written in July, to the producers of Lipton's Tea, and he had already given up hope when he received an encouraging reply from the board of directors. They said he could have the money needed to build the boat provided he named her *Sir Thomas Lipton.* And so Lipton's Tea became the first big sponsor in the Transatlantic Race. After all, ships were a natural adjunct to the firm, for over the centuries they had carried the produce of the tea gardens of India and Ceylon. Furthermore, the founder of the firm, Sir Thomas Lipton, was associated in the mind of every sailor with his famous races in *Shamrock* against the American holders of the America's Cup.

Geoffrey Williams' dream was at last coming true; he wanted a real thoroughbred and this was the specification:

> ... the minimum freeboard necessary to stop water coming over green, and its high ballast ratio and uncluttered decks would give me a clear and stable working platform ... no auxiliary engine, no W.C., no wash basin, no hanging lockers, no standing headroom, and its berths are made up of Pirelli webbing stretched across aluminium tubes.

The only concession to comfort below deck was a very big chart table facing the galley, so that he could prepare a meal without leaving his seat.

While the boat was being built he worked full time at the boat yard, picking up a very necessary knowledge of the odd jobs about a boat, of which he knew nothing. During the winter of 1967-68 he started on his physical training. The programme included weight-lifting and three or four training runs each day, each followed by a cold shower. Tense and weary, he was unable to sleep at night and tossed about in bed for hours until:

> The only remedy was to get up, put on shorts and a sweater and run along the beach and the pier. After running into the teeth of the gale with the wind tearing at my hair and the rain soaking my body I would feel better and return home exhausted and ready for sleep.

His first trial run in *Sir Thomas Lipton* was on 28 April 1968 and he had no difficulty with the 500-mile qualifying cruise. But there still remained the other big problem of navigation. Being an intelligent man he set about solving it in an entirely original way.

He proposed to use a computer to help him follow the most advantageous course across the Atlantic. He knew that the only way to make tactical use of meteorological information was to have access to sufficiently detailed weather maps in order to select the

The 56-foot Sir Thomas Lipton *close-hauled in a fresh breeze. She was the biggest English yacht in the third Ostar, with a flush deck and no top hamper so as to provide a clear and stable platform for handling the sails*

Geoffrey Williams taking in a jib on the foredeck. It took three years to get the Lipton into racing trim and elaborate the necessary computer links and

best course at a given time. That would mean having a facility on board to decode and reproduce the daily bulletins from shore stations, which would not only be extremely expensive but, even more important, would consume too much electrical power. He then hit on an idea that was to be the subject of much discussion at Plymouth: he would maintain contact with a shore-based computer which would use meteorological forecasts to work out the various possible courses, and the efficiency of the performance of the boat on each course, at the times when he was able to transmit his position.

Williams elaborated what amounted to a veritable order of battle. Early each morning the KDF computer at Bracknell was to compile a forecast chart for the next forty-eight hours, which would be transmitted to English Electric in London and fed into a second computer. At 0800 GMT Williams would radio his position to David Thorpe of the *Daily Telegraph*, who would pass it on immediately to English Electric. Taking into account *Lipton*'s course and speed, the second computer would pinpoint her on the Bracknell chart.

This computer would then work out all the possible courses for *Lipton* to steer in relation to the predicted wind force and direction, a sort of fan radiating from her present position and with a midrib along the shortest route to Newport. Furthermore, for each of these courses the computer would estimate the probable speed of the boat and the time to go for arrival in Newport from that fix. At 1100 GMT *Lipton* would again make contact with London and the computer would read out for Williams the three shortest routes to follow from his indicated position and the courses to steer. It would only remain for him to choose one of them, according to the tactics he had decided to apply.

In spite of all this meticulous planning, the start of the race on 1 June 1968 found Williams in a state of utter panic – that was something that he had not anticipated. He was getting himself some coffee and bread and honey when all the misgiving that had built up during the past months blotted out everything else. Overcome by nausea he was unable to stand and after an hour of misery he collapsed. His friends had to help him get the boat ready for the start. It was only after he had cleared the starting line that he completely lost this sense of fear, as he says:

I felt as if the worried mask I had been wearing for the past nine months was swept away and I smiled despite myself. I am sure that colour came back into my face as I realized that all the hectic preparations were over . . . no more telephone calls, no more bills, no more wellwishers and no more crises . . . At tea time I was happier than I had ever been . . .

When the deep depression set in over the race on 12 June the fleet was decimated but Williams, well-informed from London, made a slight northerly detour and avoided the Force 10 winds. He didn't let up for all that, and he had his bad moments. The boat

Spirit of Cutty Sark, *sailed by that genial giant Leslie Williams*

Geoffrey Williams, delighted with his victory, though it was already being contested as a result of the assistance he received from the land-based computer

failed to pay off when he was going about in a fresh Force 7, as he modestly describes it in his log:

> The jib starts to flog and I must rush forward to the halyard winch again before there is any chance of it being backed . . . as I crawl over the sail which has already fallen to the deck, a stronger gust of wind catches the jib and rushes it back up the stay. I am whipped off my feet and feel myself rising in the belly of the sail. I grab desperately for the guard rail and fall back to the deck . . . Little incidents like this frighten me more than anything and chastise me for leaving this sail set for so long.

And that very day he changed sail sixteen times. Next day Williams, who was still giving his position, was reported to be definitely in the lead, ahead of another Williams in *Cutty Sark*. But this Leslie Williams was gradually being overtaken by a twenty-nine-year-old South African student in the 50-foot ketch *Voortrekker*, while behind him the fifty-year-old American Tom Follet was showing that the multi-hulls also had a chance in the race; he finished third, ahead of Leslie Williams.

As the days went by, Geoffrey Williams was seen to be more and more clearly in the lead. Twenty-five days, twenty hours and thirty-three minutes after the start he crossed the finish line and won. The first criticisms of his 'over-ingenious' method were immediately heard; *Yachting and Boating Weekly* called it 'armchair navigation'. Williams himself estimated that his computers had saved him almost two days sailing. He had set out upon an intimate personal adventure and he knew that never again would he experience the sensations of that voyage.

Williams returned to Britain and took up his intended post in a sailing school, the Ocean Youth Club. It was a modest affair with only a few old cruising boats, but was unique in being financed and directed by the young people themselves; the adults were only there to supervise things. He found a little house in Cranborne Chase in Dorset, not even in sight of the sea.

> No longer can I feel a catch in my throat when I remember winter storms beating against the North Cliffs in Cornwall. Now I can go secretly at dusk and watch the deer, the badger and the hare, returning to my dark and lonely home and no longer notice that I am alone. It seems that I have reached the island in the granite pool of my boyhood.

Eleven

1972: Alain Colas Plymouth to Newport in twenty days

Long before Geoffrey Williams reached Newport Eric Tabarly was back in France; he had failed both in the race and in his design for a boat. Before the start he had been convinced that a trimaran could win but he had not been able to prove it; yet he was sure that *Pen Duick IV* was the best boat in the race, as he said to Jean-Paul Aymon of *France-Soir*:

I have been involved in this thing for the past four years and that is why I sailed across the Atlantic again single-handed in 1966 in *Pen Duick II*; it was to improve my chance of winning that I had the schooner *Pen Duick III* built for me last year and she carried everything before her that season.

I knew there would be half a dozen multi-hulls in the race when I started work on my 20.5-metre aluminium alloy trimaran at Lorient last January, and I knew too when it came to trying out her sails that I would need a lot of luck to get to Newport first, or even to finish the course.

Then after a couple of months I met with a series of setbacks, delays due to unforeseen problems associated with an entirely new design and delays due to strikes. I had been promised *Pen Duick IV* by 15 April at the latest but I was not able to sail her until a month later. In fact it only left me eight days to get her ready for the race.

And yet what an extraordinary experience it was to be on this trimaran. Her performance was all that I had expected; at last I could make more than 20 knots, a speed that no mono-hull

could reach. All might have gone well if I had not been the victim of a collision with a merchant vessel on the first night of the race and I didn't know how much damage had been done until I put into Plymouth again for repairs.

As I said when I got back to Lorient today, the welded connections between the hull and the floats were showing signs of increasing weakness. The damage due to the collision itself prevented them from taking the strain as designed and even if, in spite of the trouble with the rudder, I had gone on my way I should certainly have had to abandon the race.

What am I to do now? I must say that I am convinced that if *Pen Duick IV* had been in good shape I would have had the best boat in the race. I am sure too that I had overestimated my rivals; out of the five multi-hulls that I saw at Plymouth there were only three that seemed much good. Even if I had been sailing *Pen Duick III* I should have had a chance of winning. I still stick to my theory – a trimaran ought logically to win, and I mean to prove it.

My boat was built to cross the Atlantic . . . I could certainly cover the 3,000 miles from Plymouth to Newport faster than the fastest boat in the race; even if she were in the lead by eight or nine days – the record won't prove anything. What I do know is

---

Alain Colas, skipper of the fastest trimaran

that *Pen Duick IV* won't finish on the scrap heap. I abandoned the race but *Pen Duick* has not said her last word yet.

On 1 February 1970 Tabarly found a purchaser for *Pen Duick IV*: Alain Colas, a young lecturer at the University of Sydney who like Chichester had gone to the Antipodes in search of adventure. Colas, from the heart of France, the son of a dealer in ceramics in the charming old town of Clamecy on the banks of the Yonne in the Nièvre, had also discovered the allure of sail. He too cherished a hope, the hope that some day he would have a real boat of his own. In 1968 the boat of his dreams was *Pen Duick IV*.

Then he joined Tabarly's team and even sailed with him for the start of the 1968 Ostar in his aluminium trimaran; the lecturer had forsaken his pupils to learn himself from that great master. He had fallen in love with the boat and sailed in her half-way round the world, taking part in races, record-breaking runs and cruising voyages, handyman, crew and cook by turns.

When Alain Colas heard that Tabarly was obliged to sell *Pen Duick IV* because an obstinate trustee refused to pay the interest on the money he had invested in the boat, he at once offered to buy her. But the boat was priceless, a unique prototype, and no doubt worth tens of millions of 'old' francs or some hundreds of thousands of 'new', and Colas hadn't anything like that. Eventually the two sailors discussed a price of 230,000 francs, a sacrifice for Tabarly but a fortune for Colas who drew on the family money and his own savings, put in what few goods he possessed and heavily mortgaged his future earnings.

For two years his 'dancing girl' never let him down, in the Indian Ocean and the Pacific during a single-handed non-stop voyage round the world in the record time of sixty-six days, Colas and *Pen Duick IV* were an ideal couple and attained a speed that had never been equalled: 305 miles in twenty-four hours. He made modifications, and said kindly of her: 'She's no longer the wild cat that Tabarly handed over to me.' This then was the perfectly matched pair that presented themselves on 17 June 1972 for the start of the fourth Transatlantic Race.

The 1968 race had witnessed the defeat of the multi-hulls; one has only to consider the numbers involved, thirteen of them out of twenty-five, or more than a third. In the 1972 race there were no more than eight out of fifty-eight; this, on the other hand, was the race of the big boats. The small boats were the exceptions, like David Blagden's 19-foot *Willing Griffin* or the Czech Konkolski's 22-foot *Niké*. Even Francis Chichester had a longer *Gipsy Moth V* and 65-foot boats were not uncommon. There was also *Second Life,* sailed by the Dutchman, Dijkstra (71 feet), *Strongbow* by the Englishman, Martin Minter-Kemp (65 feet) and *Wild Rocket* by the Frenchman, Joel Charpentier (63 feet). With her length of 70 feet *Pen Duick IV* had nothing to fear from her rivals and Colas had a phrase that pleased the reporters: he called her his 'floating tennis-court'.

The French press took kindly to her new skipper. He was fluent yet concise, smiling and patient, quite a different sort of single-hander from Tabarly the taciturn; not too tall or burly, he was well-built and muscular, yet hardly looked the sailor when not wearing oilskins. With that malicious twinkle in his eye and questioning glance, if you saw him carrying his briefcase you had a preview of the businessman and able public relations officer that he was to show himself a couple of years later.

All the same, Colas was not the star turn at Plymouth, both because they had seen *Pen Duick IV* before and because there were two other big stars on the bill, Jean-Yves Terlain in the huge *Vendredi 13* and the great Francis Chichester.

In the twelve years that followed that first race in 1960 Chichester had gathered all the laurels and broken all the records; absent in 1968, he was back again this year. On the eve of departure this most famous sailor had asked his friend Tubby Clayton to celebrate communion on board *Gipsy Moth V* with only his wife Sheila and his son Giles. The curious and the admiring kept their distance, out of respect for the man who had become more and more an invalid; he had just undergone a serious operation and onlookers said that he had almost to be carried on board – and added in a whisper 'he can't possibly win, but what a man!' Some even wished in secret that he might not return; it was unthinkable that a man like Chichester should end his days in the gloomy corridors of a hospital. 'If die he must,' they said quietly, 'let it be far from human sight, in the midst of the ocean that was his kingdom.' But the sea gods had decreed otherwise, and what came to pass was to be a shock to his friends.

In the Sound, within a few minutes of the start, *Vendredi 13* narrowly avoided collision with *Gipsy Moth V*. Gone were the days of the informal Ostar; all the world was able to follow the incident on television and they blamed Terlain. But soon after, while the cameras were still focussed on *Gipsy Moth*, they came to realize that this was only the beginning of a long drawn-out tragedy. Jean-Paul Aymon, on board the *Observer* press launch, described in *France-Soir* the sad spectacle that met his eyes.

During the second hour of the race this experienced sailor found himself in a difficult situation, close in to a rocky shore and unable to go about while grappling with one of the foresails. Like other reporters, we were horrified to see the old warrior almost groping his way on deck, losing his cap and spectacles and hanging on to a shroud. With a typically English sense of decorum our boatman steered away from *Gipsy Moth*, as if our presence might embarrass and annoy the old sea dog, and simply said, in a very loud voice, 'Sir Francis can certainly get himself out of that bit of bother – let's get back to Plymouth and wish him the best of luck.'

Clearly exhausted by the effort, Sir Francis went below, coming up again later to take control of *Gipsy Moth*; but off-shore things only got worse. Illness was taking its toll and to relieve the pain he had to give himself the injections prescribed by his doctor. As he admitted later, 'I would suddenly see the sky go black although it was broad daylight only a few minutes before.' By 5 June he was in the Atlantic, under a cloak of silence that he did not wish to break

Pen Duick IV. *She was beaten in 1968 but sailed again in 1972 with a different skipper, Alain Colas, in a race that had already changed its character*

but a silence that it was hard for his friends and family in London and Plymouth to bear.

Not that his was the only boat out of communication with the land; five others including the three favourites, *Pen Duick IV*, *Three Cheers* and *Vendredi 13*, were off the air, but they were known to be following the northern route and were transmitting no messages so as not to give away their positions.

Onlookers were horrified when Terlain barely avoided collision with *Gipsy Moth V* just after crossing the starting line. At the helm of his enormous *Vendredi 13* her skipper looked like some savage in his metal-sheathed crash helmet. She was certainly a fine boat, the work of the American designer Dick Carter, and if there was a trend towards longer hulls she certainly beat all records at 39 metres. Terlain had already made a name for himself by finishing second in the single-handed Transpacific in March 1969, only beaten by the formidable Eric Tabarly – a fine performance for the youngest entry for he was not yet twenty-eight at the time.

Although born in the town of Angers, Terlain like Alain Colas had passed his childhood in the Nièvre and only spent the summers in Brittany, where his parents most often left him ashore while they took his two sisters and his elder brother cruising with them in the 8-metre family boat *Quo Vadis*. At twelve he had hardly ever sailed although he had wanted to. He was sent to school in Plymouth, that stronghold of English sailing, but for four more years he did not even get a chance to go aboard. His dream became a passion and Terlain saved every penny to buy himself a boat. He had not saved anything like enough when, at fifteen, he met two boys who had been thrown out of the Sea Scouts for indiscipline – Dominique Guillet and Pierre English. The three of them pooled their funds, bought a derelict racer, smartened her up and made their first essay in sailing on the river Maine. That summer, having no cash, they decided to go to sea as stowaways. They were arrested as vagrants by the police at La Trinité-sur-Mer and Jean-Yves was sent off to a monastic boarding school. It gave him a compulsive longing to escape and since the sea cost too much he bought an old scooter when he was seventeen and set off to explore the byways of Morocco.

When he got back to Nantes he played the turlisiphon, a sort of slide-trombone, in the Ecole des Beaux-Arts jazz orchestra for pocket money before passing the entrance examination for the Beaux-Arts in Paris, recording a trumpet tune and then setting up as an interior decorator. In May 1968 Guy Piazzini, the Swiss who had already sailed once in the Transatlantic Race, offered him a boat so that he could sail in it too, provided only that he could get her taken overland from Toulon to the Channel. But in May 1968 there was a general strike in France. To get to Plymouth on time it was first necessary to find a carrier, persuade the crane men to offload the boat and finally get everything ready for the start.

Then there was the difficulty of putting his theoretical knowledge into practice; his dead reckoning was to say the least sketchy and he had never taken a sextant shot. Little by little he got into the swing of the race and although his radio was out of action he was one of the few French entrants not to retire from the 1968 Ostar, in which many had suffered heavily from the severe weather. Out of the thirty-nine starters only eighteen reached Newport, and he came in tenth after a thirty-eight-day passage.

On his way to take part in the 1969 Transpacific Race, Terlain met in New York the forty-three year old yacht designer Dick Carter, who had some revolutionary ideas and had already carried off a good many firsts with *Red Rooster* in the R.O.R.C. races. From the East Coast to San Francisco he had set up all sorts of projects, including one for a huge yacht to be sailed single-handed. Terlain suggested rigging her with three masts and three boomed jibs. He found his Ostar entry form waiting for him when he got back from the Transpacific and managed to establish some sort of standing with the Ministry concerned with youth activities and sport, the Minister having sent him a congratulatory telegram in Tokyo. In this way he was even commissioned to visit Dick Carter in America and together they quietly got on with planning their next boat. In February 1972 Terlain went to live in Pouliguen to supervise the work of building. Three friends, Dominique Guillet, Olivier de Kersauson and Jean-Pierre Millet, helped him to fit her out. She was launched on 18 March and made her first trip under sail on 5 April. During the 500-mile qualifying cruise Terlain discovered innumerable necessary modifications, and the work on board was never-ending. On 6 June, when *Vendredi 13* was finally fitted out for Plymouth, Terlain took on board at the last moment three big hastily made genoas to improve her poor performance in light airs.

At Plymouth *Vendredi 13* was certainly the cynosure in Millbay Dock. She was also the prime favourite, for the bookmakers were offering two and a half to one as against five to one on *Pen Duick IV*. Among the crowd that swarmed around the boat Terlain was the only one to remain calm. People admired his detachment and relaxed charm but they spoke too of his unawareness of the difficulties ahead.

Half an hour before the starting gun on Saturday, 17 June, his friends were still helping with last minute adjustments that never seem to be over; two hours later *Vendredi 13* was well ahead. But trouble began on the second day out. First the jib halyard winches jammed and Terlain had to change the halyards and use other winches to hoist sail, which, for one man, was very hard work. On the third day he found that a short circuit had left him with a flat battery which he could not recharge. That led to fresh problems; his navigation instruments were out of action and so was his radio and his met. decoder. Fortunately he had provided an alternative power source for his automatic steering which continued to function. On the fourth day the halyard blocks at the masthead, which were too small, also jammed and that made it almost impossible to change sail. On the fifth day *Vendredi 13* was struck by a heavy sea and Terlain was thrown from his bunk against the deckhead and suffered a head wound an inch or more in length. He hastily prepared a dressing for it but resolved never again, even when asleep, to be without his crash helmet. On the seventh day he sprang one of the winch pawls and the crank hit his arm so hard that he thought he had broken his wrist. Miraculously his wrist-watch saved him – and he escaped with a bad sprain. To make it worse,

---

Sir Francis Chichester sets out on what was to be his last race. He was known to be weak and ill, and during the second hour of the race reporters were horrified to see him almost groping his way on deck, losing his cap and spectacles and hanging on to a shroud

there was little wind for some days. But *Vendredi 13* remained in the lead.

On land, of course, nobody knew anything about all this, and by 27 June people were getting worried, as Gérard Petitpas and Jacques Vignes record in their account of the race, quoted in Alain Colas' book, *Un tour du monde pour une victoire* (Arthaud):

It was understood before the start of the race that Jean-Yves Terlain would report his position regularly; he had the necessary transmitting equipment and his continued silence was agonizing. As long as the weather was bad one could imagine that Terlain was too busy to bother with his radio but one hoped to hear something as soon as the weather moderated, and not a word had come through.

Alain Colas on the other hand seemed deliberately to have chosen silence. His position must indeed have been known to some, since he had a radio beacon on board that could be picked up through a satellite link to give a fix every ninety minutes, but the secret was well kept. As for Tom Follet in *Three Cheers,* he had no way of communicating with the shore. Because of this lack of contact, the big event in the race was not made known until long after it happened. It was by a most extraordinary chance that after covering 1,500 miles *Vendredi 13* and *Pen Duick IV* should meet in mid-ocean. Alain Colas was still infatuated with *Pen Duick IV* and it was in this frame of mind that he awoke on 27 June.

What a lovely day! It's much better in the cockpit than down below in the fug. Getting up on the coach roof, sextant in hand, I screwed up my eyes for the glare was already strong – and there was Terlain! There, two miles away, that strange sail lost from time to time behind the jib, it was *13*; unbelievable, not one chance in a million!

I have lashed the helm and will let this super-greyhound do the steering. Following in his wake I have raised him above the horizon after ten days at sea, almost exactly ten days and exactly half-way, 1,455 miles from Plymouth on a great circle! We have got past the zone of tacking against strong winds and I have kept level with this mammoth on his own ground. I must not let up now, even in the lighter winds we shall get between here and Newport, where a trimaran should make the difference if she does not come apart. *Vendredi 13*! I am delighted – I can hardly take my eyes off her. Nothing of the kind has ever happened before in all the history of sail. To crown it all there was a witness to our meeting; a merchant ship westward-bound crossed our track and sailed right between us. She had a blue funnel with a big letter 'T' in a white rosette.

I was able to sail closer on the wind than he and could see his three masts growing taller; then the dark hull came above the horizon and I could make out details on deck. What was I to say to him when we were abeam, perhaps something in the Stanley-Livingstone manner like 'Jean-Yves Terlain, I pre-

sume?' Or perhaps something frivolous like, 'Is this the right way for Newport?'

The sea is calm and the light westerly wind is raising little waves that reflect the sun in a thousand facets as if the ocean were strewn with diamonds. I was level with *Vendredi 13* by mid-afternoon and bore away to increase the distance between us as quickly as I could. Terlain was sitting in his cockpit. I signalled to him. He got up and went below, then coming up again strode along his deck to the pulpit, looked at his sails, and then at me. I gave him a big wave and he waved back. It was like a new start, but this time a friendly sailing match.

As Petitpas and Vignes say in their account of the race, Terlain continued to think that *Pen Duick IV* had not really outdistanced him but had gone off on a more southerly course; this was only partly true and led to the indecision that marked the final hours of the race. Colas saw things differently and wrote in his log for Wednesday, 28 June:

The heat is terrific and I am very thirsty; already badly sunburnt on the neck and shoulders in spite of the big hat of plaited pandanus that I brought back from Tahiti. I have a feeling that today will decide whether the race is lost or won. The flat calm tells me that, and I had time enough to work out a philosophy, in the Arafura Sea and the South Atlantic, on my way home.

I don't mean to give in before I am beaten. I know that a region of calm has geographical limits and that you must get out of it at all costs, without waiting for a change, by sculling, or wearing flippers or blowing into the sails! I had been over the boat with a fine-tooth comb before the start to get rid of anything unnecessary and now I have got another obsession about weight. Half the spare battens have gone overboard and a whole crate of tinned food, all the wine and spirits – and two jerry cans of fresh water by way of giving myself a good shower! I don't know if all this has made much difference to her waterline but it has some morale value and I'll get rid of the batteries too; they are flat without that damned generator that smothers me with smoke and splits my ear drums and just wastes petrol . . .

We are practically on course for Newport I'm glad to say. I only hope Terlain has been becalmed too! Anyway I would give anything to know where Tom Follet and Jean-Marie Vidal have got to in their ultra-light trimarans.

Thursday, 29 June. We are long past the early days of the race when I stayed muffled up in all my clothes twenty-four hours a day, even when I occasionally crawled into my sleeping bag. Here I am at the helm in pyjamas and slippers – slippers are just the thing for the open sea! No sleep at nights except for half an hour or so now and then, which I snatch when I can in the light clothes that are all the weather calls for. That is my rule, a little sleep when things are going well, and I have even rigged myself a real bed with flower patterned sheets and counterpane . . . Anyway I'm fed up, we've got to get the boat out of this glue pot of a sea.

In Plymouth, Newport and Paris there was still no news; to quote Petitpas and Vignes:

Saturday, 1 July: At the end of the second week we are still

After a long ominous silence a freighter by chance established contact with Chichester. He was a long way off course and his slow progress suggested he was steadily weakening. Gipsy Moth presented a sad spectacle with no one on deck and her jib topsail in the water

without news of *Vendredi 13* and *Three Cheers*, but if the hopes of Terlain and Colas who expected to get across in twenty days are fulfilled we should not have to wait much longer.

Sunday, 2 July: *Three Cheers* has been reported well behind *Pen Duick IV* and the feeling grows that the race will be fought out between Terlain and Colas, that is of course if all is well with *Vendredi 13*.

Monday, 3 July: Dramatic news – *Vendredi 13* has given her position; is she ahead of *Pen Duick* or behind? It is impossible to say, but it is clear that the two French boats are well in the lead since *British Steel* gave her position the same day as 46 degrees West 46 degrees North and *Strongbow* has reported damage: her wind motor carried away and a forward bulkhead split.

Friday, 7 July: Terlain reports that he is fifty-three miles off the Nantucket light-vessel and eighty miles from Newport; with variable winds *Vendredi 13* is making between 2 and 10 knots. Will *Pen Duick* and *Vendredi 13* make contact and finish the Transatlantic Race like a race round the buoys?

At 19.00 (Paris time) *Vendredi 13* has been reported by the Nantucket light-vessel; *Pen Duick IV* is not in sight; so Terlain now seems the probable winner. If the wind holds he expects to finish at about 0700 hours on Saturday (Paris time).

But Colas didn't mean it to end that way; this is what he says:

I shall long remember that last night on watch, in which I made good only sixteen miles . . . Freighters, coasters and trawlers kept up a dance round the almost motionless boat, bright spots danced before my eyes as I tottered at the helm. Come on Colas, an Ostar is worth it! Two or three times I felt myself swaying, brought up in my fall against the compass, the sides of the cockpit or the edge of the coach roof . . . It was an excuse for a bowl of coffee or for going onto the other tack, always trying the other tack.

In the morning the sea was ruffled by flaws of wind that increased a little and gave me some way, justifying the spinnaker. Breakfast and domestic chores helped to pass the time. Listening to the American broadcasts I was stupefied with the pop music on every wavelength. I now regretted those tens of miles to the southward, but for which I might perhaps have made Newport before the wind dropped.

A launch came up on the horizon, fishermen who asked me if I was in the race, to which I said, 'Yes of course,' hoisting my tricolour ensign in a hurry; 'but do you know if anyone else has got in?' No, not as far as they knew – the lump in my throat went away; but I must watch that big week-end schooner. I felt a wave of happiness but this was no moment to let slip for there was now enough wind to fill the spinnaker.

The big red balloon stamped with the Norman leopards pulled me along at four knots; *Pen Duick* is fantastic, like a railway

The fourth Ostar was dominated by the multi-hulls. Jean-Marie Vidal's Cap 33, *designed by Allègre, was, with* Pen Duick IV, *among the fastest*

engine; the driver has only got to shovel on the coal, a puff of wind will move her. I sighted land at 16.45; it was Block Island marking the southern entrance to the bay. A light aircraft flew over and turned for Newport and I soon realized that my brother Jean-François was on board, invited by Claude Lelouch who had chartered the plane to fly over his chicken *Vendredi 13* at the Nantucket light-vessel.

Rivetted to the helm I was doing everything I could because I was afraid that the sea breeze would die down before nightfall. The land grew nearer but no boat had yet come out to meet me. I began to have misgivings and really wondered if the fishermen had been wrong. Then I came up with the DGA buoy that marks the entrance to the Newport Channel and lowered the spinnaker, a tough job for 163 square metres of canvas is no small matter. Then, while I got it all clear as fast as possible and eased off the jib for the last leg towards the finishing line, a swarm of light aircraft started madly circling the boat while a red helicopter hovered overhead and took the wind out of my sails. But I didn't care; deafened by the buzz of aircraft and the throbbing of my own temples, I hardened in the sheets at top speed and gathered way.

The end of the story came on Saturday, 8 July, when, as Petitpas and Vignes relate, it was still the evening of Friday, 7 July, in America:

Terlain had rounded the Nantucket light-vessel at 1420 hours, that is to say almost four hours earlier, and nobody doubted that he would be in by nightfall or by dawn at the latest; they were all set to welcome him. Then it was announced that *Pen Duick IV* had been sighted, and less than two hours away from the finishing line – another dramatic development! *Pen Duick IV*, the ghost ship that had not been heard of for twenty days, had suddenly cropped up within sight of Newport. At 20.10 (01.10 in France) *Pen Duick* crossed the line. She had won in twenty days, thirteen hours and fifteen minutes. The record set up by Geoffrey Williams was just under twenty-six days.

For Colas it was the happiest day of his life:

My air cover had dispersed and all was quiet. Boats were pouring out of the bay as I steered towards a brilliant sunset, against which was silhouetted the Brenton Reef Tower perched up on its piles. There was the line – I was about to cross the line; and there was I, alone with the joy that filled my heart to bursting, alone before that bright and silently setting sun.

Sitting in the cockpit, I could no longer move and felt the tears stream down my cheeks – the years of dreaming and of preparation, the long road, the sacrifice of all I possessed, the help of friends, the joys, the frustrations – and now I was crossing the line. I had won the race. I knew it was the happiest moment of my life. I went forward to lower the sails, a loose heap of white on the deck. My movements were those of a robot and my walk must have had as much elegance as a penguin's. I was surrounded by boats and there was Téura smiling at me and my brother Jeff saying over and over again 'It's marvellous –

marvellous.' Among the siren blasts and shouting, the questioning by reporters, there I was stuck on board for everyone to stare at, laughing, shaking hands, talking into television microphones above the noise of engines, blinded by the camera flashes. I had won the race and my dream had come true.

The Coast Guard launch came alongside and the President of the Race Committee gave me his hand in congratulation. The trimaran was taken in tow amidst an ever-growing crowd of other craft to the accompaniment of hooters and fog horns, the cars following along the bank joining in the chorus. When we reached the Port O'Call marina the pontoons were black with people and to a cacophony of every sound imaginable my old war horse was tied up and I was confronted by the press . . . Twenty days, thirteen hours and fifteen minutes; it beat all records and before my eyes there danced the prospect of a race round the world, round the world to victory!

Now began the long wait for the becalmed *Vendredi 13* because the wind fell away as soon as *Pen Duick IV* had crossed the line. However, the wind got up again on the morning of 8 July and *Vendredi 13* was not more than two hours' sail from Newport. On board, Terlain turned on the radio to hear the latest news only to learn that *Pen Duick IV* had beaten him to it. At that very moment his automatic pilot packed up. *Vendredi 13* had nevertheless completed the course in twenty-one days, five hours and thirteen minutes.

At 1130 hours on Tuesday, 11 July, the Frenchman, Jean-Marie Vidal, in *Cap 33* finished third with a time of twenty-four days, six hours and thirty minutes, also beating the 1968 record and a few hours ahead of Brian Cooke in *British Steel*.

The 1972 Ostar had proved a triumph for the French, who had dominated every aspect of the race; apart from the Colas-Terlain-Vidal trio, eleven of the twelve French entries were among the first nineteen to finish. For example Alain Gliksman made a time of twenty-eight days, twelve hours and fifty-four minutes in *Toucan*, 10.5 metres overall, beam 2.14 metres, and under two tons, coming in eighth and only ten minutes behind *Strongbow*, a vessel twice her length.

Another of the stars was Marie-Claude Fauroux, the first woman to complete the course in a single-handed Transatlantic Race, although many of the other competitors thought she had no business to be in it. Marie-Claude Fauroux in *Aloa* finished fourteenth in the very good time of less than thirty-three days, a week less than Chichester's time in the first Ostar.

Brian Cooke's performance did little to console the English for a serious defeat; for them this race marked a turning point in the history of single-handed sailing. Their supremacy, threatened already by Tabarly, was now more than merely challenged and in

Jean-Ives Terlain on board Vendredi 13. *Working with the American designer Dick Carter, Terlain planned a big mono-hull for single-handed sailing, and this was the boat the trimarans had to beat*

Vendredi 13. *She had a 128-foot glass fibre hull, no mainsail and only boomed jibs on her three 25-metre masts*

the wake of their master the French had again shown themselves redoubtable sailors. It was then too that the English came to know that they had lost their great leader, struck down by age and ill health.

Ever since the start of the race it had been a very anxious Britain that had tried to follow the progress of an ominously silent *Gipsy Moth*. In London they feared the worst and it was not before 25 June that there was new hope at the RORC and the Royal Western, and wherever else there was the love of sail. It was no search operation to find Chichester, but a chance encounter that made it possible to fix his position.

On 27 June, just when Colas and Terlain met in mid-Atlantic, a freighter established contact with Chichester. It was a long way off from the two Frenchmen and on a far more southerly route that *Gipsy Moth* was making her slow progress. Sir Francis found all this worry and solicitude quite ridiculous and returned a short answer to the call from the steamer: 'I have been ill but I don't need any assistance, I'm O.K.' But that was hardly enough to satisfy his friends. RAF aircraft took off to keep an eye on *Gipsy Moth*, whose slow progress showed that her skipper was steadily weakening, until eventually the message that everyone expected came through: 'I am weak and cold. I am going back to Brest.'

On board the weather ship *France II* the tone of this message, from an old man whose reputation they all knew of, was interpreted as no less than a distress signal. The heavy weather made it necessary for her captain to come alongside without being able to lower a boat. The weather ship struck the mizzen mast about 10 feet below the truck and left the upper section hanging dangerously over the deck. Chichester was furious: 'I do not need assistance, or company, or a doctor. Thank you. *Go away!*'

France II stood away into the darkness just as another vessel arrived on the scene to render assistance to *Gipsy Moth*. She was the yacht *Lefteria*, an old converted tunny fishing boat flying the American flag and with eleven persons on board. She was not seen by *France II* because, according to the captain, the little fishing vessel had failed to show the obligatory navigation lights. In the resulting collision *Lefteria* broke up and sank almost immediately. There were only four survivors and they were picked up by the weather ship.

Next day at dawn the British frigate *Salisbury* approached *Gipsy Moth*. On board were Sir Francis's son Giles Chichester, a journalist friend from *The Times*, John Anderson, and a Marine officer, Peter Martin. They went on board with two riggers who attended to the damaged mast. 'But for this mishap I should have been able to carry on alone,' Chichester declared, 'and besides, I feel better.'

Left: Vendredi 13 *pitching heavily in a swell during trials before the race*

Right: Gipsy Moth. *Several vessels went to Chichester's assistance and seven men lost their lives trying to help him. The weather ship* France II *broke his mast while trying to help him during heavy weather. Chichester was furious, but when H.M.S. Salisbury* arrived he allowed his son Giles to have the mast mended before setting a course for Plymouth

But he allowed Giles and Peter Martin to stay on board and they sailed back to England with him. Taken into hospital at Plymouth he dictated a few words to his friend John Anderson who published them in the *Sunday Times* on 9 July 1972.

I did not know until Thursday that the crew of the *Lefteria* were also proceeding to ask if I needed help, and this news has come as a dreadful shock. I had not asked for help, but that cannot alter the fact that those who lost their lives were trying to help me. They acted in the highest tradition of the sea, and I am deeply distressed that their generous action ended so disastrously.

People are asking whether I ought to have entered at all for the single-handed Transatlantic Race, and whether I was fit for the voyage. These are difficult questions to answer, but I don't think I need to make any excuses. I am seventy. I had been seriously ill, and certainly my doctors were not happy about my

Pen Duick IV. *Her new skipper Alain Colas had two years to prepare for the fourth Ostar. He fitted a satellite communications beacon for safety, which proved useful*

after the ninth day of the race

decision to enter the race. But who finally has to decide whether a man is fit to do anything? You consult doctors, you listen to their advice, you accept their treatment.

But in the end you have to decide for yourself. No one else knows my own body as I do – I have lived with it for seventy years, tried and tested it in every circumstance of life. I knew that I was not as strong as I was, but I knew myself and I also knew *Gipsy Moth V* – after all, I had already sailed her single-handed for some 26,000 miles. I believed that I could make the passage – had I not thought this, I should never have set out. I was wrong, but at least it was an honest mistake.

At 2010 on 7 July Colas crossed the winning line, twenty days, thirteen hours and five minutes after the start, five days faster than the 1968 winner. He needed to relax after being suddenly exposed to a barrage of questions from newspapermen

At 1240 on 27 June, the tenth day of the race and 1,455 miles out from Plymouth, Colas sighted Vendredi 13 *and took this magnificent photograph*

Twelve

1972-1976: Alain Colas' Jumbo-Yacht

The curtain never really came down on that fourth Transatlantic Race. For one thing it had become more than a mere sporting event: it was something that all Europe continued to talk about through the long days of that summer. Also, preparation for the 1976 Ostar began for some of the contestants almost as soon as they reached Newport. These were four years during which Alain Colas was to divide the world of sail with the wildest project ever put forward for single-handed sailing. They were marred by one accident, to Colas himself, and by the tragic loss of Brian Cooke. And those four years were to open with the terrible ordeal of Francis Chichester, who had yet to end his last long voyage of silent suffering.

Hardly a month and a half had gone by since Chichester had come back to England to recover from the last painful hours of the 1972 race. Again he felt some of that human warmth of feeling that his countrymen knew so well how to show towards him. At the Royal Hospital in Plymouth, where they were trying to restore some of the strength that his body now seemed less able to sustain, the windows opened on to a bay of happy memories and within a stone's throw of his room was the unchanging setting of some of the great moments in his extraordinary life, like the scene that was enacted at exactly ten minutes to nine on 28 May 1967.

Three hundred thousand people had assembled on the wide expanse of Plymouth Hoe to see the man of sixty-six who had sailed his little white yacht across 29,630 miles of ocean. Francis Chichester had come back, alone in *Gipsy Moth IV*, along the traditional route of the big ships that once sailed to Australia for cargoes of wool. It had taken him 107 days from Plymouth to Sydney and 119 days back from Sydney to Plymouth. Like them he had rounded the Cape of Good Hope and Cape Horn, allowing himself only a few days' rest in Sydney. He took 226 days in all, very little more than the time taken by those clippers at the beginning of the century with their crews of forty able-bodied seamen.

At four minutes to nine, therefore, the gun that saluted *Gipsy Moth IV* as she passed the breakwater let loose a tumult in the Sound. The sirens and horns of hundreds of vessels of all sizes began to sound and the two-shilling Union Jacks bought by the children waved all along the quays as they tried to catch a glimpse of *Gipsy Moth*. In the pubs people raised their mugs of beer, and the admiral's barge with Sheila Chichester and his son Giles on board, as well as several bottles of good champagne, came alongside *Gipsy Moth*. The television spotlights shed a harsh light over the 57-foot ketch. Putting the helm over to starboard, Chichester's slight figure under his yellow sou'wester could be seen calmly handling the four sails. The onlookers already knew that he was going to be awarded the K.B.E. and that he would be given the accolade by Queen Elizabeth II with the very same sword that Elizabeth I had used to dub Sir Francis Drake.

Above: Brian Cooke, the first victim of the fifth Ostar

Right: Five years before his misfortunes in the 1972 race Chichester was knighted by the Queen at Greenwich on 7 July. The sword is the same one used by Elizabeth I to dub Sir Francis Drake

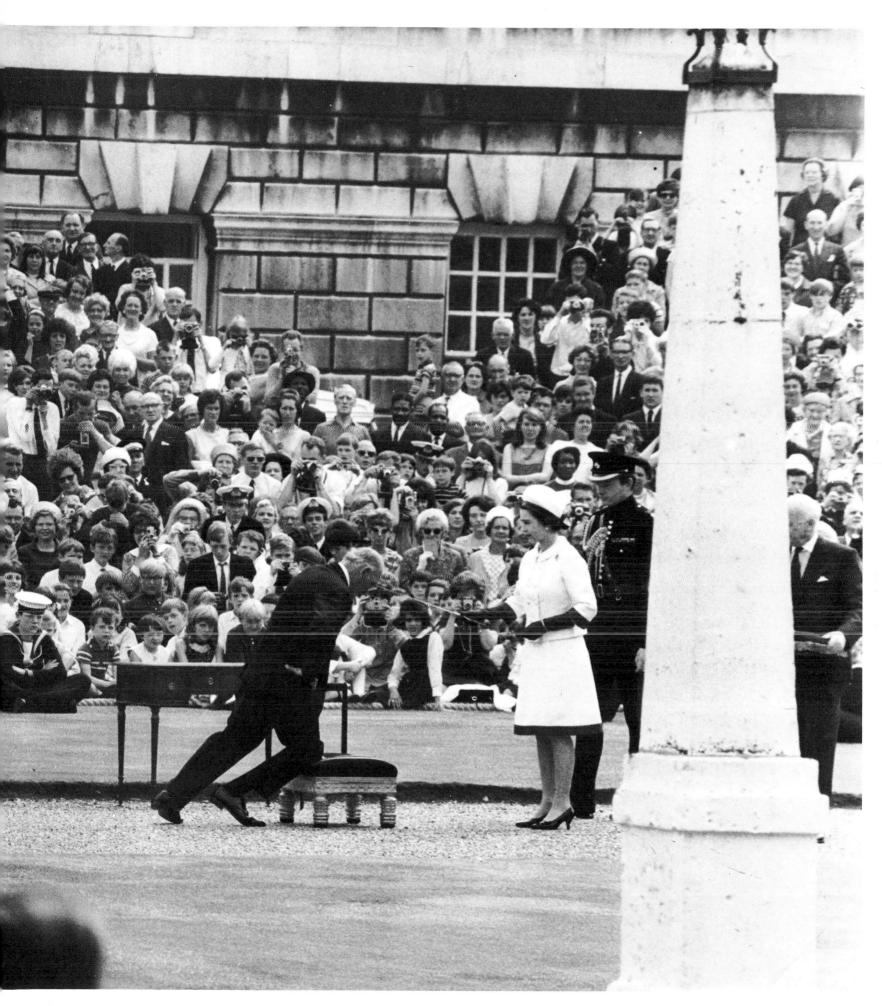

Sir Francis remembered all that from his bed in August 1972. On 25 August Giles and Sheila were summoned to his bedside. Death, though England did not wish to believe it, was now at hand. It had been held at bay only by the will power of the old man. Next day the unequal struggle was over, the 'Great Sir Francis', as the English called him, was dead. Not far away on the famous quay-side at Millbay Dock he had said a good many years before: 'I have had my share of life. That I am alive at this moment is a miraculous gift that has been granted me, and if I set out to sail the seas it is because I feel that that is the best use to which it can be put.'

In that month of August entry applications for the 1976 Ostar were already pouring into the *Observer* office. Almost all those who had taken part in the 1972 race were already thinking about the next, like Terlain for example, who was thirsting for revenge, or Colas, who was planning his fantastic yacht.

The chance encounter between *Vendredi 13* and *Pen Duick IV* was to count for a great deal in the history of racing, and on the future career of Colas, who was still amazed at it many months later:

In theory, there is really no chance of finding a 39-metre vessel in an ocean, not one chance in however many, but I saw *Vendredi 13* with my own eyes. I saw too that she was under-canvassed, that is to say that with a better sail plan *Vendredi 13* could have gone much faster. However, Terlain's *Vendredi 13* finished only nineteen hours behind me, just nineteen hours. But if Terlain had the equivalent of ten ocean crossings to his credit, Colas the sea-dog had the equivalent of forty-three! Moreover, Terlain did not have time to try out his *Vendredi 13* and at the start of the race he had not even found out where his bunk was. Compared with him I was a man determined to win, who had already covered 43,000 miles in my trimaran – man and machine were as one. I am convinced that if this under-canvassed boat finished only nineteen hours behind my trimaran it proves once again the old rule of sail: that the theoretical speed of a ship is proportional to the square root of her length along the waterline – in a word, the longer the better.

Arising from that encounter Colas had conceived an enormous boat, a sailing giant, and embarked upon a nautical and financial campaign that, far beyond the scope of the 1976 Ostar, was to divide the sailing world. Some people even think it presented a danger to the Transatlantic Race itself and perhaps to all races under sail.

The winner of the 1972 race was good at coining words and was at no loss in finding names for his mad new project: 'Jumbo-Yacht', 'Cathedral of the Seas', 'Sailer in Capital Letters'. In fact it was the longest boat in the history of the race, twice as long as Terlain's 'folly' and almost four times as long as *Pen Duick IV*.

During the week Colas, the expert, the all-rounder, struggled to find financial backing for his Jumbo; at week-ends he went to sea to keep himself fit. On one of these week-ends, not to waste a second of the time that was becoming more and more precious, he took a party of journalists with him so that he could expound his revolutionary ideas. I was one of those on board his glorious *Pen Duick IV*, now renamed *Manureva* after another voyage round the world gleaning yet more single-handed records. That day was to change Alain's life and leave a dark shadow on the Atlantic waves.

That Whit week-end he had allowed himself a little cruise 'to roughen his hands', because even if his life's work made it necessary to spend most of his time in shipyards, banks, publicity agencies and ministries, Colas the perfectionist knew that he must also watch his physical fitness.

When he sailed for pleasure he liked to take his friends with him, and in the charming little Breton port of La Trinité-sur-Mer he met Christian, who was in charge of a local boat yard and kept an eye on *Manureva* when Alain was away on what he called his 'Paris voyage'. He also met Maurice, an old street vendor who happened to have settled in Saint-Malo and had made good selling carpets. They joined us on board.

Téura, his Tahitian girl-friend who had just presented him with a sweet little baby daughter Vaïmiti ('little ocean wave' in Tahitian), was also there. She decided to join us as the weather was fine and our destination bore the inviting name of Belle-Ile. Jean-Claude Deutsch, the *Paris-Match* photographer, and myself were the two journalists on board. 'Come along, whether you have got your sea legs or not,' Colas had said. 'Come on board with us, it's quieter there to take photographs and have a talk about this Jumbo-Yacht that I am building: 71.5 metres long, four 33.5-metre masts and 1,200 square metres of sail!'

The statistics took us back to the days of the old Cape Horners, but it then needed twenty men to handle a clipper like *Cutty Sark*. Nevertheless, some of the experts thought Colas capable of sailing such a boat across the Atlantic; he had proved his ability by winning the 1972 Ostar and later by breaking almost all the single-handed records in every ocean in *Manureva* – one record for the Indian Ocean, one in the Pacific, three in the Atlantic, the record for 1,000 miles, for 500 miles, for the longest day's run, the week's run, and so on.

On Sunday evening, the day before we set off for Belle-Ile, he had shown us the film of these exploits and we saw what perfect harmony could be established between a man and his boat – the exact timing of each movement on board, nothing left to chance, nothing left undone. From the steering position he had command of a whole array of halyards and worked the sails with absolute precision like the conductor of an orchestra, never a loose end; he was a maniac for organization with the efficiency of a perfectly adjusted machine. Sitting comfortably in an inn on the coast the film let us share with him the unbelievable events of the year before: Cape Horn, the storms, the hours of trying to keep awake. And also the mishaps, the mainsail that fouled the mast in a squall as he was going into Sydney Harbour, Colas climbing the mast to free one of the halyards and get that damned mainsail down. We all found it very amusing that Sunday evening.

On Monday morning at 10 o'clock the little band of would-be sailors boarded *Manureva* in good order. When she changed her name *Pen Duick IV* also lost her unpainted metal hull, which was

---

Sir Francis Chichester in a Plymouth hospital, only a few steps from the Sound where all his great voyages began. Sir Francis died in hospital on 26 August 1972

now dark blue. Christian and Maurice acted as crew. Téura was busy in the galley and we with our cameras and tape recorders.

It was just after 11 o'clock when *Manureva* got out of the harbour at La Trinité. With her sails pulling nicely, as always with Colas, it was a tricky operation, but perfectly executed. There was a good land breeze, quite fresh, up to Force 5 at times. *Manureva* put one float out of the water. Five knots, sixteen knots, eighteen knots, it was fantastic. In less than an hour we were off Belle-Ile. Then the wind fell and Colas decided to set the spinnaker, and coolly told us about his life-work. He said:

When I had crossed the finishing line at Newport in 1972 I knew that I would not be able to resist the wish to feel once more that fantastic thrill whose culmination is in the moment of victory, the moment of self-realization. I thereupon resolved to try and retrieve that special moment. But once again it would be necessary to find the means to bring it about. My encounter with *Vendredi 13* had convinced me that it would have to be a big boat and the result of the Ostar strengthened that conviction. I decided that to win in 1976 it would be necessary to cross the Atlantic in less than eighteen days, and knew that only a big boat could possibly beat the record.

At 12.30 we were at the harbour mouth of Palet, a little town tucked away below the imposing fortifications of Belle-Ile. Colas came in under sail, as always. The harbour is fairly narrow and the tide was carrying *Manureva* toward the jetty. Without starting the very small auxiliary engine, Colas handled the ship to the delight of the bystanders waiting for the ferry. Jumping on to the quay he put his arm round Téura and off we went to a little bistro. Over lunch he had more to say about the 1976 Ostar.

He did not see how he could get any more speed out of a trimaran; it would have to be a mono-hull at least as long as Terlain's – not just a few centimetres more but something quite different. 'What we need,' he said, 'is the courage to aim high. If we don't somebody else will. Progress is an irreversible process and man progresses because he is the expendable servant of the implacable machine.'

He and the designer Michel Bigoin immediately saw things in a big way – 55 metres. And then their calculations showed them that even that ridiculous length would not be sufficient. To put three masts on a 55-metre boat and still not be under-canvassed like Terlain would call for very high masts and a phenomenal amount of sail on each mast. 'From what I know of my own strength and ability,' said Colas, 'I could not allow for so extraordinary a height.' He and Bigoin concluded that only a four-master would make it possible for them to deploy the sails so that they could be handled by one man alone. But with one more mast they would need a greater length of deck to provide sufficient clearance between the masts and to maintain the efficiency of various sail plans. The boat got bigger and bigger – up to 71.5 metres (236 feet).

Even at the most conservative estimate the Jumbo-Yacht was

Returning to La Trinité-sur-Mer after a trip, Colas' mainsail jammed and to avert a collision he hastily let go the anchor. His foot caught in the cable and was almost severed

going to cost at least five million new francs. Working with Bigoin he drew up the plans for his 'Cathedral of the Seas'. 'I knew what I was up against,' he said, 'but I am by nature a fighter and it was an act of faith.' Colas the apostle was able to arouse enthusiasm for everything to do with himself and his project. A Dieppe firm spontaneously offered to build the boat at cost price, but when they saw how much work it would entail the directors had to withdraw the offer so as not to delay the completion of all the trawlers under construction in their yards.

To collect five hundred million centimes he made the rounds of all his friends, relations and admirers. Gaston Defferre, the deputy mayor of Marseilles, was one of them and promised the support of his newspapers to finance Colas; he brought in with him all the Provençal dailies, and for once their proprietors were unanimous at their general meeting about their willingness to help. Colas promised exclusive rights to the dailies and they in turn offered him a certain amount of the space normally devoted to advertisements; he could sell this to a firm, or to anyone else who wanted to put an advertisement in the papers.

We finished our lunch of sea food quickly for the tide was falling. Getting out was quite a complicated manoeuvre but by four o'clock we were clear of the harbour. We were in the lee of the island and *Manureva* was tossed about, but we made some way.

The value of the unused space offered by the Provençal dailies added up to a huge sum, 2,300,000 francs, but Colas had asked for 3,000,000 from Gilbert Trigano and Jacques Giraud, the patrons of the Club Méditerranée, to pay for the first instalment of his Jumbo.

At first Giraud refused: '3,000,000 francs for a boat; it's quite out of the question!' But when he met Colas he was carried away by the sailor's determination and made over 2,300,000 francs from the publicity budget of the Club Méditerranée to the Provençal press. He added the further 700,000 francs that Colas had asked for so that he could take part in what he considered to be 'an exciting challenge in the philosophy of holiday clubs'. Colas still needed two of the five millions of his original estimate.

To make the model of the boat Alain appealed to the Renault information department. It would be necessary to apply the most up-to-date procedures in body work to the construction of his yacht. The plans of the hull were squared off on basic sections and each point of the profile was assigned three mathematical coordinates by a computer. This computer smoothed and adjusted the curves, memorized them and fed them into a second computer which controlled a milling machine that carved the three-dimensional model in thick fibreglass. It was a costly process but thanks to it an almost perfect 'maxi-model', one-twentieth full size, was completed within three weeks. 'Our first record!' Colas remarked.

In the model tank where it was tested its precision won the admiration of the naval architects; moreover, its performance in all conditions showed that the Colas-Bigoin Jumbo was no Utopian dream.

Colas persuaded the government department responsible for alternative sources of energy to place their experts, technicians and facilities at his disposal. Already, quite apart from the Transatlantic Race, at a time when the keynote in France was 'We haven't got petrol but we've got ideas', people were thinking about giant cargo ships without engines. Colas had it in mind to provide the power for his automatic pilot (and perhaps even for the galley) from solar cells. Wind motors would supply current on board and for the navigation lights. The waves themselves would furnish the necessary energy to sound the sirens. He also did some research on hydrophones; the rules prohibited the use of radar but not the detection of other vessels by listening to their propellers.

'Every day I have to improve my knowledge on all sorts of subjects,' he said, 'and I have to fight for every centime to build a boat for five million francs that ought to cost at least two or three times that. For example, I shall need seven tons of paint. Each sail can only be seen properly from one position and it's impossible, alone, to keep an eye on four sails on a 72-metre boat.' With support from Thomsons and an astonishing surveillance system devised by CISI, Colas had made his Jumbo into a fantastic laboratory.

We were approaching La Trinité and Maurice was making coffee. It was after seven and the day was drawing in. We laughed and sang. Téura had snuggled down at Alain's side, and he was happy. 'With this wind,' he said, 'we shall do very well, right up to our mooring. The course is right and everything is fine. We'll only have to get the sails down. Are you ready?' 'Aye, ready,' replied the crew. 'Lower away!'

The genoa came down but not the mainsail. The sheet had jammed in the block, or the halyard at the masthead, as had happened at Sydney and as we had seen in the film on Sunday evening. The huge sail just wouldn't budge.

The boat was coming too fast into the little harbour at La Trinité-sur-Mer. Alain left the helm, rushed to the bows and did the only thing that could be done if *Manureva* was to avoid ramming head-on a 16-metre at anchor to port. He let go his anchor and *Manureva* spun round.

The ninety-pound anchor went to the bottom while the inboard end of the chain cable made a loop in the air and wound itself round his foot. The blood and bone and raw flesh presented a terrible sight. Colas was helplessly dragged towards the side as the cable ran out, still running through the fairlead. 'Help!' he cried, and then, 'my leg, my leg.' Maurice rushed forward and threw himself down to grab Colas.

Ten seconds may have gone by, or perhaps a hundred times as many. Colas shouted for a knife. Silence, and then, 'My foot, my leg, it's awful,' but never a groan. We knew that he was aware what this meant for him and for his way of life, those few seconds that had carried us from happiness to horror; before our unbelieving eyes a white streak protruded from a big red gash on one side of his leg, and on the other another red stain. It was Colas who held them together. Then Maurice suddenly remembered something of what he had learned as a medical orderly in the Algerian war – a tourniquet.

At La Trinité, *Manureva* coming in was something worth

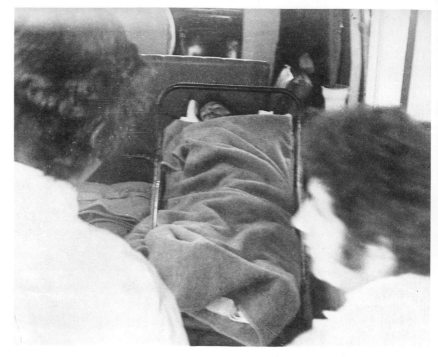

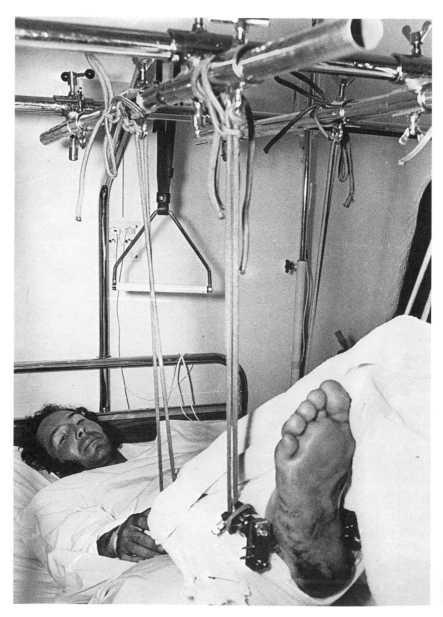

Colas a few hours after the terrible accident

watching. Keen sailors never missed it. On the quayside they began to understand what had happened when they heard Téura let out a cry that echoed across the suddenly silent bay. Only Alain seemed to keep his head; he did not even seem to be in pain but went on directing the operation to save *Manureva* and avert a further accident. A man who said he was a doctor came out in a boat and took Colas ashore. The minutes went by. Téura kept saying, 'Alain, always so careful. No, no, no, it isn't possible.' Then all at once she went to the stern and found things to do. 'Alain said we must take care of the boat.'

Then we heard the siren of an ambulance; the little dinghy came back and Téura was taken ashore. Alain was put in the ambulance. He was perfectly clear-headed, asked us to be sure to find out where he was being taken for treatment, asked for his notebook and telephone numbers, said that he must let people know; but never a groan. For him the accident was already just something that had happened. He wanted above all to save his leg, and also the enterprise in which he was engaged.

An hour later Alain Colas was admitted to a nursing home in Vannes, where Dr. Moquet soon realized how serious the injury was. Extensive work was required – saving the arteries, getting the blood flowing again and restoring the tendons – and he lacked the necessary facilities. Téura got in touch with Gaston Defferre in Marseilles, who contacted his own hospital and the nursing home at Vannes; Dr. Moquet had to cope with the telephone as well as the foot he had to save. The Paris hospitals said that they could not admit Colas because on a Whit Monday they could not lay on the team of specialists that would be needed to save the foot. Minutes counted – and Moquet had to take a decision. He chose Nantes, which could provide two specialists and where there was a very modern hospital. Colas went on his way, asleep now and with Téura always at his side. At 11 o'clock at night the two surgeons, Dupont and Bainvel, were waiting for him at Nantes, the one a cardio-vascular specialist and the other in orthopaedics, a well-matched pair. In Paris, Professor Guilmet, the great heart transplant specialist, was in contact with the doctors at Nantes. It was 11 o'clock when the operation began; it was seven in the morning before it was over.

Maurice, his hands and yellow sea boots still marked with the same dark brown stains, kept repeating, 'With his strength of will he will pull through; I tell you so and you will see.' Téura added, 'You must explain in your magazine that everything will go on as before and that Alain has told Maurice and me that nothing has been changed. Make them understand that.'

For six months Colas was to continue an heroic struggle to keep alive something that even some of his friends considered from now on to be a lost cause – a huge boat for a maimed single-hander. Almost alone now, apart from the invaluable support of his family and a few faithful friends, Colas carried on even as he asked himself, 'Why continue the struggle?' He answered that question in an article I published in *Paris-Match* when he left hospital after six long months of purgatory:

I went over that manoeuvre every night during my first weeks in hospital. A picture of the accident was ever before my eyes and I kept asking myself the same question: how could I who am always so careful have been so stupid? My only comfort was when I came to know that the manoeuvre itself had indeed been perfectly successful. My friends told me afterwards that the buoy to which I was about to moor the trimaran to stop her was barely a couple of yards ahead. When I saw that the mainsail had jammed I was therefore quite justified in dashing forward and letting go the anchor to bring her up short with her stern near the buoy. Once I had let go the anchor I immediately turned toward the mainmast to lend my friends a hand as they had not yet managed to get the sail free. When I had already half turned round and was almost off the foredeck a loop in the cable twisted round my foot like a lasso.

I found myself pinned to the stern with my shin bone in the air. The cable was still biting into the flesh and rubbing along the bone. I twisted round to get the knife out of my pocket; I cut the line and it was a great relief to see my foot again but it was hanging by three or four ligaments. I turned on my back and compressed the artery as well as I could. Having got my foot back it remained to stop the boat; therefore, in spite of what had happened to me, I was not guilty of any 'professional error'.

It is true that I had made one mistake, in using an ocean racer for coastal navigation. Although I knew the harbour at La Trinité off by heart and had been in under sail any number of times, it was a mistake to have tried it in *Manureva* when the harbour was crowded; I wouldn't have gone shopping in a Formula One.

I was well aware of the possible outcome, for I had seen hands amputated as a result of similar accidents, and I struggled to remain conscious long enough to say to the surgeons, 'Save my foot!' The mind works very quickly at such times and I remember saying to myself, 'If you can get that foot into competent hands soon enough, medical science will restore it to you.' I was sure of that even from the very first moment, even when I could see the rope biting into the flesh. I am one of those people who really believe in modern science. I am the first to apply modern methods and modern materials in my sailing and it would be illogical if I were not also the first to accept them in relation to my own body.

When the surgeon came I said, 'Above everything else, don't amputate if there is any chance.' Then followed the first of those black gulfs until I awoke thirty-six hours later in Ward 3 in the orthopaedic wing of the hospital at Nantes.

The surgeons at Nantes then had before them a leg which had suffered 'a considerable loss of substance'; that is to say, the warp had stripped the flesh from the shin bone for a good six inches. The fibula had disappeared, only the Achilles tendon remained, along with, as Colas said, 'one or two of its colleagues'; a vein and two arteries were in sad state, and must be saved at all costs by transplanting the necessary tissues from the other leg. Dr. Dupont removed three small sections of vein from the left leg to make the connection where there was now only a gaping wound in the right leg. In the shoes and stockings that Colas was still wearing the doctors found various fragments of the fibula which they threaded on a rod. Dr. Bainvel also recovered part of the ankle bone from the stocking and attached it to the tibia. All this remained open and unsupported; the flesh grafts were to come later.

It was a day before I at last came round. There were familiar faces around me and I experienced a wave of joy to see a foot within my vision, my arms were immovable because of the transfusions. I did not then know what I would have to endure in the weeks to come.

But they did not keep back the truth and the doctors painted a black enough picture, explaining what I would have to put up with if I wanted to save the foot. They even suggested amputation as a remedy, but I knew that if I chose that easy way out I would surely one day regret it.

In the week following the accident Colas had to make one major decision in spite of his wretched state of weakness – whether or not to go on with his Jumbo-Yacht. It was hard for him to keep a clear head even for a few hours each day, but he stuck to his plan.

I spent much of my time under anaesthetics; the most serious problem was the fight against infection and they had to cut away with a scalpel anything that might start it and make sure that the irrigation of the wound was functioning properly. For example, they had to remake the junction of the artery twice. Up to the end of June I was anaesthetized every two or three hours and the time it took to recover from each operation got longer; they did not conceal the fact that this itself endangered the system and, in particular, presented a danger of heart damage. Fortunately my strong constitution, due to a life of sport and clean living, enabled me to survive the shock. Of course it could not go on too long and I saw that the orderlies found it less and less difficult to lift me on the trolley for the operating theatre; by mid-June I weighed no more than ten stone and I had since lost a stone more. They would have to administer the anaesthetics less frequently.

Colas often refused even local anaesthetics in spite of the pain, often almost unbearable, and he tried to keep his wits about him in dealing with the people with whom he had to work. When the telephone rang his voice grew stronger as if by magic and only his face betrayed the suffering. His cheerful voice misled people who spoke to him, for only a few seconds earlier they might have seen him clench his teeth to suppress a gasp of pain. He never admitted defeat.

I had made up my mind; there could be no question of giving up the task in hand. Even if my body presented a problem there was no reason why the rest of me should not go on, although as much as lifting a book had become a feat of strength.

The memory of those early weeks is still rather blurred. I could be quite clear-headed for a while, I could take a decision on the spot in reply to a letter or a phone call, but a week later I might just as likely not remember ever having got the letter; I had to go over the whole file again every time. Yet hardly seventy-two hours after the accident I had sent a telegram to say that work on the boat must continue and had immediately instructed Albert Coeudevez, the mast maker, to cancel my order for mast ladders and to substitute leads for supplementary halyards, so that in case of trouble I would not have to go up the mast to put it right. I would then only need the two stand-by halyards already envisaged for each mast.

There was a period of crisis at the end of June and I may be wrong but I thought I detected some indecisiveness among the medical team; they had detected symptoms of necrosis, that is to say a gradual death of the tissues. Fortunately there was never any question of infection. They had been able, and with a reasonable margin of safety, to avoid the use of drugs in case it should become necessary to deal with some unforeseen development. Nevertheless, the spectre of an amputation again seemed very near. And now I too had in a way to play my part; I was trussed up even more securely and had to do more exercises, and the irrigation was increased. I asked for weights and a harness and took it upon myself to stimulate some activity in the system.

After forty days and forty nights of pain (Colas would not use the word hell) things reached a turning point on 14 July with the arrival of the plastic surgeon. It was no longer a matter of small skin grafts, of which he had already undergone a whole series, but of repairing the gap between the ankle and the middle of the tibia. It was necessary to remove a strip of flesh from the left calf, and for Colas the worst part of it was about to begin.

The 'cross-leg' procedure involves crossing the legs so that a strip of flesh from one can be grafted on the other. For three weeks they had been preparing me for it, that is to say they had cut round three sides of a flap on my left calf, half an inch thick, six inches long and four wide. Then they bolted the left leg to the right with a dozen pins, some of them going right through the right leg to screw it into the left tibia, so that this flap could be applied to the other leg without even a hundredth of a centimetre of play. This was stitched to bruised flesh where there was nothing but a broken bone, and then for a matter of weeks the base, through which it was joined to the left leg, was gradually reduced as it drew its blood supply from the right. Then came the day when it was possible to separate the two legs. It was still necessary to transplant small pieces from the right thigh to fill the hole they had made in the left calf.

By the end of August Alain Colas had spent three and a half months on that bed of pain. He rose from it exhausted, emaciated and played out. By mid-September he had begun to convalesce and for his thirty-second birthday on 16 September Dr. Bainvel made him a superb birthday present – he could leave his bed and learn to walk with crutches.

It was my first birthday on land for a good many years. First I had to learn to use the left leg, which had also suffered a lot since it had provided a source of flesh and veins for mending the right. The blood vessels were distended and movement was painful. Learning to use the left leg took almost a month, but meanwhile I was again working seven days a week on my four-master.

Since I would have to make the best possible use of my head and my arms I decided to adapt the deck and sail plan to the new factors in the problem. For example, I had intended to have genoas, which with their big area considerably overlap the mainsail. Handling them would be quite an acrobatic feat, so we replaced them with boomed jibs which would be easier to manage. More spectacular was the relocation of the steering, usually well aft, which we moved to the waist of the ship to give me a more direct check of the sails. The foredeck was no longer at a distance that would call for a 100-yard sprint or a running fight every time. The chart room, chart table, galley, bunk and food locker were all grouped on deck near the helm so that I need not go below. I may have lost something aerodynamically, but this flush deck-plan put my living arrangements on the same level with my navigation. And, if I did not get my sea legs back at first, I had access to other cockpits at the foot of each mast where the various sheets and halyards were grouped. Finally we made a covered way with handrails inside the hull, which I could use rather like the firemen in a modern fire station.

Late in October the doctors immobilized his right ankle, which was to make it impossible for him ever again to flex the ankle backwards or forwards.

This immobilization, which fused together the tibia, the ankle bone and the outer part of the fibula, was to consolidate the foot; it was a question of stability at the cost of mobility. Altogether I had lost too many of the tendons, ligaments and minor muscles in the course of this affair to be able to shore up what was left of that mast. In action my foot was riveted to the end of my right leg; when at rest I had a right ankle that had lost its mobility and a left leg missing one of its two major veins, a piece of the calf and some strips of skin. When walking I had to use my hips, as a lot of other people have to do, to compensate for the foot being stuck at right angles to the leg. I might consider myself lucky to have got off so lightly.

Almost six months to the day, Alain Colas left the hospital at Nantes for the Club Méditerranée at Vittel, where he started a programme of physical training with the facilities that had been provided for the forthcoming Olympic Games. At the end of November his first visit to the shipyard showed him that the immense energy he had expended from his sick bed had not been wasted.

In a way this accident has led us to improve the very techniques that we were evolving to make it possible for one man to sail a 72-metre boat. Michel Bigoin and the whole team have surpassed themselves because the four-master is now even easier to handle.

I have often asked myself during this six months' ordeal: 'why, why go to those extraordinary lengths to put a foot on the end of my leg?' These months of well-nigh unbearable pain, this uncounted expenditure of energy and precious time given up to the extremity of a limb; I must find some purpose in it. Telling you today of what happened after that accident has helped me to feel that it has not all been unwarranted and useless, even for those others concerned, insofar as through what I had to bear the surgeons themselves may have made some advance in their own special field. More still, I hope that I have shown that the outcome of an operation must depend largely on the quality of the material upon which it is performed; I mean my physical condition as an athlete which made it possible for the treatments to be tolerated by a perfectly fit body. If that should lead some people to reconsider the misuse of their faculties through an indulgence in alcohol, tobacco, or any other unwholesome way of life, my struggle will not have been altogether in vain. If this can persuade anyone to take care I shall be glad, but I wouldn't do it again just to set my fellow men an example. But, like anybody who has spent some time in hospital and seen children in distress who have done nothing to ask for it, I realize how much it means just to be alive and lead a normal life. That is why I do not wish to see myself as a martyr; it will take more than a sore foot to make me give up the vocation of ocean racing.

If Alain's physical battle was the most painful part of the lead-up to the race, it was not perhaps the most difficult. With his new handicap he still had to get his boat off the drawing board. He did not need suppliers or helpers now but allies. Michel Bigoin took charge again when Colas had another spell in hospital.

The first real miracle came from Usinor when some of the staff of that big French steel business were able to show the directors the film of Colas' voyage round the world. The management almost immediately agreed that their technicians should undertake studies for the highest possible specification steel for the hull. They in turn got special ingots cast, in spite of the economic crisis, with the result that the hull of Club Méditerranée was to weigh 243 tonnes instead of 300. Next the Atomic Energy Commissariat 'donated' the ballast for the keel, 56 tons of spent uranium, which was ideal because of its very high density. It was 'donated' because under French law it was illegal to sell the uranium, which should theoretically have cost 37 francs per kilo – making a present therefore of two million francs! The handsomest gift of all was from the best rope maker in France, Henri Lancelin, who gave 4,200 metres of cordage, hand-made by him in Mayenne. It was the equivalent of one tenth of his annual turnover.

What Colas appreciated most of all was the disinterestedness shown by the people he asked for advice. Albert Coeudevez had to devise a new way of stepping the 32.5-metre masts. Victor Tonnerre took over from another sail-maker and completed in four weeks the foresails that would normally have taken months to make. Bernard Mercier refused to make a penny out of what was indeed his monopoly, the controls for a rudder that weighed seven tons. The management of Guimard not only supplied pumps for 10,000,000 old francs but persuaded their associates, Radiotechnique, to provide the solar batteries needed to operate them. Safety at sea called for huge inflatable lifeboats and Angeviniére sent life rafts.

For all that, the estimates kept on increasing and the bills from the Toulon Arsenal grew bigger in an alarming way as the vessel took shape. Colas went to live on the spot. Fortunately, a number of people, some of whom he hardly knew, generously came to his help. The Arsenal engineer-in-charge did far more than his naval

duties required and some sixty anonymous volunteers from all over the place lent a hand. Work went on night and day.

The crew included Robert Laugier, who came to work at nights and at the weekend to instal the eleven kilometres of electrical wiring, forgotten in the estimates and brought to light in the course of the days' work, and Camille Dunaime who, although paralysed in the legs spent his yearly month's holiday in a hut on the quay at Toulon to superintend the installation of the hydraulic steering. Michelle and Simone, the 'hostesses' at the Club Méditerranée, abandoned their *pareos* and holiday beaches to lend Colas a hand, while Michel Dixmier and François Landrin put their small concern, Cap Industrie, at his disposal. As Colas said: 'Without these volunteers and crew and all this help the amazing quantity of stuff that had to go into that one yacht would never have been got in order and that veritable floating laboratory *Club Méditerranée* would never have put to sea.'

It was the 'floating laboratory' aspect that attracted the most adverse criticism. Some felt that an electronic liner under sail was quite out of keeping with the spirit of a race intended for a sailing élite. Others saw it as a valuable contribution to yachting, just as that famous challenge to the race had prompted Chichester and his rivals to perfect a self-steering gear which otherwise might never

have been invented, or Tabarly to design *Pen Duick II*, which led to remarkable advances in the construction of popular types. We all know that Hasler created the Ostar partly in order to try out *Jester*'s strange rig. One could quote some of his own remarks and recall that he wanted to make the Ostar a severe testing ground, although he had abandoned that concept four years later. 'It is strange to see how little progress there has been in yachting and I hope that the Transatlantic Race will make single-handed sailing much easier and more comfortable. In this respect *Vendredi 13* was a fascinating experiment, in the wrong direction.'

At the Royal Western Yacht Club of England the 'liner under sail' was to disturb the organizers of the race. Once again the rules (or absence of rules) proposed by Blondie Hasler made it impossible to limit a boat's size. Certainly there was nothing that could disqualify a sailor on the grounds that he had been the victim of an accident. As for the great Hasler, he was no longer interested in an Ostar where there were now to be 140 starters.

Under the watchful eyes of Colas and designer Michel Bigoin, Club Méditerranée's hull is turned over in the Toulon dockyard. For technical reasons the 72-metre hull had to be built upside down

Jack Odling-Smee and his colleagues, faced by an exceptional situation, therefore required Colas to submit to a further test. As well as the usual 500-mile qualifying run he would have to sail 1,500 miles single-handed in the North Atlantic. This was not within the spirit of the Ostar; it was not even in accordance with British traditions. It was selective and discriminatory – but still it was reasonable.

It shocked and annoyed Colas who was losing his sleep to get the Jumbo-Yacht finished and complete his physical training but, angry as he was, he would sometimes add, 'At least it will make us get ready in time and I shall have to put on the finishing touches for the race all the sooner.' On 4 May 1976 he set out alone to face the Atlantic in his Leviathan, just six months after another candidate for victory in the fifth Ostar, Brian Cooke, had also put to sea to complete trials with his *Triple Arrow*, a fast and very light trimaran. Unfortunately Brian Cooke was to have even less luck.

His fragile multi-hull was found at sea, capsized and with nobody on board, on 22 February, its life raft half inflated. Brian Cooke, the modest champion, smiling, likeable and admired, had disappeared. For several weeks the English refused to believe that there had been a tragedy for he had too fine a record as a sailor to end so badly.

When Cooke first took part in the race, in 1968, it was almost in the capacity of a 'regional delegate'. In *Opus* (sail number 4) he was the torch bearer of the thousand members of the National Westminster Bank Sailing Club and its moving spirit. Deputy manager of the Poole branch of the Bank, vice commodore of his club and a former merchant navy officer, he had covered the course that year in an ordinary 32-foot cruiser lent to him by a Mr. Austin. And he did not disappoint his friends; after a fine passage he was sixth across the line at Newport, and fourth on corrected time.

In 1972 he was in the race again with *British Steel*, a fine mono-hull, and beat the record set up by Geoffrey Williams in 1968. His time was twenty-four days and nineteen minutes, but that was not good enough; he only came in fourth, behind the French trio with Colas at their head. He was however first of the British entries.

In 1974 he shook England when he sailed *Triple Arrow* in the Round Britain Race and seemed likely to win until the trimaran was capsized by a big wave. Cooke managed to get back onto the upturned boat; the English considered him well nigh immortal.

In December 1975 he was, like Colas, sailing the Atlantic alone, but with a different object: to set up a new speed record for the course pioneered by Chichester between Africa and South America – 4,000 miles in twenty days. That was his way of preparing for the 1976 Ostar. He meant it to be his last race before he 'retired' to sail gently round the world in his 10-metre sloop.

On 11 December *Triple Arrow* was reported 250 miles west of Lisbon. Then followed two long months of silence, broken at last by the sad news from a freighter. On 22 February 1976 they had seen the three upturned hulls, some 540 miles off the Canaries. The rigging was intact and the sails set, the inflatable dinghy half-inflated and stuck, the escape hatch for use in the event of a capsize shut, and the hull empty.

With the loss of Brian Cooke went the main hope of the English for the 1976 Ostar; there were few others to match the French

favourites, of whom Colas was now one since he had completed the supplementary trial imposed by the Royal Western.

Colas made Le Havre on 12 May after covering the 1,500 miles required by the organizers, a first major success that ought to have silenced the critics. He had shown that, alone and handicapped, he could handle his sea monster, but he also showed an optimism that was premature. He almost thought himself invincible. His critics accused him of trying to ensure his victory through the enormous sums of money being invested in his boat. They envied him too the sole possession of a ship that was to cost more than a billion and a half old francs of other people's money.

In reality, on the eve of the race Colas was more heavily in debt than any other sailor in the world. He owed 250 million old francs on a boat that was virtually unsaleable because it had only a sentimental value. His friend Michel Dixmier remarked:

Perhaps some rich colonist or an oil sheik, as keen to possess a white elephant as one might be to own Brigitte Bardot's bath or Paul McCartney's shirt, may some day offer a million and a half for the yacht; but first she'll have to win the race. After all, Colas is not the first sailor who has had to look round for backers. His only fault is perhaps that he has been more successful at it than others.

Certainly nobody can say that he was the first sailor guilty of appealing to a sponsor. Nothing is more difficult to decide than the point at which generous support becomes big business, whether it be well-meant help from a sports federation, a national subsidy, a philanthropic donation, or an advertisement campaign. However, sixteen years after the first race the Ostar was to give Plymouth a very different look on 5 June 1976 than it had on 11 June 1960. In that unspoilt setting – not a single skyscraper and only the two blocks of modern hotels among the usual 'bed-and-breaktasts' – the yachts of the fifth Ostar were to splash a sophisticated pattern in the gaudy and iridescent colours of the sponsors for whom they spread their sails.

Just before the 1976 Ostar Brian Cooke put to sea to make final adjustments to his Triple Arrow, *but she capsized and Cooke drowned, a victim of the fifth Ostar before it had even begun. He had made fourth place in the 1972 race in* British Steel *and was the British hope for 1976*

Thirteen
1976: The Fifth Ostar

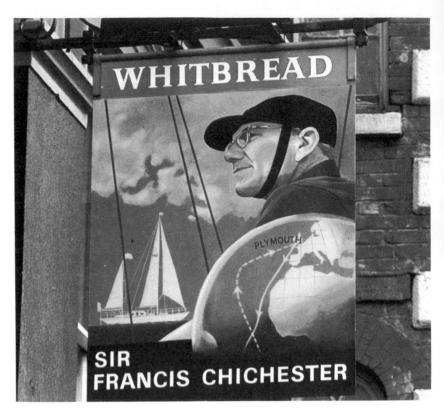

Along the quays at Millbay Dock, running their eyes over the names painted on the hulls of the finest boats in the fifth Ostar, the spectators who had come in thousands had the curious sensation that they were thumbing through the pages of a commercial catalogue. After invading the Grand Prix and the football grounds, publicity and sponsoring had succeeded in making its mark on the Atlantic without anybody really having been aware of it. As older sailors in England and America pointed out, the idea was not a new one, even if the smart publicity men present at the start of the race might think that they had invented what they called 'a new approach to communications'. Getting a boat paid for by a firm was no new thing; it did not begin yesterday or the day before, but in the last century.

After their extraordinary race in 1891 Lawlor and Andrews challenged each other again; it was a double challenge involving both the time for the crossing and the size of the boat. Lawlor started first but had to give up. Andrews set out in a tiny boat on 20 July 1892, succeeded in getting to Spain and set up a new record for the smallest sailing boat to cross the Atlantic; she was only 14½-feet overall. He had been sponsored by a soap-maker and her name was *Sapolio*. That record remained unbeaten for seventy years.

Not long after, in 1894, an American magazine was the first to commission and follow up a mad escapade in the Atlantic: the crossing under oars by the two Norwegians, Harbo and Samuelson. Jean Merrien relates the story in *Les navigateurs solitaires*:

George Harbo and Frank Samuelson have been called the 'giants of the Atlantic' and their achievement was certainly spectacular; it showed to what lengths human strength, endurance and will-power could be carried. It is only to be regretted that their avowed purpose should have been so lacking in higher motives, though it was not without its simplicity. They were doing it to make their fortunes by exhibiting the boat after the crossing.

Harbo and Samuelson were both of Norwegian stock, but were naturalized Americans. Their home port was Sandy Hook a few miles south of New York and like Johnson they were fishermen on the Banks and like him they lived on board their dories. Harbo is always spoken of as the navigator and it seems that he was once a pilot.

It was in 1894 that the idea occurred to them. They thought it over and found a sleeping partner in the news magazine *Police Gazette* and their dory bore the name of the manager *R. K. Fox* – so much for publicity!

The two oarsmen left New York on 6 June 1896 at five o'clock in the evening with the ebb tide before a large crowd gathered together by the *Police Gazette*; Mr. R. K. Fox must have been delighted that his publicity had reached so wide a public. It didn't matter if the idiots drowned themselves, some wreckage would be found and that would make a nice headline; launching a fund-raising campaign would boost their circulation.

Heading East by North, if the wind were not against them they should reach the Channel within sixty days. It took them fifty-five. But the skin of their hands very soon marked the count of oar strokes and in spite of all precautions they had much to bear. Another immediate difficulty was that their oil stove was quite useless in a blow and throughout the voyage they had to

Chichester was one of the first to set an example of modern sponsorship

make do with what they could eat raw or cold; it was fortunate that their supplies included eggs and biscuits.

They were given their position by another Norwegian ship on 24 July when they were 400 miles from the Scillies, and they made land in that group of islands on Saturday, 1 August, after fifty-five days at sea – fifty-five days of galley slaving. It was far worse than a galley. In the wind and cold, and often soaked through, they slept in their oilskins, which raised blood blisters on their wrists. But they were no more content to stop at the Scillies than Johnson was at Abercastle and they went on to Le Havre, reaching there on 7 August 1896 at nine in the morning.

There can be no doubt about their crossing the Atlantic, thanks to the many ships they met with on the way, but their dreams of wealth were never realized. At Le Havre their exhibition closed after four days. Then they rowed up the Seine, but hardly covered the cost of their stay in Paris. Nor were they any more successful in England, and in their own native Norway they had a very poor reception because, as naturalized Americans, people did not like their flag! They went home in a passenger steamer – to find themselves totally forgotten. Later they came back to Norway; Samuelson died there in an asylum in 1946.

For the first Ostar the question of sponsorship simply did not arise. The race interested nobody. But with his win in that race and his second place in 1964 Francis Chichester became a sound investment. When he was preparing for his famous round-the-world voyage and paying for a fourth version of *Gipsy Moth* was becoming a problem, he was one of the first to set an example in modern financial methods.

Despite his popularity Chichester had to admit that it was not so easy to find somebody willing to lend £30,000 to an ailing hero who had decided to build himself a boat and sail alone across the roughest seas. Fortunately for him a distant relative, Lord Duverton, then made the first move. The international wool syndicate was pleased with the idea of following the old sailing route along which wool used to be brought from Australia and undertook to get the project under way. Their publicity agents remembered that Chichester was still a great name in Australia after his famous Croydon–Sydney flight in 1929. They paid two thirds of the cost on one simple condition: Chichester was to wear no other underclothes or sweaters than those of pure virgin wool, branded like the sheep with the 'Woolmark'. Even his white *Gipsy Moth* was soon to bear the same mark.

Chichester still hadn't enough and turned to Colonel Whitbread who was one of the principal brewers in the country and who agreed to advance him a considerable sum. You could see what he got in exchange when Chichester came back to Plymouth in triumph after his circumnavigation; the town was covered with posters saying 'Drink a toast of Whitbread's Beer to Sir Francis who has drunk it himself all the way round the world'. Journalists were also told quietly that he had some Nescafé on board. And that was not all; a businessman, Basil Charles Dean, was engaged to commercialize his success with plastic busts, reproductions of photographs and models of *Gipsy Moth* on sale at £5 each. They estimated that they had contracts worth a clear £50,000 at least, plus the dispatches to *The Times* and the log of the voyage sold to *Paris-Match* and *Figaro* as well as, of course, the rights to a forthcoming book. It was a technique that was to become a classic of its kind.

In the 1968 Ostar Geoffrey Williams gave a fine demonstration of intelligent financing with his 'floating teapot'. *Sir Thomas Lipton* also had the backing of an information bureau and the support of the *Daily Telegraph*, which made space available to him.

This Ostar was in its way a thirst-quenching experience for the English. Lieutenant Leslie Williams R.N. was in *Spirit of Cutty Sark*, a tribute to that grand old three-master, but also to the brand of Scotch whisky that made it possible for him to enter his fine sloop. One also drank to the health of Captain Martin Minter-Kemp of the Royal Welsh Fusiliers and his trimaran *Gancia Girl*, in a glass of Italian Asti Gancia of course. There were also some new brands of beer in the race: Watneys sponsored Colin Forbes, and the Australian Bill Howell in *Golden Cockerel* was backed by Courage.

It was in that year that Jean-Yves Terlain, quite unknown and without a penny, was also trying desperately to get help in conveying his boat across France during the general strike, from Toulon to the starting line in England. In 1972 the same Terlain found himself faced with the problem of financing the construction of the giant designed by Dick Carter, not just a few thousand new francs but a million. The plans had been ready since the autumn of 1970, two years before the race. Terlain sent off four hundred letters to as many potential sponsors and the answer was almost always the same – 'your proposal is attractive but far beyond our budget'. Some were really interested, like the Renault management, which contemplated shipping one of their new R5's across in his yacht to show how light it was, but six months later Terlain still had not received a penny from Renault toward the project.

It was then that his friend Karin suggested that he should get in touch with the film producer Claude Lelouch. She flew to the Cannes Festival, got an interview with Lelouch and suggested that he should make a film of the crossing. It was an original idea but it had one flaw: it presupposed that Terlain would win the race. After a dinner two weeks later Lelouch agreed to finance the boat; it was all kept very secret and they decided on a name: she was to be called *Thirteen* for the thirteen letters in the name Claude Lelouch and because it was his lucky number that he used as a name for his productions and his film club.

At the *Observer* and the Royal Western they were beginning to get worried about the devious publicity. They did not forbid it but they tightened up the rules. After Geoffrey Williams' victory in 1968 they had prohibited shore-based electronic navigation. This time they objected that the name *Thirteen* could be confused with the race number, so she became *Vendredi 13*, but that did not bring him any luck either!

In matters of business, not to win is unforgivable. When Colas snatched the prize from Terlain at the finish in July 1972 he unwittingly consigned to a pigeonhole the Lelouch project for a film to celebrate the unbeatable yachtsman. Terlain found himself smothered in debts which he had to repay by chartering *Vendredi 13* for luxury pleasure cruises in the Caribbean. He now needed an agency to find takers and there were two men who undertook to do this for him by including *Vendredi 13* cruises in their lists. They were Jacques Giraud and Gilbert Trigano of the Club Méditerranée. But if Terlain was to go on with his ocean racing he had to find another skipper; he chose his friend Yvan Fauconnier. All three were to meet again for the 1976 Ostar.

The victory of Colas the 'amateur' over his 'sponsored' rivals in *Vendredi 13, Cap 33* and *British Steel* soothed the nostalgia of the gentleman-sailor; if a Colas could win, anyone else might hope to win, even if *Pen Duick IV* was worth 300,000 francs. For them the Jumbo-Yacht was a betrayal; Colas had brought businesslike professionalism to the point of perfection.

Having promised the written narrative to the Provençal newspapers he arranged with the French radio network, Europe 1, to talk about his travels. From his sick bed, and at a time when he sensed a certain uneasiness among some of his sponsors, he found encouragement in the attitude of Jacques Giraud and Gilbert Trigano who never even mentioned giving it up, and made them a thanks-offering over and above the terms of his contract. He gave his Jumbo the name *Club Méditerranée*. That did not, however, pay the untold costs of the undertaking so he covered himself with labels. With the knife at his throat, he allowed his name to be used to advertise men's toilet requisites. He never stopped recording his impressions for the newspapers or the French radio, preceeded perhaps with a little speech about the Thomson cameras for watching the trim of his sails, or followed by some slogan about the personal hygiene preparations he used. All this did not go down well with the Race Committee.

At Plymouth before the start of the race people remembered Blondie Hasler, its originator and what he had to say about sponsoring in Frank Page's book *Solo to America* (Adlard Coles, Ltd, London): 'I would hate to be sponsored and paid for,' he said to an *Observer* reporter. 'For me it would be horrible to start on a Transatlantic Race knowing that I had to do well to give my sponsor his money's worth.' Reading that one can well understand why he no longer entered the race.

To get as far as the starting line for the 1976 Ostar was itself something of an achievement because finding the necessary sponsors was not easy. Some got held up at the last moment, like Alain Gliksman whose big trimaran *Grand Large* had been considered a possible winner but now lay shut up and rotting at Toulon; the sponsor had suddenly found another helmsman for the single-handed race, Pierre English. Rather than sort out this complicated double-thinking Gliksman preferred to withdraw altogether. Chay Blyth, although the mainstay of the British hopes, had to give up too. His *Great Britain III*, damaged but repaired again in time for the race, stayed at her moorings because the insurers had suddenly discovered that the risks and the money invested in fitting her out were too much for them.

But many did succeed, including Jean-Yves Terlain. He had the fastest boat of all, the lively catamaran *British Oxygen*, which had won the Round Britain Race and was well-known to everyone in England. However, she was deemed over-fragile and a Beaune wine merchant had to take on the risk of chartering her for gold before she was allowed to start – on condition, of course, that she was repainted in the French colours and sailed under the name on the bottles with which she was so generously rebaptized: *Kriter*. Moored alongside her was *Vendredi 13*; Yvan Fauconnier had not had time to clear away all the luxury charter fittings on board, so she was rather less lively than she had been in 1972. With the baths and first-class state rooms she looked quite genteel. She owed her second youth to the little I.T.T. Océanic television sets whose name was now painted on her hull.

There was also a magnificent 'cigarette boat', *Gauloises Longues*; an odd name to be sure but without the backing of the State Tobacco Company she would still have been lying idle in a field in Valais in Switzerland. The list of starters also included a 'yoghurt-boat' *Nova*, and a 'beer-boat' *Cap 33*.

The news editor of the *Financial Times* admitted that he would not have been able to enter his *F. T.*, a trimaran painted as pink as his own newspaper, but for its backing. The veteran Olivaux in *Patriarche* thought the help of the wine concern of the same name in fitting out his little boat a veritable miracle when it came at the last minute. As for Clare Francis, that brilliant British yachtswoman and favourite target of the photographers, she looked charming in a well-fitting white T-shirt embroidered with a sweet little black golliwog, the trade mark of the marmalade makers who had sponsored *Robertson's Golly*. The two French ladies also sported the colours of their backers. Aline Marchand hoisted a splendid spinnaker stamped with the name of the spectacle maker who had given her his support. Dominique Berthier found it more difficult to display the name of the 5100 Computer that had fitted her out. As the use of numerals was forbidden they had recourse to a pun and called the boat *Saint Milcent*. Amidst the crowd of spectators the dignified publicity officers of the *Observer* were seeing to it that hawkers were well-supplied with their T-shirts and hats stamped with the emblem of the 1976 Ostar, and they sold like hot cakes. For that British newspaper this was not so much a bonus as a necessity and went toward recovering part of the costs of organizing the race.

It deceived nobody, except the people in charge of French television, who told their commentators not to mention the name of any boat associated with a trade mark. It apparently never occurred to them that without those damned 'sponsors' their cameras might have surveyed an empty Millbay Dock. For a good few of these sponsors their only reward was to be a wreck lying at the bottom of the Atlantic, or a few lines in one of the specialist magazines announcing a place well down the list. All the same, Millbay Dock at the start of the fifth Ostar was a very different place from the Millbay Dock of 1960. Some of the sponsors showed very bad taste and many spectators were rightly shocked by the mock bride being photographed on board *Pronuptia* on behalf of the store that sells gowns for other more modest brides-to-be.

In the middle of all this noisy excess the taciturn Tabarly stood out the more clearly as the true racing man – Tabarly the silent, who had refused to change the name of his *Pen Duick VI* in spite of the attractive offers made to him, a Tabarly who was to become unwillingly anti-Colas. The silence of the forty-six year old Pépé was to fetch a cold wind across the 1976 race, and soon an air also of anxiety and distress.

Aline Marchand's 'spectacle-spinnaker'

Fourteen

1976: America Celebrates its Bicentenary

It was just a hundred years since Alfred Johnson set off alone across the Atlantic to honour in his own way the first centenary of the American nation. During the hundred years that were to follow, the mother country of Johnson and his little *Centennial* had become a world power and, in June 1976, with its almost unlimited resources, it was going to give its sons the biggest holiday of their lives.

From coast to coast the country was swept by a prodigious wave of emotion and the focus of it all was the conservative little town of Newport. To celebrate the 200th anniversary of their independence on the Fourth of July, the United States of America had chosen to pay homage to the ocean across which their people had come. Newport was waiting for those most beautiful ships in all the world, the Tall Ships, the three- or four-masters which the great maritime nations cherish and maintain with an antiquarian zeal. Their final landfall was to be at New York on the Fourth of July for a splendid procession round Manhattan Island with its skyscrapers, but Newport was to be their mustering point and the spark that was to set off an explosion of bicentennial celebrations. The little seaside resort was preparing for its biggest invasion in a history already rich in glory.

Apart from its significance as the finishing line for the last three Transatlantic Races, Newport stood for the 'mansions' built on the immense fortunes of the Rockefellers and Vanderbilts of the last century, or the Bouviers, the parents of Jackie Kennedy-Onassis. F. Scott Fitzgerald wrote about them in *The Great Gatsby*. Here they kept up the traditions of the twenties and contested that most exclusive of all races, the America's Cup. It was also a town of little weather-boarded houses, in wine-red or olive-green, that enthusiastic societies zealously protected against the encroachment of developers, the godly village where the spotlessly white church reared its steeple like a starched collar against the deep blue sky. Newport was the bastion of the white American aristocracy, Anglo-Saxon, Protestant and rich. This was the Newport that had put on a holiday air and was giving a great ball for the commanders of the Tall Ships and their cadet crews, with their spotless pea-jackets and knife-edge trouser creases. And here it was that the heroes of the Transatlantic Race were to step ashore, bearded, exhausted and covered with bruises and half-healed wounds.

As if to resist the temptations of that pleasant waterfront, the *Observer* had set up its headquarters at the new marina discretely pushed away on Goat Island, commanding a view of a Newport that now seemed to go to bed later each night. Goat Island was at the end of the long causeway connecting it with the gay town; it boasted only one new hotel, a bar and the two little offices installed by the newspaper. After 5 June the time they kept was European time, the accents were those of Oxford or Marseilles and, there only, 'tall ship' meant the *Club Méditerranée*. They listened not to the American short-wave stations but to the news from London and Radio Saint-Lys.

They knew very early that the 1976 race would be the hardest of all, with its storm-force winds and the likelihood of unavoidable drama. But in spite of contrary winds and rumours of shipwreck, Goat Island on Sunday, 20 June, was preparing itself for a celebration too. Only fifteen days after Plymouth had witnessed the start of the race they were ready to welcome the victor, with the Atlantic crossed in record time.

Above: Eric Tabarly, alone at the helm for twenty-four days in a yacht designed for a crew of fourteen

Opposite: The Third Turtle, *designed by Dick Newick and skippered by Canadian Michael Birch; she finished third in the fifth Ostar*

After that day, special correspondents for the most influential newspapers in the world were to swell the little colony, already increased by the wives or families of the participants. Since that Sunday Alain Colas' friend Téura and their little daughter had been staying at the new hotel and Eric Tabarly's mother had taken a room there soon afterwards, while during the following week, well ahead of the yachts, there were to arrive the parents of Tom Crossmann and Clare Francis and Michael Kane's wife. On 20 June Goat Island began to buzz with rumours from here, there and everywhere and they expected at any moment to see *Pen Duick VI* come up over the horizon. Those with local knowledge were well aware that it might be difficult to pick out Tabarly before he crossed the line because of the notoriously poor visibility in these waters, so bad that Baron Bich was lost here in an America's Cup race. Even with radar it is impossible to pick out a yacht with any certainty unless the skipper makes some signal. Besides, Eric Tabarly was not the talkative kind, he had never liked radio and had quite enough to attend to single-handed to make up for *Pen Duick*'s normal crew of fourteen men.

On the night of 21 June the first regular watches were kept, which seemed quite unnecessary since it was only the sixteenth day of the race and Colas, who had broken all records, had nevertheless taken twenty days, thirteen hours and fifteen minutes, and in favourable weather conditions too. But as for Tabarly and conditions, 'impossible' is not a Breton word!

This situation lay at the root of a gross misunderstanding that was to create an atmosphere never before experienced in a Transatlantic Race. It was to divide the most competent judges, perhaps even throw the race itself into confusion, create an air of suspense that was both fantastic and distressing, and estrange lifelong friends. It led also to groundless charges against some careful reporters due to others meddling in matters which were not at all their concern, and provoked some to the point where they lost all sense of reality in setting themselves up as prophets, or birds of ill omen. Worst of all, it was to make, and ruin, two true heroes.

From Plymouth on, the fifth Ostar seemed a race between two men, Eric Tabarly and Alain Colas, master and pupil. It brought them face to face, with their totally different styles, weapons and physical attributes. Tabarly the Hercules, the gentleman-sailor, had become a Tabarly David confronted by the sea giant *Club Méditerranée* that concealed within itself, like one of those sets of children's dolls, a false Goliath – Colas who seemed even the more diminutive within that 'liner under sail'.

Newport knew all about Colas, his day-by-day progress, and the trouble he had had with his monster ship in a storm-swept ocean. Newport knew all about him, but nothing at all about Tabarly after a last fix that put him well ahead when south of Ireland, one or two days ahead of his rivals and perhaps more. But nobody was surprised at anything Tabarly did. After 1964 he was beyond question the foremost sailor in the world, and one of the best yacht designers too – but alas an architect with no other client than

June 1976, Newport, a focus of the American bicentennial celebrations and the rallying point for sail training ships from all over the world

himself and with no source of income apart from his pay as a Lieutenant-Commander in the French Navy.

From 1964 onwards Tabarly had been continuously at sea, in the clear waters of the ocean but at sea too in the troubled waters of finance that participation in any big race involves. In France he had become a national institution, but we all know that France is too proud of her institutions to think that they stand in need of so vile a thing as money. So France, which has no yacht museum, chose Tabarly as a symbol and *Pen Duick II* as a national monument. The *Pen Duick II* that had won the Ostar, bought from her skipper for 100,000 francs, was set up as a memorial on the quay at Beg Rohu near Saint-Pierre-de-Quiberon. But Eric Tabarly needed money rather than fame to go on sailing and pay for his new cruiser *Pen Duick III*.

Tabarly sailed *Pen Duick III* in six big races in 1967 and won them all. But when at the end of the year he wanted to enter for the Sydney-Hobart race, the great one in the Tasman Sea where no Frenchman had yet challenged the champions of Oceania, he was hard put to it to find the first penny towards shipping his boat out in a freighter and buying the air tickets for his crew.

He soon came to be known as 'the poorest yachtsman in France'. The Ministry of Sport, the big firms associated with his projects and the makers of sails and fittings all helped a little, but he had to draw on his pay as a Lieutenant-Commander and on the royalties from *Victoire en solitaire,* written after he won the race in 1964 and now the bedside reading of a hundred thousand sailors. It was just enough to keep him and his crew alive on sandwiches and potted meat. Tabarly, past master at surviving at sea, had learned to serve spaghetti in a thousand different ways.

The legend that had grown up around him already spoke of him as a man that anyone would follow to the ends of the earth. In fact his crews not only went into it with their eyes shut but with their stomachs empty. Among them were his father, Guy, who missed none of the big events, his brother Patrick and his faithful companion Gérard Petitpas.

Together they challenged the supremacy of the Australians. Tabarly, who always hated the radio, cursed the rule that required them to give their positions three times a day and inform their rivals as well. But *Pen Duick III* won all the same. He was first, but on handicap he was only first in his class, the top class. He was disappointed by the category distinction, but the Australians made no mistake – they named him 'best yachtsman of modern times'.

On 20 January 1968 France shuddered when cyclone 'Brenda', one of the worst ever experienced in the Pacific, swept across the Antipodes. It did great damage on land and blew with hurricane force where *Pen Duick III* was making her way home. In the absence of any news of him France, acting through the Governor of New Caledonia, put the emergency plan ORSEC into operation. Then Tabarly turned up again; with his crew he had weathered the fury of the storm. His companions on board were Olivier de Kersauson and Alain Colas.

Pen Duick III had admirably fulfilled her assignment but Tabarly, never satisfied, was dreaming of a new and radically different boat. With the help of *Paris-Match, R.T.L.* and *France-Soir,* who argued among themselves about exclusive rights, he set about building the Trimaran *Pen Duick IV*. She cost 300,000 francs, more than twice as much as *Pen Duick III*, which was retired with dignity to become the training ship for a yachting centre under his direction.

Social unrest in the spring of 1968 held up the new project and forty days before the Transatlantic Race his trimaran was still not ready. He had no time for proper trials and had to abandon the race soon after the start following a collision and the breakdown of his automatic steering.

This did nothing to improve the sad state of his finances, and things got worse when he got back to France. A zealous tax inspector discovered that the Lieutenant-Commander, on a salary of little more than sixty thousand francs, was sailing a boat that must be well worth five times that figure. He immediately put in a supplementary tax demand based on what the newspapers had given him towards building the boat. Tabarly appealed, explaining that none of the money had gone into his own pocket but into building a ship to carry the French colours. But it was in vain; nothing could be done. *Pen Duick IV* was threatened with an order of attachment and Tabarly, with his back against the wall, had no alternative but to sell her. He left for the Pacific in search of a rich purchaser, and also to show her paces in order to get the best possible price.

When he reached California for the big Los Angeles-Honolulu race Tabarly discovered that it was restricted to mono-hulls. He could only follow the race unofficially – whereupon he broke the record just set up by the winner, who immediately wanted to buy the boat that had beaten him. The American was astonished to behold a racer stripped of all comfort, and without even a single coat of paint on her hull. But perhaps it was not her uninviting appearance that made him give up the idea; *Pen Duick IV* had too deep a rudder for cruising among coral reefs.

For Tabarly the situation was becoming more than difficult. In debt, ruined, he still found a way of building his fifth *Pen Duick*; he applied for funds to the promoters of Port-Saint-Raphael who paid for '*V*' while retaining the ownership of the boat. While waiting for her to be completed Tabarly won the single-handed San Francisco-Tokyo race in *Pen Duick IV*. His time was fourteen days and the next man to get in was ten days behind him. That man was Jean-Yves Terlain.

Tabarly went back to Honolulu, always hoping to find a buyer; and he found one, a member of his own crew, Olivier de Kersauson. He had all the qualities that would make him a fit successor except for one great failing – he hadn't a penny. All Tabarly could do was to get *Pen Duick IV* back to France; he hoped to persuade a naval vessel to take her as deck cargo. There, perhaps, this fine thoroughbred that could do 20 knots and whose only black mark was her failure in the 1968 Ostar might find a new master at some yacht auction, like an old cart-horse. There was one man who did not let the opportunity slip, for he too had sailed with Tabarly in that superb trimaran. It was Alain Colas, and he offered a little more than 200,000 francs for Tabarly's crack boat.

Tabarly with Pierre English, Philippe Lavat and Gerard Petitpas during the 1967 Sydney–Hobart race. That year Tabarly won all the races for which he entered and was acclaimed by the Australians as 'best sailor in the world'

Pen Duick VI *under full sail with her crew of fourteen. Tabarly considered her marvellous for round the world racing with a crew, but she was far from ideal for*

Tabarly's Pen Duick III *in Sydney Harbour*

In January 1969 Tabarly exhibited his *Pen Duick V* with her new ballast system and she was the sensation of the Paris Boat Show. But all was not going well with the Port-Saint-Raphael promoters and Tabarly had never been an ideal public-relations man. That didn't surprise anybody; he had never preferred cocktails and social functions to the open sea. He was also busy working on his next project, a sixth *Pen Duick*.

By now, '*II*' had become a museum piece, '*IV*' had been sold to Colas, '*V*' had been taken over by the promoters and '*VI*' was still on the drawing board; he had only *Pen Duick III* left to race with. He modified her, but badly; she wouldn't go. On top of all that Tabarly, always clumsy on land, filled in his application form incorrectly for the only race he went in for in 1971, the Cape Town-Rio, and found himself disqualified.

Next year he was back to Los Angeles with the old *Pen Duick III* to win the Transpacific for which he had not been allowed to enter his trimaran three years earlier. France struck a medal with his effigy, but didn't give him much help apart from that. But Tabarly was already dreaming about the recently announced Round-the-World Race.

Pen Duick VI would be the ideal boat for it and past experience had taught him that he would do better to let someone else take over money matters. Gérard Petitpas, a former merchant navy officer and a regular member of his crew, therefore cast aside his oilskins and sea boots and set about 'Selling Tabarly'; but barely eight months before the race he had still not raised the necessary cash. Sponsoring was already recognized, but the sponsors preferred cars and bicycles, or a game that could be shown on television, to a yacht that was being raced far from the eye of a camera.

When *Pen Duick VI* was about to be launched in July, 1973, Tabarly became 'the bankrupt captain of a millionaire's yacht' in the eyes of the journalists. To quote *Figaro*:

> The Navy, with its abundant resources and manpower, agreed to build the boat in the naval yard at Brest. The keel was laid on 20 January and they got on with the job. Now, on the eve of launching, a difficulty has cropped-up — whose boat is she? She's ours, says the Navy, and asks Tabarly how he expects to repay the 150 million old francs for work done on the hull.

At the very last moment, when *Pen Duick VI* was about to be slipped they offered Tabarly a contract; the Lieutenant-Commander was to become the owner of the vessel and would reimburse the Navy by instalments, over a period of ten years! On top of these obligations the summer manoeuvres in 1974 made it impossible for *Pen Duick VI* to take part in any of the big races that year.

In spite of all his efforts there were still unpaid bills amounting to 700,000 francs, what with the designer, ship chandlers, insurance

---

Pen Duick VI's *masts did not stand up to high winds; dismasted off Rio she is under jury rig*

premiums and so on. He decided to form a limited company and, under the direction of Gérard Petitpas, commercialized the *Pen Duick* label in the form of T-shirts, gramophone records and posters. But it was no good; Tabarly's financial problems remained unsolved.

On 18 September 1973 Tabarly got off to a good start in the Round-the-World Race but fifteen days later was dismasted in storm force winds and put into Rio, where the French Air Force rushed out a new mast for him. Reaching Cape Town just in time to do the second leg of the race he nevertheless beat the record. On 2 January 1974 he was dismasted again, leaving Australia with a locally-made mast and after a delay of thirty-five days.

Gérard Petitpas was finding the bills came in faster than the money to pay them and the dismasting off Rio had not helped matters. The insurance company paid for the mast, rigging and sails and the Air Force didn't charge anything. But the billeting of the repair men in Rio and their air fares back, because the military plane had not been able to wait for them, had cost Tabarly another 100,000 francs.

However, a Minister sent Tabarly a telegram: 'To win is good, to keep on is better.' It was signed by the then Minister of Finance, Valéry Giscard d'Estaing. But with a broken topmast spreader he had to abandon the race on the last leg. And alas that was not all. He only came third in a race to Bermuda and after 'at last' coming in first from Bermuda to Plymouth, racing with a crew this time, he was dismasted for the third time. The problem may well have been not in the mast itself but in the way it was stepped.

To avert financial shipwreck Petitpas put 'Tabarly sportswear' on the market, marked with the name of 'Pen Duick' and in the colours of her spinnakers, orange and black. There were T-shirts, slacks, windcheaters and oilskins, not to mention caps and sea bags. A further sales campaign was arranged for Christmas and journalists were surprised to see Tabarly, 'the last of the die-hards', put his label on everything. As Jacques Nosari wrote in *Figaro*:

This Christmas we expect to see a 'Round the World' game that the experts are now devising, a card game where the Jacks, Queens and Kings have been replaced by the heads of famous yachtsmen (they haven't yet dared to substitute Tabarly for the ace), and there will be puzzles, posters and, obviously, little boats that will float, all called *Pen Duick*.

So far Eric Tabarly's nerves have proved stronger than his financial position. Now he must stop a gap of 80,000,000 old francs, quite apart from repairs and upkeep on *Pen Duick VI*. It's too much, far too much if one wants to stay pure and undefiled, unlike the others in the big events whose yachts have been turned into sandwich-boards.

The 'sandwich-board boat' had indeed taken the place of the romantic ship, but Tabarly tackled the problem the other way round; he made the placard carry the name of the boat.

These commercial ventures along a wide front fell far short of yielding the anticipated profits. It was only in the fields in which Tabarly himself excelled, the accounts of his voyages and designs for yachts, that he was able to build up capital. His little 6-metre,

the 'Pen Duick 600', was formally given its name towards the end of 1975 by the daughter of Valéry Giscard d'Estaing, and within six months 380 of them had been sold. But they needed much more money now because Eric was planning to build another quite revolutionary boat, a huge trimaran hydrofoil that at a certain speed would rise clear out of the water, a boat fit to win the 1976 Ostar. At that point he had neither the time nor the money to carry out the plan.

For the 1976 race Tabarly was therefore left with *Pen Duick VI*. It seemed that he had at last solved the mast problem, as was shown by his spectacular win in the Portsmouth-Capetown-Rio-Portsmouth race in which he had again broken several records for the course. *Pen Duick VI* had again shown her form – but with a crew of fourteen.

Now, in a storm-swept Atlantic, there were few indeed who would envy being at the helm in a boat so apparently ill-suited to single-handed sailing. Nevertheless, Tabarly was the favourite. People said that he was determined, angry and exasperated by the way this race was shaping, and by Colas, who had become a big name in the sailing world with his 236-footer that Tabarly regarded as a floating scandal. He would have liked to put things straight for once, and felt that at forty-six the man whom his friends had been calling 'Pepé' rather too soon might still have something to say for himself. But what he had to say would be said in action by being first across the finishing line, for words were not his strong point. After he had given his last position off Land's End he was lost in a silence which was to remain unbroken, and throw every Frenchman into a frenzy of doubt and anxiety.

From the first week the pattern of the race was clear. Colas, who spoke over the radio with the regularity of a metronome, described how his Jumbo-Yacht was behaving herself almost from hour to hour. He said the halyards were not standing up to the heavy weather. Some sceptics doubted if it could be as bad as all that, but they were wrong: the 1976 Ostar was a hard race, very hard indeed, and the *Club Méditerranée* that they didn't think much of was behaving very well, at any rate better than most of the others. It didn't need much to restore Colas' usual self-confidence; he soon claimed to be well ahead and that still further annoyed the growing faction of anti-Jumbos, particularly as nobody knew what had become of the other favourites, *Spirit of America* and *Three Cheers*, who still remained silent, and above all of Tabarly himself. The race was living up to its promise and the Atlantic to its reputation. It even shook Tabarly, who was on the point of giving up, but nobody knew that yet; he only confided it to his log. As he related it to the special correspondent of *Paris-Match* when he reached Newport:

Monday, 7 June. I think the weather has been favourable for the multi-hulls and tell myself that if they have followed the northern route they should be ahead; if they have gone southward they will have made only moderate progress. I have taken advantage of the lull to cook myself a new dish of spaghetti and eaten it to the last morsel. Never have I felt so hungry. Perhaps as one gets older one's muscles need more calories. I was hardly back in the cockpit when the wind increased and the wind gauge needle registered 40 knots. There was just one thing to do – take in the genoa, and do it quickly. Hurrying forward I cursed my labours for they were not getting me anywhere. Since yesterday evening the barometer has been falling steadily; the depression is on its way. During the night the wind rose to around 50 knots and there was a very heavy sea.

The wind was blowing great guns and *Pen Duick* ploughed heavily into the troughs of the waves, making me glad that I had strengthened her bows at the Brest dockyard. As for me, the icy spray drove incessantly in my face like needles. Out of sheer obstinacy the self-steering gear kept on disengaging. Normally when she luffs, that is to say goes up into the wind, it should put the helm over to make her pay off. As it is, the helm remains a-lee and she heaves to. I had to take over from the defective steering gear but there can be no question of staying at the helm indefinitely; it would be far too exhausting. The cockpit is constantly filled with spray and I have never felt so cold; I have to go below now and then. Sometimes the hull shudders when she hits a wave . . . it's like a thunder clap.

Early in the morning, under a dismally grey sky the wind was up to 69 knots and there were overhanging crests to the waves. It was an awful job getting in the mainsail. I had just secured it, a difficult job too with the deck lurching in every direction, when I made a shattering discovery: the propeller of the auxiliary generator had been carried away, the crank connecting the propeller to the driving shaft having broken. So now there will be no power for the automatic pilot and we are only four days out. The situation is anything but bright and I feel exhausted and demoralized. All of a sudden I remembered the trouble I had after my vane gear was damaged in the 1964 Ostar, and in a state of utter dejection decided that I would never be able to make Newport. Shall I retire from the race? I do not know what to do.

Confused as I am I know that if I mean to go on I shall have to give up the too difficult northern route and look for better weather further south. I am forced to this conclusion by the need to find some sunshine to warm up the solar batteries in the cockpit, which might make it possible to use the automatic pilot from time to time.

That decision taken, I went on to the other tack with my staysail hard in and at 60 degrees to the relative wind. I am now making five or six knots south-east and I am not labouring under any illusion; I have practically given up the race. However, I shall give myself one last chance and before I really turn back I will get some sleep so that I can think more clearly.

Wednesday, 9 June. When I woke it was already late. I feel rested and see the race in quite a different light. There can be no question of giving up and I am furious with myself for all the miles of easting that I have just made, furious with my feebleness. There is time for a cup of coffee with bread and salted butter. When I went up to the cockpit the wind had moderated and gone round to south-south-east. I am going over onto the other tack, but this time towards America.

The weather is breaking up again. After another not very deep depression I am now almost immediately faced with a third and this one is nastier, but come what may I must stick to the northern route.

There is nothing I like better than the sight of the sea and clouds flying across the sky but in this greyness there is no time to take it easy; with one depression following another I am always changing sails, hoisting them when the wind drops and getting them off again in no time when it blows again, and I'm always tacking. Physically, I have recovered my nerve but with the sky almost always overcast I have not been able to get a fix. There is nothing but rain, drizzle and fog and never has *Pen Duick* been so damp; the bunk is wet and my clothes are never dry.

Four days later on Sunday, 13 June, the news reached Newport of the first important retirement from the race: Michael Richey in *Jester* had given up 'in favour of an Irish cruise'. This was sad tidings for the organizers on Goat Island because it marked the first occasion on which *Jester*, the most famous of all the boats in the Transatlantic Race, would not be one of those to cross the finishing line. Sailed by Hasler she had made the passage in forty-eight days in 1960 and in thirty-eight days in 1964. Michael Richey had taken fifty-seven days in 1968 and fifty-eight in 1972, but long and arduous though these voyages were he had never abandoned the race. 'It's the end of an era,' said one of the members of the Royal Western, and as if to bear that out it was known soon afterwards that Valentine Howells, the only skipper who had sailed in the first Ostar, had also retired, with head injuries. And that was only a beginning; the 1976 race was indeed to give cause for apprehension. Even Tabarly, at grips with that wild weather, was using language that one seldom heard from him and spoke of the folly of single-handed sailing, although of course only to himself.

Sunday, 13 June. A fourth depression of exceptional violence swept down on us and now at 8 o'clock the sky has suddenly cleared. I have taken the opportunity to get a sun sight and just had time to work out the fix, which commits me to the northern route.

Late in the afternoon the wind made it necessary to take in the genoa and I set the No. 1 jib but it split while I was hoisting it and I lowered it at once. That was not the end of my labour; after setting the storm jib I have been tearing the skin off my hands to put a reef in the mainsail because the wind is now up to 40 knots and still rising. Then I lowered the mainsail, and the storm jib too because the sheet had parted. Finally I lowered the mizzen. The wind gauge is stuck at 60 knots. The sea is white with foam, a 'violent storm' as they would have called it in the old sailing ships. There is nothing I can do so I am lying ahull and I shall try to get some sleep. She is lying broadside-on to the sea and drifting at about 2 knots downwind. I tell myself that it's silly to sail alone; the boat and I can only wait till the storm abates. I had another nasty surprise this evening; the rudder would not answer the wheel because the steering lines had parted. Regretfully I see that I shall not be able to mend it and it will be a sad loss because it made for much more accurate steering than is possible with the hand tiller, which always has some play.

On Monday, 14 June, the worst fears were confirmed; if the 1968 race had been characterized by the tragi-comic retirement of the 'amateurs' it was now the best sailors who were in trouble, and

'The radio wastes too much time and there is enough to do on board after a blow, navigation for example, or splicing a sheet that has parted in the gale . . .' Tabarly

the silent stuck to his customary rule

serious trouble too. Marc Linski had a struggle to keep his boat afloat after an accident and the French girl Dominique Berthier, after seeing her *Saint-Milcent* sink after a collision with a freighter, was back in Paris. The Englishman, Tony Bullemore, was rescued by a Liberian tanker after suffering superficial burns; his boat was ablaze. Joël Charpentier in *Wild Rocket,* who had seemed at one time to be in the lead, had broken his foremast and abandoned the race.

Alain Colas was having more trouble with *Club Méditerranée;* his halyards, unequal to the violent winds, were not standing up to the work. As he said over the radio:

The wind is up to force 7 or 8 with squalls up to 45 knots and with hail that cuts one's face and hands.

Last night was bad. At dusk the No.1 jib halyard, the one nearest the bows, parted. The deck is narrow here and the sail, blown aft and with the weight of its battens, fell into the water and dragged along the side like a trawl: full of water it weighed a ton. Bracing myself not to fall overboard I had to get it in inch by inch. The waves were up to ten feet high and the deck rose and fell like a lift. It took me hours to get it all in, gathering up the heavy canvas and gripping the reef points. Then I was able to get it up again. I had foreseen such an eventuality and had three jib halyards on each mast.

At dawn the same thing happened again, and to the No. 3 jib as well, which came down on top of the steering gear. As Colas says:

I waited until the wind dropped a little because I had only one spare halyard for the No. 1 jib. Bereft of so many sails the boat lost some of her way but was still making 10 knots. In all this confusion there were several tears in the sails which will require hours of cross stitching, like they used to do in the old three-masters.

In light airs I grumble at not being able to set all sail and feel that she is not making her proper speed. As the wind dropped I set all the sail I could except the No. 1 jib, which is now definitely useless. It is very hard work and the broken halyards and the spares have all got tangled up inside the fourth mast, so I shall have to scramble up and cut away the sections of halyard with a saw blade; it will take two hours at least.

Then I must mend the No. 3 jib so that I can get it up. She'll go better then and I shall be in a better temper.

But during that week-end the bad weather did nothing to cheer him up.

I spent the night taking in one sail after another. The weather's been rough again but this time I have taken precautions and there has been only one mishap – the eighth halyard has parted. I can still manage but this sort of thing is very exhausting. The whole sail comes down every time a halyard

The 236-foot Club Méditerranée *ships a heavy sea. The halyards did not stand up to force 10 winds and it took Alain Colas five hours to recover the jib that had gone overboard*

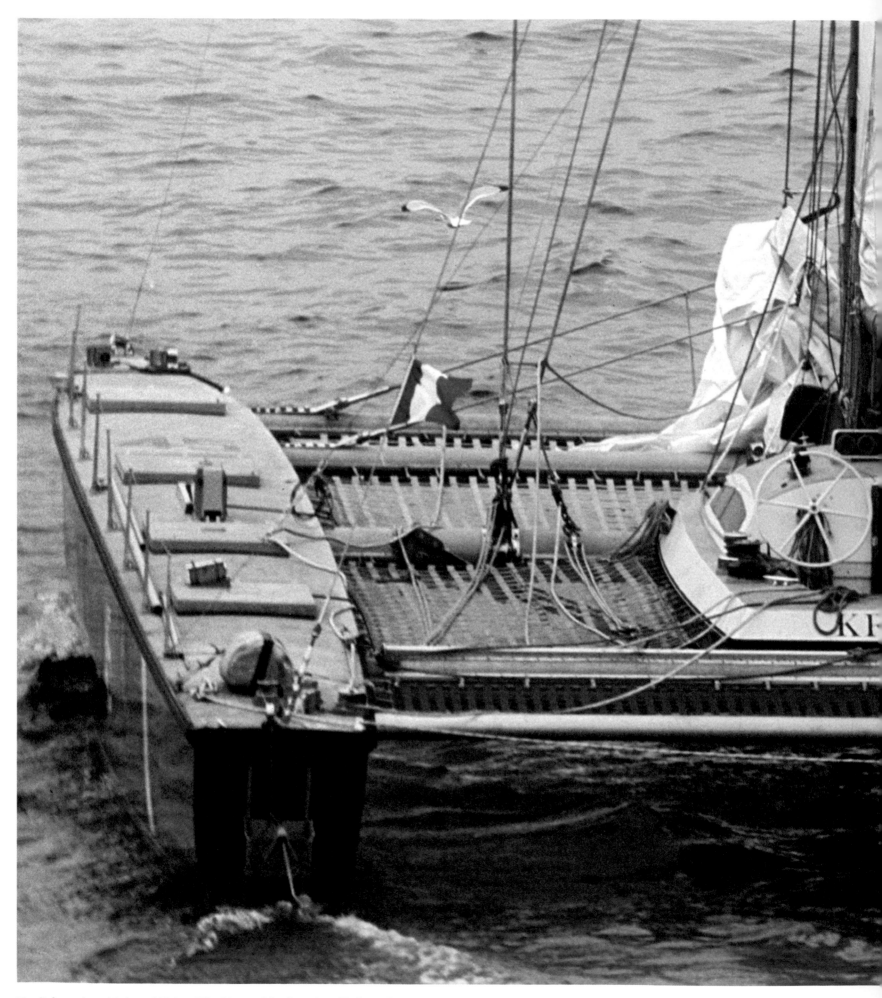

The light and sophisticated Kriter III, *skippered by Jean-Ives Terlain who came second in the 1972 race, broke up in heavy weather*

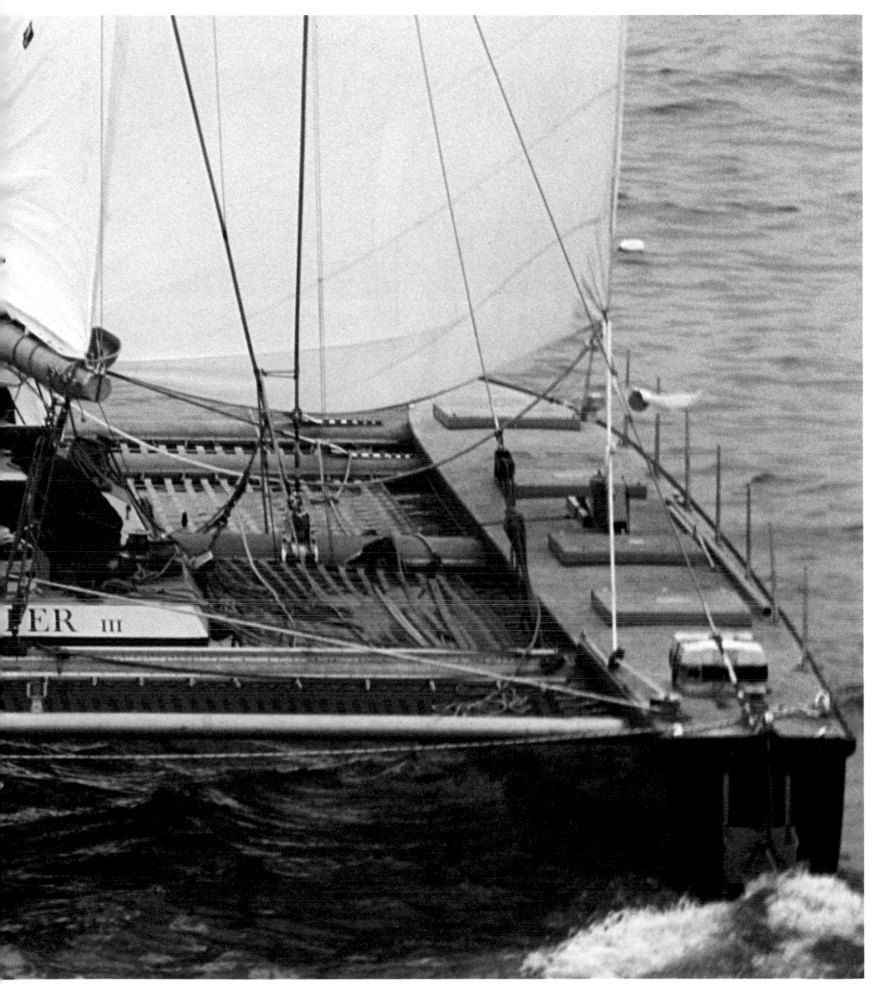

goes and you have to jump to it to save what you can . . . A broken halyard is the physical equivalent of eight rounds in the boxing ring.

It's blowing hard now with a very heavy sea. Twenty-foot waves and a Force 10 wind make navigation difficult. Walls of water crash over the boat. Fortunately this 72-metre can heel over 35 degrees; had I been in the trimaran I sailed in the last race and round the world I should have been under bare poles in this wild sea. As it is I have been able to shorten sail in time and carry on.

Even that dignified newspaper *L'Equipe* forgot its usual reserve with the headline 'Panic winds at sea'. Patrick Chapuis wrote the following commentary on Colas on 16 June.

This is the second gale of this severity since the start of the race and the meteorologists predict a third. Force 10 on the Beaufort scale is what even sailors call a storm, with wind speeds 48 to 55 knots and 30-foot waves. This only confirms what reports we have had from those at sea.

We have heard Alain Colas regularly on Europe 1 ever since the race started, but in the message that came through last night and which has not yet been broadcast one could discern a real note of dismay in his voice. He has broken two more halyards. It is the enormous press of the wind against his sails that causes the damage and he can now use only three of his four masts. He can hoist no sail at all on the foremast. In that wild weather, surrounded by breaking seas, it is an incessant struggle to handle his yacht to meet the onslaught of wind and wave. A struggle also to assess the situation and try to choose the best course to steer in the light of the weather reports. Alone on board he has to do all that and attend to his daily needs as well. But to sleep or eat, or even get a cup of hot coffee, is a difficult matter in a cabin tossed about by the sea where one has lost all sense of the horizontal.

Colas has not been able to get an accurate fix, but gives his estimated position and this is a long way above the optimum route, which implies that he is going off course and is not able to keep the vessel heading the way he wants.

This Ostar is taking a dramatic turn and one almost forgets that it is just a race when one thinks of the fate of men and women in distress.

On the other hand the Tabarly mystery may soon be resolved. The position of *Pen Duick VI* has been the big question mark ever since the start. Now an Air France plane has reported a large mono-hull two thirds of the way across, off Newfoundland and well ahead of Colas. This would confirm a report received three days ago.

If this really refers to Tabarly it puts him some thirty hours ahead of the others, but there is no way of verifying it. He expected to take eighteen days and it is now the twelfth day of the race, so the estimated position seems reasonable.

We have interviewed Gérard Petitpas, master mariner and close associate of Tabarly, who in his Paris office is also beginning to get worried. 'I wish I knew more,' he said, 'because what Colas says is really alarming. But I am sure that if Eric were in distress he would have let us know . . .'

What we do know is that Tabarly's ketch is well able to stand up to bad weather. We know he had trouble with the mast on his round-the-world voyage, but she is nevertheless a well-tried boat and anything likely to fail has done so already. While many of the boats in this race were only fitted out at the last moment and had covered no more than the 500 miles necessary for them to qualify, *Pen Duick VI* has already been through it all, and come out on top. At forty-six Tabarly is a tower of strength and a very experienced sailor. We are eagerly awaiting further news.

All the same Gérard Petitpas did not deceive himself and regarded most of the news as mere fantasy, knowing that it would be almost impossible to make out the race number on a hull at an altitude of 10,000 metres. Three days earlier there had been another false report of the same kind. It was part of the game in this race, as the contestants were not required to report their positions. Under normal conditions that was one of its attractions but in 1976 it could only be a source of anxiety. The French papers had front-page headlines such as: 'Big Trouble in the Transatlantic Race' or 'The Atlantic Hecatomb'. In cottages in Brittany and Cornwall people trembled to open a newspaper. Then on Monday, 14 June, Yvan Fauconnier in *I.T.T.-Océanic*, the fine three-master that had finished second in the 1972 race as *Vendredi 13*, sent a message to Yves Devillers, editor of the magazine *Partir*, that sounded very much like an S.O.S.

The situation is critical. Wind velocity is about 55 knots and there is a very heavy sea. Wave height six or seven metres and a crossing swell. As I tried to take in the middle jib, because the wind was still rising and we were making nearly 9 knots under that sail alone, I was unable to hold the winch and was struck several times by the handle on the arm and thigh. I think my arm is broken and I find it painful to move about.

The force behind that winch handle is hardly imaginable; it tore the steel buckle from his safety harness, which may have averted an even worse accident, before striking his arm and thigh. Within a few hours the limbs had swollen to three times their normal size. Fauconnier could barely drag himself on deck and, with one side paralysed from shoulder to foot, had become incapable of managing his sails.

A second and even more alarming message was received that same Monday afternoon:

Things are going badly. The forward and port-hand lifelines have gone and I can no longer think of going on deck. The outer jib has shaken out and is rapidly tearing itself to pieces, but I can't do anything about it. The boat is beam-on to a heavy sea which is getting worse all the time.

An enormous breaking sea has swept over *I.T.T.-Océanic* and knocked her flat with the masts in the water, shattering the side-lights on the port quarter with a noise like thunder, and the deck lockers too. This sent everything flying through the air in the cabin and alleyway, including the batteries which spilt acid everywhere. I am making water and the wind velocity is over 60 knots. I am fixing things as well as I can but I don't know where to begin. The very robust deck lockers were simply swept away by the breaking sea and everything that is not made fast threatens to fly in my face. Think of something quickly because if I am knocked down again and make a lot of water I don't give much for the chances of the boat.

That night the state of the sea allowed them all to get some rest, but the ocean still had its surprises in store, even for a Tabarly exhausted by the weather he had had to endure:

Tuesday, 15 June. I must heave-to again; even though the wind has dropped it's still blowing 40 knots and the sea is still high. Just as I was getting ready to hoist sail I saw that one of the slides on the mizzen mast was broken. It's only a minor repair but by the time it's done I shall have lost a good two hours. I am aching all over as if I had been unloading ten tons of flour; with the boat rolling like this everything is difficult.

The glass is rising and the sky clearing. I can see the sun again and it's too good an opportunity not to take a sight. I went below to fetch the sextant and came on deck again. The horizon was clear but masked at times by the wave crests; then all at once I was deluged in a sheet of spray and the sextant was soaked. I laughed at my own clumsiness, got the sextant dry and promised myself not to make that childish mistake again.

In the afternoon a Norwegian freighter with an orange-painted hull forced me to alter course. I had seen her a long way off, steaming slowly into a head sea and pitching a lot. After a while it was clear that we were on a collision course or at least heading for a close encounter. I waited for him to alter, but he stood on unconcernedly so I took the helm in case I might have to avoid him. It was a wise precaution because not to rub noses with him I had to go about and pass down-wind under his stern, and was astonished to see the two men on watch just looking at me. The visibility was perfect, the freighter had therefore deliberately refused to allow me priority and this is inexcusable. However, there are more and more of these merchant navy captains who ignore the Rules of the Road with vessels under sail. Their conduct is despicable for they rely on their tonnage and their immunity to punishment, for one may well ask how I could have lodged a complaint, most of all if I had been sunk – and they can't say that their size restricts their ability to manoeuvre.

It took me a long while to recover my temper and I began to wonder if after the four depressions we had had we were now going to run into a fifth. The answer came next day, at 4 o'clock on Wednesday, 16 June, when the wind whistled in the rigging at 55 knots. I set about lowering the mainsail in all haste – five depressions in eight days is a pretty rare event. *Pen Duick* and I are making our way through a very heavy sea, with almost a free fall into every trough of the waves. She's never had such a terrific pounding before and she has certainly seen bad enough weather in every ocean. Now one of the crashes has sent all the crockery flying – well, perhaps this depression won't last long.

But these five depressions had already accounted for some of the best of them. On Tuesday, 15 June, Mike Best found that his trimaran had lost one of its floats and become alarmingly unstable. Alain Colas, who kept a daily count of the number of halyards he had left, found that he was now running into the red. He was still breaking halyards and would soon have nothing to keep the sails on his giant masts. Nevertheless, he offered to assist Fauconnier until he heard that a Russian tug had got permission from the Soviet authorities to go to his help. In Paris race watchers were able to breathe again, but not for long, for now Terlain in *Kriter III* was the one to transmit a despairing message:

The boat is breaking in two. This morning when I stripped off the shreds of trampoline forward that had not stood up to the successive storms I found that the two forward beams had split. It will be impossible to tow *Kriter III*. If you pull on the starboard hull, then the other, which I have not been able to bail out and which is two thirds flooded, will collapse and sink. If you pull on both hulls at the same time the broken beams will literally stave in the port-hull. Nor can I rely on my mast; it is unsupported forward and at the first pitch it will come down aft and destroy what little solidity *Kriter III* still has. There is even some play in the two main beams and she is leaking through the gaps. The cabin is breaking up and the side-lights have burst under the pressure.

On 17 June it seemed almost certain that *Kriter III* might founder at any minute, but fortunately the storm had held him at a position not far from his friend Fauconnier and the Russian tug was asked to rescue both of them. The suspense could not go on for long and it was important that the Russians should make contact that day. But the first news to reach Newport on Thursday, 17 June, was a laconic signal concerning Pierre Szekely in *Nyarlathotep* which said, 'Picked up by Spanish vessel *Touro*, only the skipper, boat sunk.' The Swiss, Pierre Fehlmann, with his smart *Gauloises Longues*, was to meet the same fate. Even Colas had lost some of his assurance; he admitted that it was no longer a question of making the passage in eighteen days but perhaps twenty, as in 1972, or even more. The day closed on another note of distress; Plymouth Radio was informed by the Coast Guard that an S.O.S. from a vessel somewhere in the Atlantic had been picked up by an aircraft; they were trying to fix its position.

But the date that was to mark the turning point of the race was Friday, 18 June. Fantastic reports came in one after another at ever shorter intervals and the Paris dailies had to reshuffle their front-page stories.

The day began with the usual quota of casualties but Paris, London, Plymouth and Newport were waiting in suspense only for the rescue of Fauconnier and Terlain. For twenty hours the Russians had been manoeuvring round the two Frenchmen and determining their exact positions. The fact that two boats so close together had to be rescued led to some confusion. Fauconnier recounted the episode later:

The Russians gave us twenty hours of radio contact with radio bearings every twenty minutes, and it was difficult to understand what they said; it was always the same dialogue in French and English – 'Your position 48.51 N 31.35 W.' 'No that's *Kriter*, go

over to *Kriter*.' Then Jacques Timsit would come in jokingly from *Arauna IV*: 'This doesn't sound like single-handed sailing!' I switch off to get some sleep at 2.30 in the morning while Jean-Yves Terlain takes over the radio watch.

I rouse myself at 4 o'clock, fix my position and think they should be here by now. I go on deck – and here they are. 'Do you see me?' I ask. 'Da.' 'I have two lights at the mast head.' They circle round once, and then round again. The transmitter is too close and I can't hear anything. 'Are you going to send a boat?' – 'Can you repeat the message?' – 'Are you going to send a boat?' – 'Da.' – 'When?' – 'In the morning.'

I go back and lie down to gather my strength. Then, all at once, I hear the sound of running footsteps on the deck, wellingtons and leather boots, a stampede of Vikings, and hardly awake I realize that it is six o'clock. They are everywhere, their boat bumping against *I.T.T. Océanic*. The Second Officer and the doctor with his bag have come below. I suppress a laughing fit to see the doctor looking for somewhere to put his bag. Then I go on deck to supervise the job of fixing a stay to the mast. Then I get into their boat; it's like a lift up to the tug, with 10-foot waves. I ask where we are in relation to *Kriter* and we try the direction finder. Jean-Yves quietly gives us the bearing and in five hours we are up with him. It's half past four in the afternoon and this awful experience had overtaken us both within fifty miles of each other.

On board *Kriter III*, Fauconnier found Terlain making his last rounds as owner. 'The floats are in constant movement,' he said, 'and every little incident has its repercussions. It's like a piece of knitting where any stitch that gives can soon start an enormous run. The port-hand hull is almost under water and the gap between them is getting wider all the time. The wreck is breaking up minute by minute.'

Terlain had as much as possible of his gear put in the boat where Fauconnier was waiting for him. Not seeing him come back Fauconnier went on board again and asked what he was doing. 'Phoning Paris,' he calmly replied. The tug showed its impatience with loud blasts on its siren. Terlain's last telephone message sounded like a modern version of Cambronne: 'I see my ship sink and it makes me truly . . .'

Terlain rang off. Between them they had dismantled the radio and were taken over to the tug *Besstrashnyj*, where a bath and the sick-bay awaited them. 'Such men indeed deserve to be called heroes and I raise my glass to them,' said Nikolai Butnik, the captain of the Russian tug, not concealing his surprise that such yachts could be sailed single-handed. 'The word hero applies just as much to your ship's company in *Besstrashnyj* whose life work is the safety of your neighbours,' replied Terlain, and drank a toast to their rescuers.

For them the race and their long anxiety were now over. For the general public the race was that very day to take an even more extraordinary turn in two dramatic events that not even a novelist would have dreamed of.

Yvan Fauconnier's I.T.T.-Océanic, June 1976

At 12.00 GMT on 18 June Europe 1 broadcast to a France that was just sitting down to lunch the news that Colas could no longer manage his *Club Méditerranée*. His sails were torn and he hadn't enough halyards left to hoist what sails he still had. He had announced that he was making for Newfoundland and would put in to St. John's for repairs; he needed new halyards and the help of a master sailmaker.

In Paris that marked the start of another race for his 'crew', Jean François Colas and Michel Dixmier, to organize a relief expedition to Newfoundland with about half a ton of halyards and sails. Since there could be no question of getting new sails made in forty-eight hours they used the sails from *Manureva*. Alas, there were no flights to Canada available because of a strike, so they had just twenty-four hours to get *Manureva*'s sails up from Brittany and charter a plane to fly them over.

Not far from the corner of Paris where Michel Dixmier was organizing his 'Operation Sails' the telephone was constantly ringing in the office of Gérard Petitpas. At the other end of the line a reporter from the French Television Second Programme was telling him that the Canadian Coast Guard at Halifax had reported sighting *Pen Duick VI* sixty miles south of Newfoundland. This made it clear that Tabarly was not only two days ahead of Colas but that he would shatter the 1972 record if he kept up the same speed. Before broadcasting this sensational news, however, the reporter wanted a confirmation that Petitpas was hardly able to give him. He knew that Eric would not report any position until he was practically over the finishing line. Trying hard to control his feelings he hastily consulted a chart; to this former merchant navy captain and member of Eric's crew the position seemed a reasonable one, taking into account Tabarly's fantastic start from Plymouth and the time it had taken him to clear Ireland. If the report was correct he must have kept up an average speed of 7 knots. 'Yes, it's possible,' he replied over the telephone. 'It's optimistic but it is possible.' At 4 o'clock the television put out a news flash which came through just as Petitpas reached the Europe 1 radio station.

The radio station, which until then had held the exclusive rights to news from Colas, was all of a flutter; they were trying to find out if the television news could be true. Petitpas suggested telephoning the base at Halifax. One of their reporters was back in a few minutes. Halifax had indeed received a position for the yacht with the race number 141. There could be no mistake it was *Pen Duick VI*. At five o'clock Europe 1 broadcast its own news item and immediately arranged for a meeting with Tabarly in Newport to negotiate exclusive rights for the story of the future victor. If he kept up the same speed the radio would not have long to wait to welcome their new star.

At Newport the *Observer* officials were pinning two bulletins on the notice board, two hours apart:

15.30. The France-Presse agencies in Paris and New York report Tabarly 110 miles off Newport and estimated time of arrival Monday or Tuesday. Possibly this should read Newfoundland. The report is unconfirmed.

17.43. The Halifax Coast Guard confirms the report. Tabarly 93 miles south of Cape Race. Wind favourable (20 knots) 850 miles still to go. Probable date of arrival Monday 21st or Tuesday 22nd June.

From now on the matter was settled. Tabarly had won the race magnificently. Colas and his Jumbo-Yacht had been beaten and, worse still, made to look silly.

But that was the exact opposite of Tabarly's thoughts at sea; he was not listening to anything, not even a transistor. He was actually three or four days' sail away from the reported position and judged that he had never been so slow:

Friday, 18 June. Since the start of the race the boat and I have had only one good day – that was June 6 to 7 when the day's run was 210 miles. I am not really a pessimist but I think that if *Kriter III* and *Spirit of America* have chosen the southern route and avoided the depressions it's quite likely that I'll find them at their moorings in the anchorage at Newport. As for Colas, I do not think that the rigging on *Club Méditerranée* will see him across the North Atlantic with its storms without giving trouble. After thirteen days *Pen Duick VI* is fifty miles behind my position in *Pen Duick II* in 1954: it's not the boat's fault but the unusually bad weather and almost incessant head winds. We have been warned of the presence of big icebergs in the area I am now approaching. The boat is not going very well now with helm lashed and I have to spend more time in the cockpit than I would wish because the nights are bitter. With the temperature down to 4 degrees C, holding the tiller is cruel on one's hands. The fog is getting particularly thick and if I had the bad luck to have an iceberg ahead I wouldn't see it, I'd feel it. In anticipation of these long watches I checked my heating system but that was another disappointment; it won't work. It always used to work very well and quite recently, coming up the Channel at the end of the Atlantic Triangle Race, it gave out a good heat. Probably it wouldn't take long to put right but I don't feel like wasting my time examining the damned thing. In this race I seem to have been denied every modern convenience that might make life comfortable; it's no better than life on board in the old days of sail. There is just a chance however that the wind may stay steady during the first half of the night. I have set my alarm to ring every hour and I am going to doze in my wet sleeping bag.

Unlike Tabarly, Colas was in constant communication with French radio and Tabarly's reported position suddenly made his struggle with the giant, now bereft of its working sails, seem futile and unrewarding; the race was over. At best he might finish second, but although beaten it would be an honourable defeat. He would get his sails mended and finish properly at Newport.

On Saturday, 19 June, the *Observer* made an official announcement at Newport: 'Europe 1 confirms that Colas is putting into St. John's this evening. Jean-François Colas is on his way from Paris with the sails off *Manureva*.'

There was a lull over the weekend; nothing of importance could happen before Monday when Newport would be waiting for the greatest winner in the history of the race. Meanwhile there were 120 men and women still at sea in the storms which succeeded each other almost daily.

On that Saturday, Yann Nedellec retired with injuries after his *Objectif Sud II* had been dismasted and was picked up by *R.F.A. Olma*. Doi Malingri was run down by an unidentified vessel; his masts were down and the boat was holed. Lloyds gave an unconfirmed position for the American favourite Michael Kane indicating that his *Spirit of America* had fallen back. This was a report from the German ship *Blumensthal* and could mean that he had turned back, unless the German had misread the race number.

Further reports on Sunday, 20 June, confirmed those of Saturday. Michael Kane had indeed turned back for England and Alain Colas was in sight of Newfoundland. There was one more retirement as well; another fine single-hander, the Dutchman Gérard Dijkstra in *Bestevaer* had turned back too.

It seemed now that after ten days of storm the Atlantic was experiencing an unusual period of calm, immobilizing Tabarly a week's sail from Newport where they thought he would appear the following day.

Sunday, 20 June. The day began with a fine athletic performance but by midday it was a flat calm. A lot of birds have come by but like me they are waiting for the wind. The glass is very high and I'm whistling in the hope that the calm won't last too long. My average speed has certainly not been remarkable and I am falling still further behind my 1964 passage, although for the past twenty-four hours I have been on quite a different course. I am beginning to think about the others again. In spite of the day I turned back and the day I was hove-to I think that there should be nobody ahead of me on the northern route. On the other hand the multi-hulls should have met with more favourable conditions if they went further south. In the early afternoon a little breeze sprang up and, unlike this morning, everything has come to life around me; the birds have taken wing and the rigging that hung lifeless is beginning to clatter. The boat glides silently through the water in a woolly air, for the fog is lifting with the wind.

On Monday, Newport awoke to an atmosphere of expectancy. The early news was good; there was word from Valentine Howell's wife that he had got back home in spite of his head wound and that his giddiness was wearing off slowly. The news of Doi Malingri was equally reassuring. He had been sighted by an American ship and although the yacht was badly damaged her skipper was confident of making the Azores. Late in the morning a light aircraft took off for the first time to see if there was any mast in sight off-shore. It was indeed still rather too soon for Tabarly to be in view, but the weather was clear and it was not unreasonable to think that he might have beaten the most optimistic forecasts. But the single-engined aircraft had to turn back when hardly clear of the bay; there was a thick bank of fog all along the coast and even if they had gone further they would have had very little chance of finding what they were looking for. Tabarly was sailing in thick fog, as he notes in his log for 21 June:

In this fog and cold I find it hard to believe that this morning is the first day of summer. We are on course and the boat is going well with a light breeze over a sea as smooth as a skating rink.

Sailed through a big school of grampus – they presented an extraordinary sight; I have never seen so many. Yesterday I saw two whales rubbing themselves along the length of the boat. The fog is very thick again this afternoon but the boat is going well and I have taken the opportunity to get at the sails and mend the No. 1 jib, which is torn. While I was sitting cross-legged at this tiresome sewing I thought I heard a fog horn and went on deck at once. The visibility was down to fifty yards and I could just make out a ship close to and for one long moment she seemed to stay exactly abeam to port.

In Newfoundland Colas was busy sewing too, working fast but not too fast, since the minutes mattered less now that he could no longer win the race. Jean-François Colas had brought a team of

Above: Terlain and Fauconnier in the Russian boat that rescued them both
Right: Terlain reunited with his fiancée in Newfoundland, where I.T.T.-Océanic was towed. Kriter III *broke up and had to be abandoned*

volunteers and a sail-maker who was already working miracles. Colas wanted to keep up appearances, using only one of *Manureva*'s smaller sails, and so as not to spoil the look of *Club Méditerranée* most of the mainsail was resewn.

Gérard Petitpas reached Goat Island very late that Monday evening and was immediately plied with questions by those who had been expecting him since noon. They thought he might somehow have news of Tabarly but it was he who put the questions; his plane had also been delayed by the airline strike and he was afraid that he might have missed Eric's arrival.

Tuesday, 22 June, was a particularly quiet day at sea for Tabarly: 'No sail changing and no navigation by chart because the fog has been thick all day. The only sound is the hiss of water along the hull. I like having a crew but I like sailing alone too.'

At Newport, however, 22 June had been one of the most exciting days. Since the early morning, with the change-over to Summer Time, bad news continued to pour out of the *Observer* telex. One series of bulletins made one think it had now become a race back to Europe. Gérard Dijkstra was expected back in Holland next day, Michael Kane in *Spirit of America* had been sighted off the English coast with a hole punched in his boat as if it were a used railway ticket. Yann Nedellec was in hospital at Portsmouth with cracked vertebrae.

But the main event of that day took place in Newfoundland. As Michel Etevenon, the owner of *Kriter III,* describes the sad affair Colas had scarcely left the harbour before he met the Russian tug *Besstrashnyj.* At 08.15 *Besstrashnyj* came into the fairway towing a ragged three-master with all sails down – it was *I.T.T.-Océanic.* There could no longer be any doubt that *Kriter III,* that superb racing catamaran with such a fantastic record, had gone to the bottom of the Atlantic.

At Newport the day ended on a note of suspense. Still no Tabarly; watchers were posted at the mouth of the bay and very generously the sponsors of *Spirit of America* maintained a permanent radio watch at the marina although their protégé had abandoned the race; the special correspondents hung around the little Coast Guard wireless station.

At dawn on Wednesday, Olivier de Kersauson, to make the most of a clear patch, took off in the single-engine aircraft he had chartered each day, only to return after a four-hour flight with no news about Tabarly. Gérard Petitpas went out soon afterwards in a little launch, appropriately named *Solitude,* hoping that he would spot his friend, for had not Colas himself told Téura that very morning that the race was now over? Speaking over the radio to the hotel on Goat Island he said:

I have cleared Cape Race, the southernmost point of Newfoundland. We are doing 10 or 12 knots, which is very fast. My God! If the wind holds it will only take me four days to make Newport. I am going below to find the coastal chart and study the tidal streams. At some states of the tide they could push me along and give me a bit more speed. I haven't any false hopes because it will take me three days to get within sight of Tabarly. Still, the second place is worth having. Of course he should be profiting by the same weather conditions too, so that he could well reach Newport today.

Petitpas took a few journalist friends with him in *Solitude,* which led some people to think that he had some special news for them. The French and English television teams also hired a launch. The launch skippers at the marina began to rub their hands with glee: at fifty or a hundred dollars a day their cash registers were ringing a merry tune every morning now. But outside there was little wind and Tabarly after his stormy passage still had a flat calm on 23 June.

The light airs make it necessary for me to trim the sails pretty often to keep on course. Now it's abeam I have to set the little staysail to be able to steer. I soon hoisted the spinnaker, but after an hour the wind dropped again and I had to take in that big balloon and hoist the genoa – all that labour to very little purpose. *Pen Duick* and I have now been eighteen days together and on my estimate we should have been in today, whereas in fact I have still 630 miles to go and unless the wind picks up it will take at least four more days to get there. But for my turning back, and the storm on 14 June which lost us three days, I could have made the passage in nineteen days. Once again I wonder if *Kriter III* and *Spirit of America* have not already finished the race. I had a look in the stern locker because the automatic pilot was not working and I have found out why: the metal plate that supports the steering line pinion is badly damaged.

I am beginning to feel tired this evening. I have to pause for breath now and then when I am doing anything, and with all this handling of snaphooks, ropes and sails my hands are in a bad way. The glass has fallen a bit, a shallow depression but nothing much, and the fog has come down again.

Petitpas was back in the evening with no more luck than Kersauson, but there was a surprise waiting for him. R.T.L. Radio had found a loophole in the exclusive rights enjoyed by its great rival Europe 1. With France all agog about the race, R.T.L. had sent Tabarly's mother to Newport with a reporter who snapped up everything she said. Petitpas had no news for her, good or bad. It was eighteen days since the start of the race, the eighteen days that Eric had predicted and which the report from Halifax had made to seem possible. Petitpas could only reassure her that he would surely get in that night.

The watches and reliefs were tightened up. Some were waiting at the point some miles out of Newport, some at the *Observer* headquarters, others with the sponsors of *Spirit of America,* listening to an all too silent radio; some were at the Coast Guard Station where they could do nothing since the Coast Guard launches had not sighted any boat with a race number and some snatched a few hours' sleep within reach of the telephone at the marina.

Throughout this night of watchfulness cliques were forming and reforming: there were those in favour of a 'race for normal boats' against those for 'electronic giants' – two concepts for the same race represented by two great sailors: Tabarly and Colas.

Next morning Mme. Tabarly stepped quietly onto the marina terrace, her hair as white as the white blouse she was wearing. Nothing had been heard of Eric. There were further retirements from the race but nobody was interested now. Pierre Fehlmann was happily back in Newport where the story of his foundering filled the columns of the papers and shook even the coolest reporters. As Gilles Pernet in *L'Equipe* of 28 and 29 June reported, Fehlmann told them:

My 17-metre *Gauloises* had always given me every satisfaction and I had come through the first three storms easily although they were exceptionally severe. All went well until I discovered water in the bottom of the hull. I did not at first realize what it meant and just started to pump her out. Then finding that the water was still rising I downed all sail. The wind was up to Force 10 and the waves almost thirty feet high. I was under bare poles, and looking over the coach roof I saw an enormous wave sweeping towards me.

The boat was knocked down and I was thrown back into the cockpit, which was lucky as I had had about a ton of water over me. Getting up again I found that the mast was broken; it was then that I sent out a distress signal. Only later did I discover the cause of the trouble: in shipping a heavy sea the forward cockpit had burst open. It had big outlets and could empty itself in twelve seconds, but it was such a confused sea that it filled for the first time when the boat was thrown from the crest of a wave into a 15-foot trough with the outlets open. When the boat filled again I was really scared; I thought the end had come.

By chance my message was picked up by a big container ship, the *Atlantic Convoyer,* whose captain told me afterwards that he had come to render assistance but with little hope of being able to do anything.

Imagine this gigantic 700-foot ship trying to rescue me from my half-submerged boat in a raging storm with waves up to thirty feet high. These ships have a very high freeboard, forty feet from the waterline, and the yacht was in danger of being smashed against that wall of steel at any moment. After some hours of manoeuvring in the dark I managed at last to get a rope round me, thrown from the ship, but that was not the end of the story because the ship was rolling so heavily that I myself was in danger of crashing against her side.

By a miracle I managed at last to hoist myself on board; I think they must have hauled me up. I have done most of my sailing on lakes and was never really aware of the seriousness of the situation. Far from it; it had never occurred to me that I would ever have to get up the side of one of those monsters. This Ostar will go down in history; from weather averages over the past twenty years we might have expected to encounter one and a half depressions during the passage, whereas I experienced four depressions of unusual severity in my first race.

A light aircraft flew over the marina as Fehlmann finished his story; it was Kersauson and Chris Smith, the *Observer* photographer, on their way back. They had covered a circle a hundred miles across, a good day's sail, and were back with the same report as the others – nothing in sight.

Then the rumours started going round. Eric had missed the bay and would go on to Boston; at 15.00 hours it was rumoured that he had been run down by a freighter; at 16.00 that he had been sunk by a Russian submarine; at 18.00 that he had struck a wreck; at 20.00 that the reported sighting from Halifax was a mistake – it was unlikely that he would have been so close to the land. But as none of this could really be verified the doubts continued, and the tension grew as the nerves of the special correspondents began to show the strain of trying to pin down some possible truth out of it all. What was true was that Tabarly was having another hard day at sea.

The glass is still falling. I had to go on the other tack in a hard squall with a 40-knot wind. I was on watch all night because the wind was always changing in force and direction. Every quarter hour or so I had to adjust something or attend to some more urgent task; it was only in the early morning that the wind became steadier and I was able to get a couple of hours' rest.

On the morning of Friday, 25 June, to reduce the general atmosphere of tension somebody happened to show Gérard Petitpas a copy of one of the yachting monthlies with the premature title 'Tabarly the Winner' to an article that explained in some detail how he had beaten all records. But Petitpas did not laugh; he was superstitious and remembered that Nungesser and Coli had never reached the other side of the Atlantic after a Paris newspaper had come out with the title 'They Have Succeeded'.

Since the night before, an air of doubt had followed the euphoria of the first few days. If the Halifax report was not mistaken there were only three possible reasons for Tabarly's non-appearance: some significant if not serious mishap such as the breakdown of his automatic pilot; some serious accident such as stranding or being dismasted; or worse still, being run down in fog or being washed overboard by a heavy sea, because Tabarly never used a safety harness.

And that was not all; an unkind fate had decreed that the more concern there was about Tabarly the more likely it seemed that *Club Méditerranée* might be first across the line. This silenced the gloating of the Tabarly die-hards, to the great relief of Colas' supporters.

Even those journalists who had sailed with Eric Tabarly were demoralized by the long hours of fruitless waiting and had to struggle to maintain their composure. 'It's not possible,' they kept saying. 'When Eric says he can get across in less than twenty days it will be less than twenty days. Something serious must have happened.'

They lost themselves in conjecture and seemed a little more worried whenever there was another message from Colas. They revealed a degree of prejudice that was hardly professional, even if it was understandable in devotees who thought Tabarly invincible, implying that if Colas came in first it would mean not only defeat, but the certainty of some accident. Because this time Colas was known to be on the way and, even if the wind was hardly favourable, his friends expected to see him in Newport on Sunday.

In Paris the editor of the magazine that had announced 'Tabarly the Winner' was having some awkward moments; the headlines in the daily papers had changed: 'Where is Tabarly?', 'The Mystery of *Pen Duick VI*', 'Growing Alarm'. *France-Soir* was talking about 'Dismay at Newport' even though Olivier de Kersauson tried to convince the editor that it was still too soon to panic. He told him:

If *Pen Duick* is becalmed that would be enough to explain the delay; I see no reason for panic yet. I have been talking to Eric's mother at the marina. Upset by all these rumours the old lady's face suddenly became grave and she asked me what I really made of it all and whether the situation was really serious. I said, 'No madame, there should be no cause for anxiety before Sunday,' and she thanked me.

Kersauson and Petitpas, who had sailed longer with Tabarly than anybody else, now remembered their sea-sense. While not ruling out the possibility of an accident they tried to verify the report from Halifax that had led them to expect Tabarly during the past week. It was highly improbable that the Coast Guard had been mistaken, but one just did not know.

Petitpas telephoned the Canadian Rescue Coordination Centre which confirmed that a position for Tabarly had been reported on 18 June. He insisted that they should read him the report from the pilot who had seen No. 141. After a long wait they replied that they never received the report. Petitpas then asked to speak to the man who had taken down the information about the sighting. Then followed another dramatic development. The report, the man said, had not been from one of their own aircraft but from Paris and related to a position given by some aircraft that had nothing to do with them.

Petitpas and Kersauson now saw what might have happened. Some journalist might have worked out a theoretical position for Tabarly from the 'information' given by the French aircraft and telephoned Halifax, in less than perfect English, to ask if it was possible that Tabarly had got as far as that. With a bad line or through mispronunciation, the question mark might have got lost and with this second telephone call the question had turned into a confirmation of the report. It was in fact very near to Tabarly's actual position a week after the supposed 'sighting' at Halifax. At the time of the report he was convinced that he had already lost the race.

Perhaps I have already lost the race; we make very slow progress in these light airs and swells, and I expect another sleepless night. My hands are hard and cracked and more and more painful; it's a torture hauling in a rope. I have been tacking all night in a wet fog and getting nowhere. Below deck everything is dripping wet.

This fifth Ostar will just have to be fought out mile by mile. There is not a breath of wind. I am sick of it and will try and get a few hours' sleep. My troubles won't be over tomorrow either; my direction finder has gone wrong.

There was a remarkable change in the atmosphere at Newport on Saturday, 26 June. A reaction had set in. Those who had slept little since Monday and spent hundreds of dollars on reconnaissance flights to see Tabarly come up over the horizon at

Michael Kane in Spirit of America. *He had to retire with damaged outrigger booms and sailed back to Plymouth*

any minute had given it up as a bad job and the packed rows of watchers had thinned out. Gérard Petitpas and Mme. Tabarly had said they were going back to Paris. For one thing it was now thought that the Halifax report had been a mistake and with the impending arrival of the Tall Ships, the big training ships from all over the world that had come to mark the bicentennial of the United States, Goat Island had become a fun fair.

Thousands of T-shirts, mugs, paper napkins, polo-necks and beer cans, all bearing the Tall Ship mark, awaited those imposing envoys of the world's navies. It was their race that had captured the American imagination. The start of the race from Bermuda, in spite of an accident to two of the finest ships, had not failed to make a grand show. The finish, however, was less spectacular. There was no more wind for the Tall Ships than for the single-handers and they were late in arriving. But the millions of dollars invested in hot dogs, hamburgers and cans of beer, waiting in the sun for the two million spectators, could not be left to a whim of the wind. The commanders of the finest sailing ships in the world had been asked to start up their auxiliary engines and get to Newport on time. An emergency plan had been put into operation to regulate the movements of the thousands of little boats that had come to escort the big ships. Police officers controlled the traffic in the harbour from their launches with whistles and waving arms like the Place de la Concorde at the evening rush hour.

From 10 o'clock onwards the Tall Ships came in one after the other, as though to a railway time table, and the Goat Island bridge was closed to all traffic. It was impossible to drive through a town cordoned off by the police and would take at least six hours to get as far as the point, where they had been watching for Tabarly the day before.

Any news of Tabarly now came from Paris rather than Newport. Somebody had told his brother that he might have been lost overboard. It was thought that the French Navy was sending help. At the marina they tried to keep these disquieting reports from Mme. Tabarly, who was more than ever inclined to go back home, 'to see about selling the family home at Chalouére. My husband died last year and it's too big for a woman living alone.'

As for Colas, his hopes had begun to revive. Almost eliminated by that accident a year ago, he now suddenly found the nightmare coming to an end. He had overcome all obstacles and was on the verge of beating that fine sailor Tabarly. Best of all he had proved to all those who thought his Jumbo-Yacht a floating heresy that she was not just as good as any other boat but even better. Colas the pusher, the handicapped, the boaster, Colas the schemer, the financier, the designer, was showing them that he had been right, and above all that he was again Colas the great yachtsman, capable of outsailing any rival in the world.

On Sunday, Olivier de Kersauson, who had told Mme. Tabarly three days earlier that there was no occasion for alarm before Sunday evening, could think of nothing that would reassure her. All the same he was telling anyone who was prepared to listen that since Colas, held back by the frustrating calm spell, had not been able to get in, Tabarly could not have got lost. But he had to employ all his powers of persuasion to get his moderate views into the columns of *France-Soir* or the R.T.L. programmes in the prevailing atmosphere of panic. Very few people listened to him

except Gilles Pernet, special correspondent of *L'Equipe,* who shared his views.

While we must not ignore the possibility that Eric has met with some mishap, I have in mind particularly some problem with his self-steering gear, we should remember that of all those taking part in the race he is undoubtedly the one most able to get himself out of a difficulty. It is very significant all the same that at Newport it is only about Tabarly that everyone seems worried although there are thirty-four other yachts in the race from which nothing has been heard since the start, and the positions of thirty more have not been known for the past week. That makes some sixty boats about which we have had no news since the beginning of last week.

Should we therefore dramatize the situation or rather call to mind that sailing is a sport in which many factors have to be taken into account and that this time the weather conditions have again upset all the predictions? One thing is clear, and that is that Alain Colas' performance in 1972 was altogether exceptional in covering the distance between Plymouth and Newport in twenty days. It would seem too that conditions were exceptionally favourable on that occasion and that the record may long remain unbeaten.

But they were both preaching to deaf ears. Paris thought of Tabarly as dead – the lost hero. On Sunday Mme. Tabarly had come back with Gérard Petitpas and one of Eric's former crew blurted out, 'It's all over this time – he can't possibly win now.'

On Monday, still under fog, another long watch had begun. But this time it was different: they were waiting for Colas, who was expected at dawn on Tuesday. There was one arrival on that gloomy day that came as a surprise to the group of journalists installed at the marina, quieter now after that noisy week-end influx of tourists; Michael Kane, the skipper of *Spirit of America,* was on his way through before going back to California with his young wife. The bull-necked ex-captain of the Marines with the musical southern drawl, the American favourite in the race, was tired and worn out and still suffering from the shock of that awful voyage in which he had almost lost his life a few days before. He summed up his feelings about the race and Tabarly as follows:

Listen to me. I was out there and it was bad; worse, it was perfectly bloody. There are a lot of people out in that ocean we shall never hear of again. I sincerely hope that nothing serious has happened to Mr Tabarly because that would be a real disaster for France. He is the best sailor in the world, the best ocean racer and the best single-hander. There is no country in the world that could afford to lose a man like that.

Walking off into the fog, Kane left behind him a deeper wake of gloom. The men who had been listening to him or recording the interview hesitated to broadcast what he had said; his praise sounded too much like a funeral oration.

In the island restaurant that evening a certain coolness began to make itself felt between the tables where the friends of Colas and Tabarly were seated. The latter were leaving for a last look out at the point, where they had already spent hours peering into the haze. It was one in the morning when they saw a light in the distance that could be the black ketch that they thought they had sighted a dozen times already during the past week. But, head-on, Tabarly should have shown three lights, green, white and red, and this was only one white light. Even his best friends had ceased to hope for a miracle; they could not imagine that two of the lights on *Pen Duick VI* had gone out. Going up to bed one of them said, 'Damn it, big ships have shown lights like that for years.'

At 02.00 on Tuesday, 29 June, the duty officer at the Newport headquarters was drowsily relaxed. *Club Méditerranée* had again reported her position; she would not reach the line before 10 o'clock at the earliest. The reporters went to bed. They set their alarms for six and the first launches to go out and meet the winner had been ordered for seven. It was going to be a busy day.

It was eight o'clock in Paris and the papers were on all the news-stands with five-column head lines: 'Help for Tabarly', for the hero now really seemed to be lost. The French Navy was even sending a Bréguet Atlantic to patrol the ocean and look for Tabarly and any other of the sixty-four of whom nothing had been heard.

At 03.12.53 (or 07.12.53 G.M.T.) Eric Tabarly crossed the finishing line at Brenton Point. All he had to say was:

The night is very dark and the air humid. *Pen Duick* and I are coming slowly up the roadstead. Yesterday evening when for the first time I wanted to give the Coast Guard my position my radio only emitted a shower of sparks, so I gave it up.

He had still a good hour's sailing in front of him before entering the harbour.

At 03.15 Alain Colas, who had left his radio switched to Channel 16, the Coast Guard frequency, happened to hear that they had just sighted a boat with a black hull and the name *Pen Duick*, the *Pen Duick* that everybody thought was in distress. He asked them to give him her position as he meant to go to her aid. It was when they gave it to him that he realized Tabarly had just crossed the finishing line.

At 04.00 one of the television reporters was awakened by the Paris office that had sent him to await Colas. They assured him that he would be in by 5 o'clock. They had forgotten in Paris that sailors work in Greenwich Mean Time; the reporter thereupon roused his team of cameramen.

At 04.30 a photographer from Sygma, the Colas agency, arrived from New York to photograph their friend's triumphal entry and saw for the first time that famous bay where the Tall Ships still lay at their moorings. He looked at his watch; Colas would not be there for five hours so he decided to wait till it was light and take some pictures of the Tall Ships before going to his hotel and getting a couple of hours' sleep. In the dim half-light he caught sight of a big ketch at the end of the quay making her way into the harbour. Her black hull still bore the traces of a half-obliterated race number.

The television team stopped at the marina office to ask for further details. The duty officer told them that Colas had indeed confirmed that he would not be in before ten. Then through the window of his office looking on to the harbour he saw a strange thing. Denis Gliksman, son of Alain Gliksman, who was the first French journalist to report a Transatlantic Race and who himself competed in the races that followed, woke up in the middle of the night. He was sleeping on board his friend Gérard Pesty's trimaran. He saw a bearded man in a big yacht who was tacking about in Newport harbour as if he had lost his way. He was looking for the spot where he had come ashore twelve years ago; Tabarly did not know that the wharf where they were waiting for him was not the same one as before. Denis Gliksman, without stopping to find out what had happened, got into his rubber dinghy and steered for *Pen Duick VI*.

The Sygma photographer put an ultra-rapid film in his camera but it was no use, there was still not enough light. The television reporter thought he must be dreaming and sent his lighting technician to look for some spot lights. The duty officer picked up the telephone and began to ring all the numbers on a list in front of him. In the new marina hotel there was total confusion. Special correspondents streamed along the corridors, bare to the waist, in swimming trunks, or bare foot, hammering on every door as they passed to awaken those who had been on duty the day before. Some of them still thought they were on their way to welcome Colas when they saw Gliksman's little dinghy hail the big black ketch. Tabarly had only one question to ask:

'How many have got in already?'

'You are the first.'

'No!'

'Yes.'

Tabarly did not have long to wait for confirmation. The spot lights trained on him from an approaching launch lit up his incredulous, smiling face.

A dinghy came up out of the mist with Tabarly's former crew on board, bringing with them contracts for exclusive rights that Petitpas had left with them when he went away. 'Accept them,' they said, 'they are terrific; they will pay for all the sails you ever dreamed of for *Pen Duick*.' They had forgotten that they were all at once supporting the theories that Colas had brought to perfection. The photographers were swarming all over her as if *Pen Duick* had been parked at a road crossing. The dispatches were already pouring out and R.T.L. and Europe 1 had established permanent links with Newport. The European daily papers reset their banner headlines for the late evening editions.

At 7 o'clock Téura and a group of Alain's friends were gathered on the quay at the marina to go aboard the pilot boat that was going out to meet *Club Méditerranée*. The smiles faded from their faces at the animated scene all along the terrace and around the marina telephone boxes. Some of them, only half awake, still thought it was some nightmare when their eyes fell on Tabarly's ketch. Vaïmiti, Alain and Téura's little girl, began to cheer up after her rude awakening as Téura kept on saying, 'Come along, wake up, we are going to look for Papa.' Her tears were hardly dry when she saw a bearded devil leaping ashore who was not a bit like her father. 'Is that Papa?' she asked, and Téura burst out laughing, and so did Tabarly. On the quay all was bustle and gaiety. Some friends of Colas warmly congratulated him; at least they would rather see Eric win than see him dead.

Club Méditerranée in sight of the finishing line at Brenton Tower at 11 o'clock on Tuesday, 29 June 1976

Tabarly had had no sleep for the last four nights and asked only for a shower and a good breakfast. But that must wait; he had first to go through customs and the customs officers were still peacefully asleep.

At 9 o'clock, three hours after he had come ashore, the two customs men at last made an appearance. Half an hour later the hero of the Atlantic was having his shower. Two hours after that he was back at sea again, to please the photographers.

At the mouth of the bay *Pen Duick* on her way out came across *Club Méditerranée* on her way in; it was 10.27. From the deck of his boat Eric tried to pick out his unfortunate rival but Colas was not to be seen. Not for a moment had he expected that his opponent would be able to put to sea again just after weathering twenty-three days of storm.

When Tabarly came ashore this time Michael Kane was on the quay and warmly clasped his hand; it was 2 o'clock and Tabarly was at last to get his first square meal at the Goat Island hotel. In the big dining-room a half-open door separated his table from the one where Colas was already sitting and by one of those odd chances the two groups had reached their tables without meeting. At both tables they were quietly discussing that fantastic fifth Ostar. Neither Eric in his glory nor Alain in the bitterness of defeat had much to say. Only their faces betrayed their states of mind: Tabarly calm and relaxed, Colas stern and dejected. If they had leaned backward they could have seen each other, but they did not. Alain's friends could only hear the laughter at Eric's table, where they were reading the congratulatory telegram from the magazine that had prematurely announced him the winner: 'We were never in doubt about your victory. Thank you for justifying our hopes.'

At Alain's table his photographer friend called for the handshake that most of those present wanted to see but Colas sadly replied, 'I think that when two sailors have just crossed the Atlantic under the conditions we had to endure they would not wish to meet again for the first time in front of flashing cameras but far away from this uproar – at sea perhaps, on board ship.'

When Eric got up to leave there were those who still hoped that he would go and shake hands with Alain but some 'well-meaning' friend just then whispered in his ear,' 'Don't waste time Eric, we are going to miss the plane.' Paris and the Champs-Elysées were already wild to greet this hero who had been snatched from a watery grave and Tabarly had to take off the same evening.

But all was not yet over at Newport, where Colas had a lot to say. He could not well conceal behind a proud and aggressive manner the mortification that had suddenly overwhelmed him. It is a hard thing to be second where a man expects to be first. It is still harder to be beaten when one believes one has proved to all the world the rightness of ideas and opinions all too often laughed at. For the first time since that terrible accident in 1975 his iron will was to fail him; and perhaps it was as well for at least it made the stoical Colas seem a little more human. He too was weary after the voyage and Colas the brave was to become Colas the bad loser. He went on talking confidently about his 'Cathedral of the Seas', the huge yacht that

All that night it was thought that Colas had won the race, but in the half light of dawn on Tuesday it was seen that Tabarly had crossed the line in the dark

had perfectly fulfilled her purpose, refusing to admit defeat and peevishly arguing that he had made the best passage, that from Plymouth to Newfoundland he had made the best speed, and that nothing else mattered. But some of the things he said were even more tactless. Some reporters tried to forget them, attributing them to the distress of a man already smothered in bills and invoices before he had had a night's sleep or a decent meal. As Alain Coroller wrote in *Les cahiers du yachting:*

Alain Colas came into port a deeply injured man. Silent and limping on the quay, he had surely never felt so completely alone. There was no radio programme to record his words. The public, always preferring David to Goliath, seemed to have passed him by. He seemed to be trying to justify himself, to prove to himself that he had not really lost the race. A difference of only eight hours was too hard to bear. Now he knew how he must have made Terlain feel four years ago; in the same situation he must have been faced with the same questions. If he had known where Eric was he might have cut short his stay in Newfoundland . . . If . . .

But, alas for Colas, some reporters seized the opportunity to repeat his ill-chosen words, emphasizing them, or worse, turning them against him to settle some old score, all the while pretending to be his friends.

That night, while Tabarly was flying back to Paris and Colas slept uneasily in Newport, while Paris, London and Rome were getting out special editions devoted to that memorable Transatlantic Race, one small boat was still making her way towards the American shore. At 06.00 on 30 June the special correspondents' telephones were ringing again – the duty officer was reporting that another boat had come in. The nightmare began all over again with the race down to the quay to behold another sea horse and its rider. Those who got there first found it hard to believe that it was all not just a bad joke.

Moored near *Club Méditerranée* was the diminutive boat that had come in third, a sort of floating meccano set of the simplest possible kind. She was a trimaran less than 10 metres over-all with the grotesque name *The Third Turtle*. Sitting on one of her floats was a slight little man of forty-five with clear blue eyes and soft fair hair, looking in amazement at the crowd surging towards him. Prudent reporters were hastily consulting their lists of boats. Michael Birch, the Canadian, could not believe that he had come in third. A lorry driver, married and with two children, he was hardly remembered as the skipper of *L'Aurore* in the 1972 race. The yacht had been designed by Dick Newick who had also designed *Cheers* and *Three Cheers*. Her narrow cabin had an area of only 32 square feet and her rig, of the simplest kind, could be dismantled to stow her in a garage. Birch steered her under a plexiglass dome seated on a bench which, with his canvas cot, was the only furniture on board – it was like camping out at sea.

So much for the man and his boat. The route he had chosen was just as remarkable, the most difficult: Birch had sailed along the

When Colas came into Newport Bay, Tabarly was already at sea again, to please the photographers

173

rhumb-line. He had passed through the same storms as Tabarly and Colas, quietly asleep if the wind was above Force 6: 'because my boat was then too dangerous so I took in all sail and waited quietly till it was over, relying on my self-steering.' Michael Birch had no radio transmitter at all, just an ordinary holiday transistor on which he could hear nothing about his rivals and their progress. 'Here is the real winner,' a lot of people said. 'His race was in the true spirit of Hasler's Ostar.' Birch won the *Jester* trophy, first awarded in 1976 for the winner in the small yacht class.

Smiling and calm, Michael Birch let the wave of photographers and cameramen go by as he had done the Atlantic storms. When the commotion died down and the last of them had immortalized *The Third Turtle* on film, he quietly put up a hand-written notice – 'For Sale, $26,000. Apply to Michael Birch on board.'

The photographers had hardly put away their equipment before another sensation was to shake the little community already stunned by Michael Birch's performance. A Polish boat was the next to cross the line, less than thirty-six hours behind the two big stars – a strange red and white sloop that was not to be found in any international list of yachts. The work of Polish craftsmen, she had been designed by her skipper for the Stettin Yacht Club, of which he was commodore. His name, quite unpronounceable to the radio reporters, was Kazimierz Jaworski; his tired, bearded face and clear eyes delighted the cameramen. His story was quite different from Birch's; following the same course, his passage had been as difficult as the Canadian's had been serene. He had lost a stone and a half and had expected on several occasions to be capsized. All the same he submitted to the bright lights and camera flashes that lit up the interior of *Spaniel*. The boat was a mass of gadgets; she even had a motor-racing bucket seat and steering wheel.

When Jean-Claude Parisis crossed the line three days, four hours and forty-three minutes behind Eric Tabarly, the sea had pronounced its verdict on this the fifth Transatlantic Race. Tabarly had won the *Pen Duick* trophy, presented to the winner of the class for unlimited yachts; Michael Birch had carried off the *Jester* trophy for the small yacht class with his *The Third Turtle*, ahead of his new friend Jaworski; Jean-Claude Parisis got the *Gipsy Moth* trophy for the intermediate yacht class in *Petrouchka*; and Colas got nothing. But decisions on land were still to upset the verdict of the sea and hurt him even more.

While Tabarly was marching down the Champs-Elysées like a hero of liberty, Mrs. Jack Odling-Smee, the dignified wife of the Commodore of the Royal Western Yacht Club of England that had organized the race, was descending upon the terrace of the Newport marina with the air of an English lady offended by some new scandal. Turning her slight figure toward her journalist friends, both French and English, she said, 'Alain has done something awful and quite against the rules, but we shall not go so far as to disqualify him.'

The committee met. The charge against Colas was that he had contravened the provisions of Rule 22-2 which says:

> During the Race a yacht may put in anywhere and anchor or moor for any purpose. She may be towed for a distance not exceeding two miles into, and for a distance not exceeding two miles out of any such harbour or anchorage, provided that the

total result of such towage can be shown not to have advanced the yacht towards the finish. When actually anchored or moored other people may come aboard, stores or equipment may be embarked and repairs effected.

Colas was accused of having had his sails set by a crew when leaving Newfoundland. This constituted 'outside assistance'. The committee recorded its verdict: a penalty of 58 hours. For the committee it was one more chance to show their disapproval of the Colas giant which they had never regarded as a suitable yacht for single-handed sailing within the spirit of the Ostar. For Colas it was yet another imposition, and one too many; he flew off the handle. 'This is a shame and an injustice,' he said. 'It is also seriously damaging to me, the last of a long series of bullyings. It's beyond all measure and I shall demand satisfaction. I shall bring it to the notice of the international authorities and I shall consult my lawyer.' He forgot that he had signed the starting order in which the Committee reserved to itself the final decision in all matters.

Even if Colas did drop from second place to fifth, behind Tom Grossman who had a pleasant voyage along the southern route in his trimaran *Cap 33*, he still remained (for one more Ostar anyway) the record holder for the course and the only man who had sailed a 72-metre yacht across the Atlantic single-handed, and in less than twenty-three days under sail.

The 1976 Ostar was officially over on 25 July, that is to say fifty days after the start. After that date the last of the heroes could no longer qualify as finishers; those who had had the most to bear and whose only crime was that they came in too late. They were perhaps the bravest and most deserving of all.

Meanwhile Tabarly had come to accept his extraordinary popularity and the discreet sponsors of *Pen Duick* were vaunting their share in the race on posters and in the newspapers. They were to shock the last of the purists, but then it was easier to forgive Tabarly than it was to forgive others.

Meanwhile, Colas was discovering the hardships of being beaten and of winning back the hearts of people, who nevertheless still admired him. Tom Grossman was back in the arms of his beloved and already making plans for the race in 1980. The charming English girl Clare Francis was just getting into Newport, to beat the women's record set up by Marie-Claude Fauroux, with the comment as modest as her own smile, 'You've not missed much!' She had got across in twenty-nine days and would no doubt have done far better but for a fault in her self-steering gear, which she had dextrously put right herself. But there were also two of the best of them who never came back from the sea.

On 30 June the freighter *Nima* had found in mid-Atlantic a little yacht with the name *Galloping Gael*, but with nobody on board. The *Nima* tried to take the 38-foot yacht in tow but the hawser parted in a heavy sea and *Galloping Gael* was lost again in the fog. Her skipper, the Irishman Michael Flanagan, had meant to emigrate to the New World and would have taken up American citizenship after the race.

By 19 July, almost forty days had gone by and people in Newport remembered that Mike McMullen had only taken on board stores for twenty. It was McMullen who had lost his wife two days before the start of the race and whose trimaran was considered as lively as she was fast. He never kept the appointment he had made with his friends and in the months to come that brave sailor never came back to land.

On 25 July the 1976 Ostar was over, dreams for the race in 1980 were beginning to be dreamed, and the critics were brewing up a storm as violent as the storms had been at sea.

Only sailors are competent to judge the matter. Others, the land-lubbers, onlookers like us at that finest of all sailing races, can only express our thanks and pay homage to these heroes of the twentieth century, whose splendid achievements recall another age.

Select Bibliography

BARTON, Humphrey, *Atlantic Adventures* (Adlard Coles, London)

CHICHESTER, Francis, *Alone Across the Atlantic* (George Allen and Unwin, London)

COLAS, Alain, *Un tour du monde pour une victoire* (Arthaud, Paris)

GERBAULT, Alain, *Seul à travers l'Atlantique* (Grasset, Paris)

GILLES, Daniel, *La Transat, un océan d'exploits* (Neptune/Editions du Pen Duick)

GLIKSMAN, Alain, *La voile en solitaire* (Editions Maritimes et d'Outre-Mer/Denoël, Paris)

HEATON, Peter, *The Singlehanders* (Michael Joseph, London)

HENDERSON, Richard, *Singlehanded Sailing* (International Marine Publishing Co., Camdem, Maine)

LUCAS-PHILLIPS, Cecil, *Cockleshell Heroes* (Heinemann, London)

MERRIEN, Jean, *Les navigateurs solitaires* (Denoël, Paris)

PAGE, Frank, *Solo to America* (Adlard Coles, London)

SLOCUM, Joshua, *Sailing Alone Around the World* (Rupert Hart-Davis, St Albans)

TABARLY, Eric, *Du tour du monde à la Transat* (Editions du Pen Duick)

——*Victoire en solitaire* (Arthaud, Paris)

TELLER, W., *The Search for Captain Slocum: A Biography* (André Deutsch, London, and Charles Scribner's Sons, New York)

WILLIAMS, Geoffrey, *'Sir Thomas Lipton' Wins* (Peter Davies, London)

Index

Page numbers in italics refer to illustrations.